# The Savvy Business Owner's Guide

# Navigating
## Through the
# Risks
## of
# Credit Card
# Processing

D1373878

# *The* Savvy Business Owner's Guide

# Navigating
## Through the
# Risks
## of
# Credit Card
# Processing

## Bill Pirtle

## with Foreword by Dan Coughlin

**MPCT**
**Publishing**
**Company**

Royal Oak, Michigan

Library of Congress Control Number: 2010926091
ISBN: 978-0-9826116-0-9

*Additional copies may be obtained by contacting the publisher. Bulk discounts are also available.*
MPCT Publishing Company
P.O. Box 904
Royal Oak, MI 48068
Phone: 734-272-6177
Fax: 888-311-6640

Edited by Rosemary Csizmadia
Cover design by Identity Graphics Design
Cover compass and iceberg illustrations © iStock.com

*Printed in the United States of America*

# The *Savvy* Business Owner's *Guide*

# Navigating
## Through the
# Risks
## of
# Credit Card
# Processing

## Bill Pirtle

## with Foreword by Dan Coughlin

**MPCT**
**Publishing**
**Company**

Royal Oak, Michigan

Library of Congress Control Number: 2010926091
ISBN: 978-0-9826116-0-9

*Additional copies may be obtained by contacting the publisher. Bulk discounts are also available.*
MPCT Publishing Company
P.O. Box 904
Royal Oak, MI 48068
Phone: 734-272-6177
Fax: 888-311-6640

Edited by Rosemary Csizmadia
Cover design by Identity Graphics Design
Cover compass and iceberg illustrations © iStock.com

*Printed in the United States of America*

*To all of the business owners and entrepreneurs
who seek good service for fair cost, and to the hard-working
Merchant Level Salespersons and Independent Sales Offices
who honestly serve them*

# TABLE OF CONTENTS

# FOREWORD

Every great teacher in any field has mastered his or her understanding of the content and can explain it in a practical and user-friendly manner. When you reflect back on your life between the ages of five and twenty-two, my hunch is you will recall one or more extraordinary teachers who truly influenced you a great deal. My favorite teachers could take the most mundane topic and bring it to life and make it seem extraordinarily relevant and exciting.

Bill Pirtle is that kind of teacher. His book, *Navigating Through the Risks of Credit Card Processing*, is a masterful performance by a great teacher. Not only does he demonstrate an extraordinary understanding of credit card processing, but he explains the information in ways that any reader can quickly understand what he is saying.

Bill first explains the core concepts of credit card processing and then moves into in-depth descriptions of the costs involved and the relative value you can expect for your investment. He doesn't hesitate to share his opinions on fraud, error prevention, sales agents, processing needs, and credit card processing contracts. He also provides his detailed thoughts on what Congress and state legislatures need to do when it comes to credit card processing.

Business owners and managers are primarily focused on improving sustainable profitable growth by enhancing the customer experience and increasing effective innovation. Issues surrounding topics such as credit card processing seldom make it to their priority list. However, costly mistakes connected to credit card processing can dramatically reduce the business owner's or the business manager's chances for financial success.

I encourage you to carefully read Bill Pirtle's master class on every conceivable issue related to credit card processing. It will be well worth your financial and time investment over the long term. It can make a critically important difference for you in terms of improving the profitable growth of your organization.

Again, read *Navigating Through the Risks of Credit Card Processing* carefully and apply the ideas in it as soon as you can.

Dan Coughlin
Author, *The Management 500: A High-Octane Formula for Business Success*
www.thecoughlincompany.com

# ABOUT THE AUTHOR

William (Bill) Pirtle has been in the field of credit card processing since 2004. In his business, Merchant Processing Consulting & Training LLC, Bill has coached business owners on credit card processing procedures, security compliance, and other good business practices. In 2009, Bill founded MPCT Publishing Company to publish *Navigating Through the Risks of Credit Card Processing*.

Like many beginners, Bill also had experiences with bad companies early in his career, but now he has great partners to work with. He currently writes for Clearent and Electronic Payments, Inc., two check processors, a gift card processor, and is an independent reseller for eProcessing Network (ePN).

Bill is an active participant on the Green Sheet, a credit card industry forum, which is sponsored by *Green Sheet* magazine. He was interviewed in the column, "AgenTalk," in the April 13, 2009 issue. On February 24, 2010, Bill was featured in an interview with Lisa Mininni on her blogtalk radio program, "Navigating Change" (to hear a recording, go to www.blogtalkradio.com/navigating_change; the program name is "Credit Card Processing in a Nutshell").

Prior to working in the credit card processing industry, Bill worked for 10 years in retail management with

Woolworth, CVS, Arbor Drugs, and in several management positions with CompUSA. An expert in loss prevention, he has trained many cashiers on proper cash and credit card processing procedures.

Bill has a B.A. in Multi-disciplinary Social Science (economics, history, and political science) from Michigan State University. While attending Michigan State, he was an intern at the office of State Senator Jack Welborn.

Active in several networking organizations, Bill is a member of the Downriver and Detroit Business Association (DADBA), Local Business Network (LBN) Bloomfield Hills Blue Marlin chapter, Michigan Business and Professional Association (MBPA).

You can contact Bill by phone: 734-272-6177, email: Bill @creditcardprocessingbook.com, or via his website: www. creditcardprocessingbook.com.

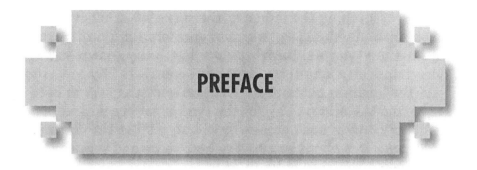

# PREFACE

## HOW TO USE THIS BOOK

*Navigating Through the Risks of Credit Card Processing* is not intended to be read cover to cover. Each chapter was created to answer specific questions regarding processing credit cards. To get the most out of this book, readers are advised to use the table of contents and index to find specific topics of interest.

## PURPOSE OF THE BOOK

Processing agents are mostly independent contractors who are responsible for signing, maintaining, and retaining current clients. By keeping our clients happy, we receive a portion of the monthly fees.

There are many good and honorable processing sales agents in this country. Unfortunately, there are many dishonest agents and even some dishonest processing companies. After several months of investigating ways to self-regulate or license sales agents with fellow members of an online industry forum, I began planning this book. It is intended to give entrepreneurs, business owners, and accountants concrete information to better understand, negotiate, and make the best decisions regarding credit card processing contracts.

In researching the industry, there is a lot of misinformation, misunderstanding, and misrepresentation on the part of its many players. Such conduct has been known to lock merchants into long-term, expensive contracts. My goal is to give the business owner the education and information needed to find the best pricing for the type of service desired.

This book is not necessarily about getting the cheapest contracts. It is about getting the best value and service. The "cheapest" contract is likely to have hidden costs and fees that are not necessarily apparent at contract signing. Experienced professional agents who recognize their financial responsibilities not only to themselves and the companies they represent, but to their customers, will be the most successful in delivery of value and service.

## THE BONUS CHAPTERS

The bonus chapters began as an idea to get a few business experts to contribute ideas for hiring someone in their line of work to match my suggestions on finding a good agent for your credit card processing needs. I found that there were a lot more categories for experts than I originally thought.

If you think about a struggling business, there are only three ways to increase income and prevent the business from folding. Those ways are cutting costs, increasing productivity, and increasing sales. So, I recruited 20 experts I know and requested that they write chapters to give tips to business owners and entrepreneurs and inform them on how to hire people in their fields of expertise. Their combined 22 bonus chapters can help you cut costs, increase productivity, and increase sales to help make your dream business become a thriving reality.

# ACKNOWLEDGMENTS

I would like to thank the following individuals:

- Dan Coughlin (speaker and author of *The Management 500* and other business books) for writing the Foreword
- Bob Hererra and Liz Scavnicki
- KS&A, for providing a forum to inform us and share issues with our condition and work through the accompanying ADD, dyslexia, and other issues
- Chuck Gifford (co-author of *Networking Your Way to $100,000 and Beyond)*, founder and owner of Local Business Network (LBN), where I met 17 of my contributing authors
- Minesh Baxi (co-author of *Networking Your Way to $100,000 and Beyond* and others), a business coach who inspired me to begin writing this book
- Joe Gregory (www.bookshaker.com)
- Bill Kleist, for creating a great cover along with giving me branding advice
- Steve Hyer, for writing three of the "bonus chapters"
- Al Crawford who instructed me on how to use LinkedIn
- Debbie Bone
- My contributing authors, for taking the time to write their chapters

- Jeff Fortney, vice president, ISO Channel Management at Clearent (one of my processing partners), whose belief in full transparency and encouragement of high ethics reinforced my beliefs of great companies and people in this industry
- Members of my networking groups: Local Business Network (LBN), Detroit and Downriver Business Association (DADBA), and the Michigan Business and Professional Association (MBPA)
- Richard Pausch
- Steve Sotis, owner of eProcessing Network (ePN), for giving me access to the tools to help business owners process sales the way they want or need to
- Paul Green, owner of *The Green Sheet*, an industry publication full of useful information, for creating the forum to allow sales agents, MLS, ISOs and registered processors help each other and advise on changing conditions
- My fellow Green Sheet forum members for my continuing education
- Ann Wilkes, a staff writer for *The Green Sheet*, who interviewed me based on my contributions to their industry forum (published in the April 13, 2009 issue)
- My late father William and mother Nancy for bringing into this world and not taking me out of it when I gave them cause to
- My brothers Mike Pirtle, Jerry Williams, and my sister Leslye Howell
- Rosemary Csizmadia for her time and patience in editing this book, and for putting up with me throughout the process

# ONE
# BASIC CONCEPTS

## BASIS POINTS

A *basis point* is 1/100th of a percent or 0.01%. One basis point is equal to $0.01 for every $100 in credit card sales. Basis points are used in conjunction with all credit card processing pricing.

A basis point can be used to represent savings. For instance, if a business produces $20,000 per month in credit card sales, each basis point of savings will save a maximum of $2. So, if you assume that the projected savings is 0.15% (15 basis points), the maximum savings would be $30 per month. However, "maximum" is a critical word in the example. There are a number of pricing categories on which the 0.15% savings could be figured. Focusing on the basis point savings in the example in one category could open a business owner to higher costs and fees in others.

Basis points are a helpful tool in understanding savings and costs. It would be a mistake, however, to put too much weight on basis points alone. Basis points will be discussed throughout the book to show in which categories they should be given more weight.

## INTERCHANGE PLUS PRICING

The components that make up *Interchange Plus pricing* include Interchange, Assessments, and "Plus."

## Interchange

Interchange has been in the news quite a bit, but most business owners still really do not understand how it affects the pricing they receive in their processing contracts. For most business owners, Interchange has very little to do with what they pay each month for credit card processing.

*Interchange* is a rate structure that is administered and set by the card brands (MasterCard®, Visa®, and Discover®). It is the amount that pays the issuer of the credit card for the card's use. Though competitive, it is not regulated in the U.S. Visa, for example, sets Interchange only on Visa branded cards for its 16,200 member banks that issue its cards. Without Visa setting its Interchange, each card-issuing bank would set its pricing independently. Interchange is used by the issuing bank to cover its costs of the card, including rewards, advertising, risk of loss, fraud prevention, and infrastructure (computer networks, etc.). Interchange is adjusted twice a year (April and October) by the card brands for their 36,000 member banks. Visa, MasterCard, and Discover have the right to set Interchange because it is their name on the credit and debit cards.

Most business owners' card processing rates are based on a "Tiered" system. The only thing Interchange has to do with the "Tiered" system is that it is the underlying cost paid by the processor. It is helpful to consider Interchange and the accompanying Assessments as the "wholesale" cost to the processor. For every credit card transaction done by a business, its credit card processor pays the Interchange and Assessments (explained in the next section).

Interchange currently consists of about 400 categories. Categories are still being created. They are determined by the brand of the card, whether it is swiped or keyed, risk of the card type, nature of the business where the card is used, level of detail of the information submitted, fraud detection methods used, and whether errors were committed in its processing.

Current Interchange tables can be obtained by going to www.visa.com and www.mastercard.com. The *Visa® Interchange Guide* is a six-page guide with a matrix of categories and lists the information needed to qualify cards for the best rates. The *MasterCard® Worldwide U.S. and Interregional Interchange Rates* (published in April 2009) is 115 pages with a separate matrix of categories for each card type (i.e., consumer, business, World, and Elite).

Interchange is expressed in "% + $" fashion. Visa's Reward 2 category (as of September 2009) is written as 1.90% + $0.10. The Interchange cost to the processor is 1.90% of the transaction plus $0.10 per transaction. So, for a $100 sale, the Interchange cost would be $1.90 plus $0.10 or $2. For a $200 sale, the interchange cost would be $3.80 + $0.10 or $3.90.

The Discover brand has only recently begun to be issued by banks and its Interchange is relatively new. Visa and MasterCard have had Interchange tables in effect for years. The author's experience has been with the MasterCard and Visa tables and not with Discover. American Express is not issued through banks as of this writing. Thus it has no Interchange set because the company is both the issuer and the processor, and it sets its own rates. Without the competing member banks, the American Express branded cards tend to be more expensive for merchants to accept than the other three card brands.

### Assessments

An *Assessment fee* is set by the card brand. It is collected along with Interchange from the processor and paid to the card brand. The money is used not only to cover the costs of the card and advertising, but for boosting profit in these now public companies. The Assessment fee for Visa is 9.25 basis points (0.0925%); for MasterCard it is 11 (0.11%), effective April 2010.

Just as most merchants do not list wholesale cost along with an item's price, most credit card processing statements (Tiered) do not list the fees of Interchange and Assessments. They are the processor's cost of doing business. While the rates a processor charges include this "wholesale" cost, the processor's profit cannot be determined by its customers.

Assessments *used* to be like Interchange; they were something not seen on Tiered pricing statements. That is changing. Up until 2009, processors included Assessments with Interchange as their "wholesale" cost to base their pricing on. Once Visa raised its system usage fee from $0.005 to $0.0185 per transaction and MasterCard created its National Access and Brand Usage Fee (NABU) of $0.0185 per transaction and increased its Cross-border fees, all processors had to pass this cost on to their customers. A few processors took this opportunity to begin passing on the Assessment percentage as though it was a new fee and not one that they have been absorbing for years. For these processors, this is effectively a 10-basis point, across-the-board rate increase for merchants who have a Tiered pricing structure. The increase might seem small, but if you were paying 2% and went to 2.10%, that 0.10 increase in rate just increased your total rate by 5%. Those merchants with an Interchange Plus pricing structure only saw the nearly $0.015 increase per transaction since Assessments are clearly defined in their pricing structure.

Assessments and Interchange are the true costs that all processors pay. Some processors or sales agents attempt to gain accounts by stating that they pay lower costs than other processors. Every processor pays the same Interchange and Assessment fees. Anyone who tells you differently is not being honest and their costing will likely be more expensive for your business. It is a common tactic among disreputable processors and sales agents to claim that they have better rates from the card brands. This is their attempt to confuse merchants and lure them into signing bad contracts.

## "Plus"

The *"Plus"* in Interchange Plus pricing is the gross profit. It is split between the processor and sales agent each month and is dependent upon the merchant's sales volume and number of transactions.

In Interchange Plus pricing, the benefit for the business owner is that the profit stays consistent regardless of how a card is processed. Why is this a benefit? In the Tiered pricing system, the processor makes more money by not correcting errors in a merchant's processing. "Non-Qualified" transactions have a much higher profit margin because of the surcharge. In Interchange Plus pricing, there is no such incentive to the processor. Simply put, with an Interchange Plus pricing system, the sales agent can focus on the best processing method for the merchant without worrying about what method will pay him the most.

Depending on the volume and business of the merchant and the service being delivered by the sales agent, 20–100-basis point profit margins are typical (20–45 for merchant locations where cards are swiped, 50–75 for keyed or Internet transactions, and 100 for special situations). Like the Interchange and Assessments, the Plus (or profit margin) is listed in % + $ fashion. For example, 0.35% + $0.10 is 35 basis points plus $.10 per transaction.

## THE TIERED PRICING SYSTEM

With a *Tiered pricing system*, merchants sign up at a set Qualified rate. Within this system, most categories will be assessed rate surcharges called Mid-Qualified (MQ) and Non-Qualified (NQ).

### Qualified Rate

The *Qualified rate* is the main rate listed in Tiered contracts. It is written in % + $ fashion (for example, 1.79% +

$0.25). It is considered by many in the industry to be a teaser rate. There are over 400 Interchange levels; maybe five of these levels are typically considered to be at this Qualified rate.

The tiers, or "buckets," are defined by the processor. Consider a child with 400 blocks. He has three or four buckets to place the blocks into. MasterCard and Visa provide the blocks (Interchange levels). The processing companies choose which bucket to place each block into. All processors using Tiered pricing structures use the same terms; however, each defines them differently.

Some processors include debit cards in the Qualified rate bucket. This creates extra profit for the processor, as the debit cards cost much less to process. Many processors use a special Debit-qualified category for debit cards since Interchange is lower on this type of card.

If Qualified rates were not deceptive enough, some companies will advertise rates as low as 0% or 1.39%. The small print will state that this 0% rate is for PIN (personal identification number) debit cards. Everything else will be processed at a much higher rate. If the merchant signs onto a Qualified rate of up to 1.49%, the contract will specify this rate as only for "Qualified" debit card (no PIN) transactions.

So, how is "Qualified" defined by the card brands? It isn't. The Qualified rate and its sister rates of Mid-Qualified and Non-Qualified are categories that all processors use. Again, all define them differently. They borrow the term "Qualify" from the interchange tables; for example, a Visa Rewards Card *qualifies* as Interchange level "Rewards 1" if it is swiped with no errors.

When a merchant tells a competing sales agent a single rate that she has currently or has been quoted, she is referring to a "Qualified" rate. What she may *not* be aware of is that if she has "Qualified" transactions, she also has "Mid-Qualified" and "Non-Qualified" transactions and, in many cases, is paying a lot more than she needs to be paying for credit card processing.

## Mid-Qualified Rate

The *Mid-Qualified* (MQ) rate is a surcharge added on top of the Qualified rate. For example, a MQ rate of 1.29% on top of a Qualified rate of 1.79% + $0.25 makes the rate 3.08% + $0.25 for those transactions.

Common transactions that carry the MQ surcharge are those keyed in a swipe account and Rewards cards. As previously discussed, each processor defines the Qualified, Mid-Qualified, and Non-Qualified categories differently. When compared to Interchange Plus pricing, assuming a Plus of 0.50%, the 3.08% + $0.25 MQ rate on a Rewards 1 level will be almost 0.84% higher. This means the merchant would be paying an extra $0.84 for every $100 charged on Rewards 1 cards at this level, or $42 extra for just $5,000 in transactions.

## Non-Qualified Rate

The *Non-Qualified* (NQ) rate is the bread and butter for most processors. Most Interchange levels will be classified as Non-Qualified. Many Business or Corporate cards, keyed transactions missing information, and keyed Rewards cards will drop to NQ.

Bar and beauty salon owners may have extensive Non-Qualified transactions and not understand how they happen. If a quick glance over the statement reveals EIRFs or Standards listings, those establishments need to be trained on new ways of processing tips. EIRFs (Electronic Interchange Reimbursement Fees) and Standards (Standard Interchange Reimbursement Fees) are categories of Interchange that indicate to the trained eye that there are errors in the merchant's method of processing.

The card brands prefer that the dollar amount authorized be the amount batched. In some industries, an added tip as high as 25% over the authorized amount is allowed. However, if the tip entered at night before batching is higher than the percentage allowed for that type of business, the transactions will be heavily surcharged. The NQ surcharge typically ranges from 1.59%–2.19%, but I have seen it as high as 6%. A 1.79% NQ surcharge will effectively double the processing cost. With the proper education and terminal, this surcharge can be completely eliminated. If the processor has a Tiered pricing system, it is making a hefty profit and has no incentive to help the merchant correct errors.

In comparing a Tiered system to one based on Interchange Plus, clearly there *are* still some categories that will approach 3.4% total. However, those categories carrying that pricing will be rare for most merchants compared to a Tiered system. EIRFs and Standards are caused by processing errors. A good partner for the merchant is one who will help eliminate these expensive errors.

## PCI-DSS (PAYMENT CARD INDUSTRY-DATA SECURITY STANDARDS)

In a survey I did on SurveyMonkey.com, which asked, "What does PCI-DSS mean to you?," the vast majority of respondents stated that it was something that they really did not understand. PCI-DSS definitely refutes the cliché, "What you don't know, can't hurt you." What a business owner does *not* know about PCI-DSS can *bankrupt* his business and likely himself as well.

The Payment Card Industry consists of companies that include Visa®, MasterCard®, American Express®, Discover®, and the Japanese Credit Bureau (JCB). PCI was created to unify the regulations of the card brands. This became necessary when the card brands created rules independently, which conflicted with one another. For example, company A mandated an action that company B prohibited.

Data Security Standards are causing confusion in the industry. The cause of the confusion, in my opinion, is how the merchant contracts are set up with the processors.

Buried in the fine print of all processing contracts is language stating that merchants must follow the rules of the card brands and that these rules may be found on their respective websites. MasterCard's rule book exceeds 500 pages and Visa's surpasses 100. Per a clause in the contract, the merchant is also bound by any new rules created by MasterCard, Visa, and PCI from the moment they are enacted. Further, the contract states that the processor may hold the merchant accountable for any fines that arise out of non-compliance. As the contract is between the Member Bank, its registered agent (processor), and the merchant, neither the sales agent who signs the merchant, nor the card brands are parties to it. Thus, the card brands assess fines to their Member Banks who will pass along the fines through the processors to the merchants who fail to comply. This is how the Member Banks recover any fines caused by merchants' actions or inactions.

In a March 2009 interview with Bank Info Security after the Heartland breach, Visa's Deputy Chief Enterprise Risk Officer Adrian Phillips was quoted as saying, "We've never seen anyone who was breached that was PCI compliant... The breaches we have seen involved a key area of non-compliance." (The full article is available at http://www. bankinfosecurity.com/articles.php?art_id=1309.) Should a breach (release of credit card numbers or customer information) occur, PCI sends auditors to do a forensic search of the methods used by the merchant. When a violation is found, the Member Bank is fined by PCI. The processor then goes after the merchant for the fees as it is allowed to do per the contract.

A YouTube® video by the Retail Solutions Providers Association (RSPA, YouTube contributor id: pcirisk) covers the case of Carla Yarborough. Carla's restaurant, Spanky's, in Athens, Georgia, had a breach due to its POS (point of sale) equipment recording restricted information. As of the time the video was made, she and her husband had paid over $110,000 in fees. The forensic investigation alone cost $10,000. The video upload was dated July 20, 2007.

The Data Security Standards are complex to cover. There are different standards for different methods of processing. Online processing requires security scans of the system on a regular basis.

Small merchants suffer most breaches because of their confusion over data security standards. Most small merchants, using a dial-up terminal, are under the false impression that they are safe from breaches. Breaches occur as a result of poor security methods. Whether it is a hacker online, an employee using a computer that stores credit card numbers to access the Internet for email or browsing, or having an employee record credit card and customer information from unlocked file cabinets, the merchant is held liable.

Not only has PCI-DSS laid down new rules for handling credit card information, but many processors have decided to use PCI as an ATM machine to extract more money from merchants. The contracts I have read limit the fees charged to merchants to Card Brand Interchange increases and fees *created or designated* by the Card Brands. However, many processors have begun charging fees for PCI compliance. Every merchant who accepts credit cards needs to fill out and fax to his processor a compliance form for each of the methods used (online, POS system or IP terminal, dial terminal, or imprinter) on a yearly basis. This step costs a processor maybe $2 each year for a clerk to take the form off the fax machine and key the entry into the computer. But some processors charge merchants a PCI fee of over $100 per year for this service. One company I work with only charges $8.95 penalty per month *until* the business faxes in the form or completes the questionnaire on the processor's website. Once the form is received, the penalty is no longer charged. (There is no PCI fee except for the penalty with some companies.)

Some processors have attempted to justify the PCI money grab by stating that they perform one scan per year for free (terminals using a phone line cannot be scanned). Others have an "insurance" program promising up to $50,000 to cover a breach. I have two problems with this "policy": first, almost every breach will exceed $50,000 in fines by far; second, since a breach makes the business non-compliant, the insurance policy might not be paid *at all*.

The point I wish to make clear to the merchant is that, in the opinion of this author, paying for PCI compliance is a complete waste of money. If you see a charge listed for PCI compliance, you might need to shop for another processor. If you are concerned about an early termination fee (ETF), consult with an attorney or your state's Attorney General to see whether your contract allows for this type of fee when the card brands have not created it (if it is not written in your contract).

There is a lot to be learned about PCI-DSS compliance. More information is available at www.PCIsecuritystandards.org.

## EFFECTIVE RATE

Your sales agent promised you this great rate to get you to sign with him (or her) and now you wonder just how good a deal you received. You wish there were an easy way to calculate your true cost of processing credit cards each month. Well, I have great news; there is! The method is called the Effective rate. The *Effective rate* is a calculation you can do each month to determine the total percentage of your credit card processing sales paid in fees.

A common pricing scam in the industry is to set the Qualified rate too low and to narrowly define it so that most transactions go into the much higher Mid-Qualified and Non-Qualified tiers. One way to check for this is simply to determine the total number of transactions and see how many dropped to a surcharged level; but that is just the beginning.

A sales agent (and processing company) desire to make a certain minimum level of profit from each merchant, much like you, the business owner, wish to make an average gross profit percentage on each sale. Unfortunately, there are many in the industry who will boost their profit by resorting to scams. In addition to the misleading Qualified rate, there are over 40 price points an agent may include in addition to the rates. The Effective rate will help you determine if you need someone to look over your contract.

To calculate the Effective rate, first determine which card brands are included on your statement. MasterCard and Visa will always be included but some now include Discover too. Now, find the total net sales (minus returns) of the card brands. The next step is to add all of the fees on the account: the "discount," "Interchange," "surcharges," "statement"... *all fees.* Also, check your bank statement for other fees that might be withdrawn from your account, which are not listed on the statement (although rare, I have seen companies that do this). Before you write down all of the fees, check several statements together (some companies carry fees into the next month to make their rates seem lower). Once compiled, key the total fees taken into a calculator, divide this by the total net sales of the card brands listed on the statement, and then multiply by 100. The result will look like this: 3.943658 or 3.94% of net sales spent on credit card processing.

*Fees/Net Sales × 100 = Effective Rate*

The Effective rate will be different every month as the card types and the amount charged will vary each month.

Statement fees and Monthly Minimum fees (if paid) will substantially increase the Effective rate for smaller-volume merchants. If you are paying a Monthly Minimum fee, do not include that fee or the statement fee if using the Effective rate to shop for a better deal.

Merchants finding an Effective rate that is 1% above their Qualified rate should investigate other processors (an Effective rate of 2.79% when the Qualified rate is 1.79%). But before you do so, review your statement for EIRF or Standard (or STD) listings on the card types (for Interchange Plus pricing) or Non-Qualified (Tiered pricing structures) items. If you find many of these listings, creating new cashier policies and eliminating these levels will save you much more than changing processors. If your current sales agent cannot help you, find one who can.

## OTHER TERMS DEFINED

### Acquirer

An *acquirer* is a Member Bank that processes credit card transactions for the merchant. MasterCard refers to the acquirer as the "Merchant's Bank" in its 2008 Annual Report. The acquirer is sometimes called the processor, but they are different. Banks like Chase®, Wells Fargo®, Bank of America® and HSBC® are some of the largest acquirers in the industry. Chase owns the processor Chase-Paymentech, but is also the acquirer for a number of sponsored, registered processors, while other acquirers only sponsor one processor. It is the acquirer who is listed on the contract as the Member Bank.

### Registered Processor

The *registered processor* is a processor who is registered with the card brands and sponsored by an acquirer. The registered processor will be the one listed on the first page of the merchant processing contract. Processors need to have strong financial backing; thus to protect its investors, a processor may be the one deciding the risk level (many banks retain this power though) of the merchant to determine whether a contract is accepted or declined.

### The Merchant Level Salesperson (MLS)

The *Merchant Level Salesperson* (MLS) is typically the sales agent who merchants see. Merchant Level Salespeople are typically ISOs (Independent Sales Offices) and independent contractors, but some are employees of the processors.

When you see what you believe to be a dishonest processor, remember, you actually dealt with its MLS or ISO who may have misrepresented the rates or costs. ISOs and independent contractors can only present themselves under the name of their registered processors (and sponsored bank) when discussing rates. When I speak to prospects about my processing company, I state that I offer consulting and training to businesses and that I offer processing through "company X." When you are presented with a contract, the name at the top is the registered processor. If the ISO or independent contractor has his own company, it typically will not be listed on the contract.

### Issuer

The *issuer* is the Member Bank that issues the credit cards to the customers. The 2008 Annual Report from MasterCard lists the issuer as the "Customer's Bank."

### The Card Brands

The *card brands* or "cardcos" (industry jargon for card brands) include Visa, MasterCard, Discover and American Express. Where this term is used in this book, I am primarily referring only to MasterCard and Visa.

### Credit Card Processing Flow

The top part of *Figure 1-1* presents credit card processing flow as viewed by MasterCard. The bottom of the figure represents how the flow actually is—notice that MasterCard does not acknowledge the registered processor and the companies that process for the Member Banks (acquirers), even though these are the entities that actually deal with merchants. In fact, MasterCard does not mention the MLS and this person is the individual who actually has personal contact with the merchant.

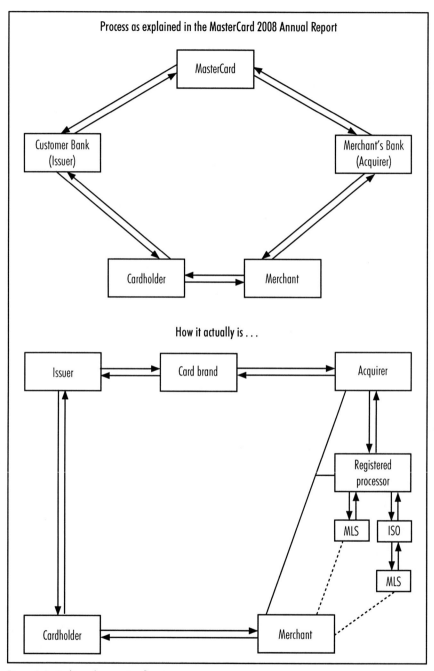

Figure 1-1. Credit card processing flow.

# TWO
# WHAT MAKES UP YOUR COSTS?

## UP-FRONT COSTS

Up-front costs in merchant processing are those costs and fees that occur at the time the contract is signed. They can include equipment costs, reprogramming fees, application fees, first and last month lease payments, gateway set-ups (for online businesses or virtual terminals), etc.

Equipment cost is the price of buying new equipment to use for processing, if needed. This would not only include the terminal, but a check reader and other accessories if included with the processing.

I have two suggestions regarding equipment. First, buy the best model you can afford so that you stay compliant and can upgrade to check or gift card services later without needing a new terminal. The second is to use the sales agent you are signing with to buy the terminal. The reason for this is to allow the agent to make some up-front money to better negotiate other costs. Buying through E-Bay® seems cheaper, but you can never be sure the terminal is new or that it will work with your setup. Plus, if the agent does not sell you the equipment, there may be a $50 to $100 fee to reprogram the terminal. Buying from the agent gets the merchant a terminal that is preprogrammed for the merchant with no downtime for reprogramming.

Small merchants should *never* have to lease a terminal. If a merchant is unable to pay cash up front, the agent or processor may accept a credit card to pay for the terminal or other costs.

If the merchant likes his current terminal and the terminal is supported by the new processor, there is no need to replace it. There may be a reprogramming fee, but not all processors and agents charge for this.

Application fees range from $50 to $200 when charged. If the fee is non-negotiable, the sales agent is likely an employee of the processor or a bank is involved. I believe that the application fee is a pure-profit fee. However, some sales agents who charge this fee use it to cover their time spent analyzing a merchant's previous statements and for other services they perform. Employee and bank referred agents need the application fee to satisfy a quota (if employee) or referral fee (if bank referred). The up-front fees and profit from equipment sales are what pay the salaries of processor or bank employees. With an independent sales agent, almost all costs are negotiable. You may be able to avoid the application fee by allowing profit elsewhere. In negotiating, if you ask for reductions in rates in exchange for paying a larger application fee, you may save money in the long term.

First and last month lease payments are often an up-front expense. Leasing companies want to have this payment before they pay commissions to the sales agent or processor because it is viewed as acceptance of the leasing contract. I only recommend leasing when a company requires multiple wireless terminals for a fleet or multiple Point of Sale (POS) systems.

The gateway is misunderstood by many business owners. Most think of a gateway as where transactions are handled in an online store. But a gateway is also used with a virtual terminal and can be used with Blackberry® devices or other select cell phones. Authorize.net® and eProcessing Network® are two common gateways. I personally prefer eProcessing Network (ePN) and use it in my business. With my ePN account, I have the ability to accept credit cards on my website. I can also access ePN's website online through a program on my desktop using an optional USB swiper or by using a special wireless unit or Bluetooth® device with my cell phone. A few years ago, I would need three or four different merchant accounts to be able to do the same things. But by using ePN and Interchange Plus pricing, I need only *one* merchant account. When I mention ePN throughout this book, I am doing so because I know the ePN products and the flexibility they offer. If you would like more information about ePN from a local sales agent, go to www.eprocessingnetwork.com.

Other up-front costs I will mention briefly are for the website and shopping cart. My company, Merchant Processing Consulting & Training LLC, only needed the virtual terminal to process an occasional credit card. If I choose to sell this book and others online through MPCT Publishing Company, I would need a custom website with an online store and shopping cart. This is in addition to a new merchant services account. While not part of the expenses of processing credit cards, the website, online store setup, shopping cart, and marketing to drive customers to the site are important costs to consider when starting an online business.

Optional up-front costs will be for other services relating to accepting credit cards including check processing or guarantee, gift card processing and printing, ATM setup, and bill pay or phone card processing.

Some agents will ask a merchant for multiple checks for their separate service partners (ATM, check processing, gift card processing, etc.). Some, like me, are registered agents of different partners and can accept one lump sum. Remember that each contract you sign is an obligation to a different company. Even if all contracts were presented by one person, the companies may not be related to one another. Signing with a credit card processor, gift card provider, check processor, ATM supplier, gateway, and leasing company means up to six different companies taking monthly payments from your account, and six different sets of contract terms and obligations.

## INTERCHANGE PLUS PRICING STRUCTURE

Many processors and sales agents refuse to offer Interchange Plus pricing structures to merchants because they say merchants cannot understand how Interchange Plus works or because it will complicate their monthly statements. I say it is because Interchange Plus pricing is straightforward and processing companies cannot play with the figures. Sales agents who truly believe business owners cannot understand or really do not want Interchange Plus pricing options are, in my opinion, patronizing the merchant. After all, the business owner **does** own and operate a business, pay employees, pay taxes, and maintain profitability.

On the flipside, some merchants are hesitant to move to Interchange Plus pricing when it is offered. But large retailers across the country pay Interchange Plus—it is how they **demand** to pay. Most processors will not allow their agents to even offer Interchange Plus pricing unless a business exceeds $25,000 a month in card processing sales. Ask the sales agent for Interchange Plus pricing if it is not being offered to you. If the agent will not offer it, find one who will. Initially understanding your statements may be difficult, but a good agent will be available to go through the statement with you until you understand it. You will definitely pay less than with the Tiered system for the vast majority of transactions.

One great advantage of Interchange Plus pricing is that the categories are listed on the statements. Many categories are "error" categories. Being able to determine how an error occurred is the key to eliminating it and saving money by staying in the lower Interchange levels.

When you go through the checkout of your grocery store and get your receipt, are you confused by the fact that it gives you a clear idea of exactly what you purchased? No.

Would you prefer reading a receipt that lists only quantities with three or four price points? Of course not. Yet this is the reason most sales agents *say* they do not offer Interchange Plus pricing. In my opinion, the real reason is they make a *lot* more money when merchants have a Tiered system.

To give you an idea of how Interchange Plus pricing works, imagine walking into your local grocery store. You see over 400 separate products (Interchange levels). Each shelf tag (see *Figure 2-1*) has three price lines that are totaled at the bottom to show you the price you will pay at checkout: wholesale (I), overhead (A), and gross profit (P).

| Visa Debit Swiped | | |
|---|---|---|
| I = | 1.0300% + | $0.15 |
| A = | 0.0925% + | $0.02 |
| P = | 0.5000% + | $0.10 |
| T = | 1.6225% + | $0.27 |
| | * $1.90 | |

| Visa Rewards I | | |
|---|---|---|
| I = | 1.6500% + | $0.10 |
| A = | 0.0925% + | $0.02 |
| P = | 0.5000% + | $0.10 |
| T = | 2.2425% + | $0.22 |
| | * $2.47 | |

| Merit III Base | | |
|---|---|---|
| I = | 1.58% + | $0.10 |
| A = | 0.11% + | $0.02 |
| P = | 0.50% + | $0.10 |
| T = | 2.19% + | $0.22 |
| | * $2.41 | |

| MC Commercial Data Rate I | | |
|---|---|---|
| I = | 2.65% + | $0.10 |
| A = | 0.11% + | $0.02 |
| P = | 0.50% + | $0.10 |
| T = | 3.26% + | $0.22 |
| | * $3.48 | |

| Merit III Debit | | |
|---|---|---|
| I = | 1.05% + | $0.15 |
| A = | 0.11% + | $0.02 |
| P = | 0.50% + | $0.10 |
| T = | 1.66% + | $0.27 |
| | * $1.93 | |

| Visa Rewards II | | |
|---|---|---|
| I = | 1.9500% + | $0.10 |
| A = | 0.0925% + | $0.02 |
| P = | 0.5000% + | $0.10 |
| T = | 2.5425% + | $0.22 |
| | * $2.77 | |

I = Interchange (dependent on type of card used and how it is processed)
A = Assessments (MasterCard = [MC] 0.11%, Visa 0.0925%)
P = Plus profit level (constant)
T = Total rate

* Cost for a $100 transaction (100 × %) + $
Rates listed in example are subject to change

Figure 2-1. Depiction of how Interchange Plus pricing correlates to the supermarket labels in the example.

You then notice while shopping around that the overhead and gross profit percentages are the same for every product you see; only the wholesale price differs from item to item. You place six total items into your cart and go to the checkout. In looking at your receipt (*Figure 2-2*), it shows two line items: the total value of items × overhead and the gross profit percentage (because these are consistent across the board). It then itemizes all of the items by product wholesale price, considering the multiples of each. Not so difficult. This represents Interchange Plus pricing.

Interchange has over 400 categories. Interchange Plus pricing has three components: Interchange, Assessments, and Gross Profit. Gross Profit, Assessments for MasterCard, and Assessments for Visa cards are consistent (within their respective brands). Wholesale price (as above) represents Interchange with one important distinction; Interchange (and Assessments) is the cost for **all** processors, regardless of their size. Returning to the example, assume that the six items represent six transactions. Your statement will show one line for profit, multiplying the percentage of profit times

| Assume that each transaction was $100 in the Six categories listed in Figure 2-1. | | | |
|---|---|---|---|
| Plus | | | |
| $600 × 0.50% | | = | $3.00 |
| 6 × $0.10 | | = | $0.60 |
| Assessment | | | |
| $300 × 0.11% | | = | $0.33 |
| $300 × 0.0925% | | = | $0.28 |
| 6 × $0.02 | | = | $0.12 |
| $100 Visa Debit Swiped | 1.03% + $0.15 | = | $1.18 |
| $100 Visa Rewards I | 1.65 + $0.10 | = | $1.75 |
| $100 Merit III Base | 1.58 + $0.10 | = | $1.68 |
| $100 MC Commercial Data Rate I | 2.65 + $0.10 | = | $2.75 |
| $100 Merit III Debit | 1.05 + $0.15 | = | $1.20 |
| $100 Visa Rewards I | 1.95 + $0.10 | = | $2.05 |
| Total Processing Cost | | | $14.94 |

Figure 2-2. Receipt for six items.

the total dollar amount of sales. Visa and MasterCard Assessments will be figured in same manner. By using Interchange pricing, the transactions will be assessed their true cost.

If you are paying 0.50% + $0.10 for the gross profit, this is equal to just $0.50 for every $100 of sale plus $0.10 for the transaction. For mostly keyed transactions, the total mark-up would be between 15% and 30%—well in line with most retailers' gross margin. Sales of $10,000 will result in card processing fees of $210–$350, depending on the card types used, with $50 in gross profit. This profit is split between the sales agent, processor and, in some cases, the person or company that referred the account. The gross profit also goes toward compensation for the processor's customer support and infrastructure, maintaining security features, as well as generating income.

## TIERED PRICING STRUCTURE

Many sales agents assume that merchants will prefer the Tiered pricing structure because it makes it easier to read the statements. The statements will be shorter, but only because Tiered pricing crams over 400 Interchange levels into three or four tiers.

Most Tiered pricing has three categories: Qualified, Mid-Qualified and Non-Qualified. Some Tiered structures add a lower rate for Qualified Debit cards and some add a special category for Rewards cards.

The term "Qualified" seems to be derived from the Interchange categories where each has defined "qualifications." The terms Qualified, Mid-Qualified and Non-Qualified are common to all processors. Unfortunately, they do not define the categories in the same way. What one processor defines as a Qualified Debit because the Interchange rate is low, another will refer to as Non-Qualified because the Interchange transaction fee is $.05 higher (remember, Interchange is listed as % + $; here, the $ is $0.15 rather than $0.10) than most credit cards.

In my explanation of Interchange Plus pricing, I asked you to imagine walking into a grocery store with over 400 different items. Now to show how Tiered pricing works, picture that same store with the same products. This time, as you walk in, you see a huge sign that says, "Everything in store 1.69% + $0.25." The good news is that the sign is accurate and the rate is decent. The bad news is that almost all of the items in this store carry surcharges in addition to the 1.69% + $0.25 (if the business was Internet or imprinter based, then all of the items would be surcharged). In this example, the merchant will get to the checkout with a surprise. His fees are much higher than expected. So he asks, "Just what items are *not* surcharged?" He is directed to a counter with just a few items. This is the sad truth of Tiered pricing.

The Tiers are set up to benefit the processor, not the merchant. At the 1.69% + $0.25, a Visa Debit card will yield a profit of about 56 basis points (bps) or (0.56%) + $0.10; a Visa consumer card will bring 5 bps + $0.15; and with surcharges, a Visa Rewards card about 120 bps + $0.15; and a Visa Business card brings about the same, 120 bps + $0.15. With only a few Interchange levels being Qualified, you can begin to see the real reason why most sales agents and processors do not offer Interchange Plus pricing. Clearly defined profit margins tend to be lower than with arbitrarily Tiered pricing.

As far as Tiered pricing statements being easier to understand, this claim just does not hold water. The Tiered statement may be easier to read, but it is not easier to understand. Using the numbers from the grocery store example (see *Figure 2-3*), the merchant will be looking at one section where all transactions are charged 1.69% times the total volume plus the number of transactions (including declines and returns) times $0.25. In the surcharges field, some processors will indicate why the item downgraded (surcharged); however, most will not. Mid-Qualified transactions will process in the example at 1.29% and Non-Qualified transactions

```
Example 1
$600 Qualified × 1.69%    = $10.14
6 × $0.25                 =  $1.50
$100 Mid-Qualified × 1.29% = $1.29
$200 Non-Qualified × 1.79% = $3.58
Total Processing Cost        $16.51
```

Rewards I is Mid-Qualified, Rewards II and MC
Commercial Data Rate fall into Non-Qualified and
many processors will not explain this in their statements.

```
Example 2
$600 Qualified × 1.69%    = $10.14
6 × $0.25                 =  $1.50
$100 Mid-Qualified × 1.29% = $1.29
$400 Non-Qualified × 1.79% = $7.16
Total Processing Cost        $20.09
```

Debit cards are also process as Non-Qualified.

Figure 2-3. Tiered pricing possibilities.

at 1.79%. These fees are totaled at the end of the statement, but are not totaled per transaction. If the processor does not clearly define why the items have been downgraded, it will be impossible to correct processing errors, which may have easy fixes.

## COMMON FEES ON STATEMENTS

Many merchants choose to select their sales agents and processors based solely on perceived costs. As discussed previously, perceptions can be only what we want to see. Just as the Qualified rate is not the only rate to look for, merchants need to realize that there are over forty (40) different price points available on a contract.

The *Statement fee* will be listed on every statement. The cost to the agent (if independent) ranges from $3–$10 per month. Some processors will include online review of statements and other features including an "account on file" and/or paper statement with the Statement fee. Agents will typically price the monthly fee at $10 to $15 per month to the merchant. You should only pay $15 per month when the fee includes online monitoring, a paper statement, and the account on file fee.

The *AVS fee* is a common fee for merchants who process online or through manual input. The Address Verification System is a fraud detection tool that compares the numbers in a street address and zip code given with the address where credit card bills are mailed. Most processors charge $0.05 for each transaction that uses AVS. Failure to use this fraud detection tool will result in higher costs.

The *Batch fee*, also known as the *Settlement fee,* is charged for transmitting credit card transactions at the end of the business day. This finalizes the authorizations for the day. It can range in cost from nothing to $0.35 per batch. For a merchant who batches every day in a 30-day month at $0.25 per day, this will add up to $7.50 per month. There is a true cost for batching, but agents do make a profit on it. Not being charged for batching might actually indicate problems with your overall pricing. In my opinion, making an honest profit on real costs is better than inflating processing costs and waiving small fees that do not amount to much.

*IVR* (Interactive Voice Response) and *Voice* (operator) approvals will cost between $1.00 and $2.00 each time they are used. These occur when the merchant chooses to call the toll-free number of the bank to verify a credit card instead of using the terminal, or when the terminal prompts the merchant to call the center.

The *Debit Access fee* is aptly named. This monthly fee is assessed for accessing the Debit Networks through the credit card processing network to enter four-digit PINs. The fee is often $5.00. PIN debits should be avoided for low-dollar transactions and sought for amounts over $50 because most processing agents set a base fee that makes them more expensive than credit card processing.

*Monthly Minimums* are normally not an issue for any but the smallest volume merchants. To find the minimum volume per month to avoid a monthly minimum fee, simply divide the amount of the fee by the lowest rate available to you. If the Monthly Minimum is $25 and the rate is 1.69%, you would divide 25 by 0.0169 to find that $1,479.29 in credit card sales is needed per month to avoid the fee. Volumes below this will result in a fee, which when added to the actual rate times the volume will be $25 (for example, $1,000 in sales at 1.69% will result in processing costs of $16.90; the monthly minimum fee would be $8.10 to take the fee to a total of $25). Some processors, however, will simply add the $25 fee on top of the processing fees for the sales volume ($16.90 + $25). Although rare, some processors require the Monthly Minimum to be their profit earned on your account.

*Wireless Activation* is a one-time fee, but it is per wireless device and applies whether the device is bought, leased, or reprogrammed.

*Wireless Access fees* are assessed monthly for airtime and range from $12.50–$30 ***per device***. If buying for a fleet, the business owner needs to shop around, negotiate, and figure that monthly cost into the return on investment (ROI) calculation. This will help to determine if the wireless cost is covered by the savings from swiping cards instead of keying them in.

*Wireless Transaction fees* are always assessed when wireless terminals are used. The fee ranges from $0.05–$0.20 per wireless transaction. This fee is in addition to the Transaction fee of the processor.

*ETF* is a much maligned fee in the industry and with good reason, in my opinion. The Early Termination fee is a one-time fee that occurs when a merchant leaves the processor before the contract expires. It can range from $195 to tens of thousands of dollars. The contract states that the merchant acknowledges that the fee is not a penalty, but is to cover the loss of profit for the processor for losing the account. If that is the case, why do many processors allow the sales agents to set the ETF or receive it upon loss of the customer? If the sales agents' promises match the results, few merchants would want to jump ship. It seems to me that the processors who lure merchants with lies and deceit tend to have the largest ETFs.

## ADDITIONAL FEES

This section discusses some of the less common fees. If you see these fees, attempt to negotiate out of the contract.

The *Authorization fee* (sometimes called a *W.A.T.S. fee*) is assessed for every authorization request. So, what is the difference between a Transaction fee and an Authorization fee? Not much, and that is the problem. The Transaction fee is accessed on transactions when approved. An Authorization fee is for the attempt to authorize. Declined transactions are only charged the Authorization fee, approved transactions face both fees. When you see both a Transaction fee and an Authorization fee, you need to put your foot down and refuse to sign the contract until one of the fees is removed.

The *Annual fee* is assessed once a year. This fee is normally a profit booster for the processor and sales agent. My opinion concerning Annual fees is much like it is on Application fees; accepting them may be good if you can get the agent to reduce your rate or other monthly fees.

*Supply Club* (or other phrasing) can cost between $10 and $20 per month for terminal supplies. For small merchants, I do not advise that they incur this monthly charge since terminal receipt tape is about $10 per package of 12 when needed. It may be "free" by participating in the Supply Club, but shipping, which is typically not included, is normally much more than the cost of the materials. If the business has multiple terminals, buying by the case through the Supply Club may be beneficial. The business owner should research supply costs before accepting this fee.

The fee I cannot understand assessing is the *Customer Service fee* (many banks also have tried them). Good customer service should be included for no cost; it is every company's cost of doing business. This fee may be included with the Statement fee, but if listed separately, negotiate it out of the contract.

The *T & E fee* is a transaction fee for a credit card being used for travel & entertainment. Try to negotiate this fee out of your contract, since interchange has already accounted for them.

An *NSF fee* is assessed for non-sufficient funds when the processor goes to withdraw money to cover processing costs from your dry account. The fee can range from $20 to as high as $50. The sales agent receives no part of this fee and will not be able to waive or negotiate it down.

The *DDA Change Form fee* is typically $25. It is for changing the DDA or demand deposit account information. In other words, there is a fee charged if you change the bank account associated with the credit card processing account. If the credit card processing application lists this fee, you may wish to pass on this processor since this type of customer service should be part of your basic contract.

*Signature Capture* actually comprises two fees, a monthly fee and a per item fee. Some new terminals allow the customer to sign directly on the terminal and the signature is transmitted as well as the card information. These terminals can be on the expensive side, and if you want to use them, the fees are normal and necessary.

## EBB AND ERR

EBB stands for *enhanced bill back* and is, in my opinion, a sneaky fee designed to hide higher fees from the business owner. The way it works is the merchant receives the credit card processing statement listing the costs for the month. However, some fees are carried over into the next monthly statement, appearing to be a recap of the previous month—until you review several statements at once. I have only seen this done once, in a case where a Detroit area cemetery was being greatly overcharged.

The enhanced bill back works because it is incredibly difficult to decipher. I can normally break down a statement visually in just a few minutes. In the case of the cemetery, I needed several statements and hours of running the numbers in different scenarios to find the formula that worked to produce the charges on the statements.

Enhanced bill back and, for that matter, any practice that allows a processor to carry over charges to the next month needs to be outlawed. EBB is used by sales agents and processors to get more profit, to confuse merchants, and make their statements so hard to decipher that most competitors will not even try.

*ERR* stands for *Enhanced Reduce Recover* and is a much friendlier enhancement than EBB, but can be misused and misunderstood. Earlier, we saw that "Qualified" transactions only brought 5 bps + $0.15 in profit using the Tiered Qualified cost of 1.69% + $0.25, while the other categories brought 56 to 120 bps + $0.15. Interchange Plus is great for almost all businesses. The only one that it is not good for is a business that swipes a vast majority of plain consumer cards (rare). ERR allows a sales agent who normally charges 50 basis points over cost to create a special rate for this category.

ERR can be problematic because instead of offering the best overall cost, sales agents can discount the one area of "Qualified" while boosting the rate in the other categories. ERR can be made to work in the right situations. My solution in most cases where the merchant has a higher percentage of swiped consumer credit cards is simply to drop my cost across the board. In other words, my standard rate is 50 bps + $0.10 over Interchange & Assessments (I&A) for key entered and Internet sites and 25–35 bps + $0.10 over I&A depending on the overall mix of swiped consumer cards.

## PCI

PCI stands for the Payment Card Industry and is comprised of the card brands.

Most business owners only know about PCI because they have seen a reference to it on their statement with an annual fee ranging from $79–$400, or a monthly fee ranging from $4.95–$19.99.

PCI fees are simply a money grab by the processors who have instituted them (not all have). Yes, there is a cost to the processors to become compliant with the new directives. And, yes, there is a cost to handle and process the required forms from merchants. But, as the credit card processing industry has been telling merchants who complain about the cost of processing credit cards, "That is the cost of doing business."

MasterCard and Visa both have specific rules prohibiting merchants from tacking on fees or surcharges to customers who use their credit cards. So, why are processors permitted to tack on PCI fees?

The fees charged have greatly surpassed the expense of following the PCI-DSS (Payment Card Industry-Data Security Standards). The processors claim that the fees will help cover potential breaches and provide insurance for merchants who have a breach. However, a single incident involving a single customer's credit card number can surpass the complete amount of insurance offered by the processor.

There are many in the industry who wonder what liability those processors who assess PCI fees might face if a merchant of theirs has a security breach. The processor is taking fees and not helping the merchant to become compliant. Before you sign a processing contract, ask the processor to explain, *in writing*, how this PCI fee protects you.

## LEASED EQUIPMENT

Merchants considering leasing need to consider all of their options. Few terminals cost more than $1,000; most are under $700. If your sales agent or processor accepts credit cards, it will cost far less to simply purchase the terminal.

Many sales agents tout tax advantages to merchants for leasing terminals. To supply a fleet or a chain, yes. Leasing a single terminal will yield a marginal tax break; however, the merchant ends up paying about five times the retail cost over four years.

Two years ago, a hot tub sales and service company signed up with a new processor and leased a Nurit® 2085 for $100/month over 4 years ($4,800) and still will never own the equipment. The business owner could not believe that the retail cost for this terminal, brand new, was under $300. Using a mailing I have received from one processor, I estimate that the sales agent made almost $3,500 on the equipment lease alone. What galls me are the other details in this case—most of her credit sales came from sales in the field. To further trick her, the agent lowered her Qualified rate and greatly increased her Non-Qualified rate (keyed into terminal). This raised her costs a great deal. A bad agent not only can cost a merchant through an expensive lease but can compound the situation by writing a contract that looks good but has high hidden costs.

Although some leasing companies now have a $50/month limit on terminals like this, I still consider leasing a single terminal to be a bad investment.

If you are looking for several Point of Sale cash register systems or wireless terminals for a fleet, leasing can make sense. Before you sign, shop around and ask your CPA for advice.

## "FREE" TERMINALS

In the eyes of a business owner, a free terminal is a terminal she receives free and can keep with no strings attached. This is most often not what the processor is offering. There are strings attached and you will not own it. For this reason, the offer processors and some sales agents make must be described as a "free" (notice the quotes) terminal. The quotes work as an asterisk, meaning the merchant needs to read the fine print.

To give away a "free" terminal, a sales agent needs to charge a minimum batch fee (typically $0.35), monthly minimum ($25–$35), and an annual fee. The agent will also face limits on what he can offer on processing costs. This means that the merchant is spending more money on processing costs by accepting a "free" terminal. So much for free!

"Free" terminals are most often used by new agents in the industry. Several large processors hire scores of new people with no industry experience and then give them a script and access to "free" terminals. Instead of trying to establish a long-term relationship with a merchant, the newbie (inexperienced sales agent) just gets the merchant to sign by offering the "free" terminal. The newbie is only paid $200 for each contract plus a small monthly residual based on the merchant's sales volume. There is high turnover of these new agents and most merchants that accept the "free" terminal soon find they have no local agent, only a toll-free number to call for customer service.

If you are using a "free" terminal and decide to turn it in and replace it by buying a new terminal to lower your rates, use caution. Most contracts with a "free" terminal require that the unit must be returned to the processor in the original box, in great condition, within 10 days of terminating the processing contract. Failure to do so will result in your checking account being hit for the value listed in the "free" terminal agreement, which is typically 50–100% higher than the customary retail price of the unit. So, for a terminal that customarily costs $500 retail, the "free" terminal contract will typically list its value at $750–$1,000.

## CHARGEBACKS, HOLDS, AND RESERVE ACCOUNTS

Chargebacks, Holds and Reserve Accounts are more closely related than many people realize. It is the possibility of Chargebacks that will result in Holds and Reserve Accounts put in place by the processing company to protect its interests.

## Chargebacks

*Chargebacks* are the forced return of a credit card purchase. This could be due to a complaint from your customer, fraud, or suspected fraud.

Complaints from a customer should be easy for you, the merchant, to control. Make sure that your return policy is clear and prominent on your website and/or on every receipt or invoice. If you provide a service or product with "Satisfaction Guaranteed" you will need to document all of the steps required to remedy the issue (for a Chargeback request on a specified circumstance). It may be prudent to create a statement above the customer signature line that says something like, "My signature confirms work (or product) was performed to my satisfaction." Please consult an attorney to create the proper wording and placement.

When products are shipped to a customer, it is in your best interest to use a carrier who requires a signature on delivery. This is one sure way to fight a complaint of fraudulent use of a credit card. Another is to use AVS (the Address Verification System) every single time and require the customer to give the address that will match his billing address or, if previously arranged, shipping address that the issuer of the credit card has in its database.

When you receive notification that a customer is contesting a sale, you must act upon the retrieval request (a request for supporting documentation) immediately. Once the retrieval request is issued, you have a limited time to locate all supporting documents and either fax or overnight ship copies (you may wish to do both) to your processor. In criminal matters, an individual must be considered innocent until proven guilty. In the Chargeback request, the customer is presumed to be wronged until you prove that you not only provided your product or service, but followed the guidelines of the card brands. Being late with documentation will have the same result as not replying at all; you will lose and cannot contest the Chargeback, and money will be pulled from your account.

Once you have been notified of a Chargeback, *do not* issue a return on that item. The Chargeback will withdraw the funds; if you issue a return, the customer may be credited twice.

Chargeback and Retrieval fees may be negotiated on your contract. Typical fees are $15–$20 for retrieval (the request for documentation) plus $20–$35 if charged back (removing the funds from your account). Business owners, managers and cashiers must be fully trained in fraud prevention and proper credit card processing procedures. Visa has some excellent training materials available through their website, www.Visa.com.

The first two Chargeback types (satisfaction and contesting validity of the charge) are typically initiated by the customer calling the issuing bank of the credit (or debit) card. The issuer of the card then sends a request to the merchant's processor via the card brand. The processor then contacts the merchant by way of a retrieval request. The issuer typically has final say (American Express will more often side with the cardholder). If the card issuer is not convinced by the merchant's documentation, it will initiate a Chargeback against the processor, who in turn will withdraw funds plus fees from the merchant's bank account.

In suspected fraud cases, the card issuer starts the process without the cardholder. This may be in cases where it appears the card is being swiped in multiple locations or where there is other apparent fraudulent behavior. The issuer initiates the Chargeback because waiting for a complaint from the cardholder could expose it to higher levels of fraud.

Consult with an attorney to see if it is legal to add language for service providers to state to the effect, "Failure to pay as agreed will result in collection of 150% (including reasonable collection or legal fees) of the original amount charged." The card brands may have the right to issue Chargebacks in their own discretion, but it is my opinion that when the business lives up to its end of the deal (giving the agreed to service or product), it should be paid as the cardholder agreed. If a Chargeback is processed and the merchant loses payment, the merchant still has the legal right to pursue payment. With the provision above, perhaps the merchant could pay 33% in collection fees and still collect 100% of amount owed. Just be sure the 150% payment comes in the form of a money order or cash. Do not use a credit card to recover fees or you risk losing the ability to accept credit cards. It is in violation of card brand rules to use a credit card to recover an amount that was charged back.

### Holds

A *Hold* will occur when the processor processes a credit card sale, but withholds the funds. Most often the Hold will occur as a result of processing a sale far higher than expected or when the volume of sales exceeds the monthly sales expected. These caps are determined on your contract when the sales agent enters the average sale and the volume you expect to process. The Hold is usually resolved by faxing the invoice to the processor's underwriting department to show it is legitimate.

Exceeding monthly sales can be more difficult to resolve. One heating and cooling company near Ann Arbor, Michigan signed up with a processor from California in May of 2004. (The numbers used in the following example are approximate only.) The business owner told the processor on the application that he expected to process $50,000 per month. The processor's underwriting department approved the business for about $70,000 per month. Well, there was near record heat in July and August that year and the business actually processed about $120,000 in the month of July alone. The business owner faxed the additional information, but was warned to limit credit card sales. After the business hit $150,000 in August, it was abruptly cut off by the processor.

Now I would have expected the processor's underwriting department to review things like orders for new equipment, talk to the customers of the business who were paying $30K apiece for commercial services, or review the company's bank accounts. The processor just decided the business was too risky and dropped it on the spot. Eventually, the company recovered its funds. To prevent something like this from happening to you, view the processor as a partner. Advise the processor when your needs change. If your sales in one season are much higher, show your new processor this so that seasonal changes are expected. Holds occur because the processor is taken by surprise and it expects a Chargeback to be initiated. The processor will hold onto funds when it anticipates a Chargeback from the issuer. If the merchant should go out of business and the issuer files a Chargeback, and the processor did not hold the funds, the processor would be on the hook for the money. Holds can be prevented by making sure your sales agent lists the true nature of your business and expected sales volume so that the processor's underwriting department can take this into account.

### Reserve Accounts

*Reserve Accounts* are like Holds, but they are rolling (consistent) and can be a set percentage of sales. Where Holds are the result of a specific action that surprises the processor, Reserve Accounts are based upon the type of business, percentage of Chargebacks expected for the industry, or concern of future Chargebacks (this may depend on the business owner's personal credit score). If a company goes out of business, then the processor is on the hook for any Chargebacks. To prevent such losses, the processor will use its right to start a Reserve Account for the merchant. This can be accomplished by requiring the merchant to send in a check initially or by withholding a set amount of card sales each month (or even each day).

Reserve Accounts are problematic for merchants though. They can cause financial hardships, especially for those with lower profit margins. The Reserve Account is held by the processor to cover possible Chargebacks until several months after the merchant either goes out of business or leaves the processor. Reserve Accounts may be dependent on the business type, sudden surges in sales (it is a growing trend that some companies going under will inflate sales through fraud before they close), or the percentage of Chargebacks to sales (for some processors, Chargebacks in the 0.5%–1% range require Reserve Accounts).

The bigger problem for merchants is at the time of this writing being decided in the Federal courts. In the bankruptcy trial of a major credit card processor (Cynergy), the problem is whether the Reserve Account can be held to be the property of Cynergy, as non-secured debt, or whether it is the property of the merchant held in trust by the processor. If it is held to be the property of Cynergy, merchants lose. If it is ruled to be non-secured debt, the merchant will lose again. If it is found to be "held in trust," who knows what will happen. No matter what the judge in the Cynergy case decides, the question will remain as other processors enter the bankruptcy process.

# THREE
# WHAT ARE YOU PAYING FOR?

## LEVEL OF SERVICE

Like many movie goers, I laughed at the scene in the hit movie, "Back to the Future" (Universal Pictures®, 1985), when the car pulled up to the 1955 Texaco® gas station and four guys ran to the car to clean the windows, check the oil, and pump the gas. I had never seen such service. (Later, I was astounded to discover that my parents had not only seen that kind of service, but actually expected it.) In 2009, we are now paying roughly 10 times the cost per gallon for gas and the only time we even see one person is if we need to enter the store. Not only does no one check the tire pressure, but if you want air, you pay extra for it.

My manager at Woolworth in the early nineties wrote in my annual review that I "spent too much time on customer service." His thought was that it was basically a "self-serve" retail store. "We either have the item or we don't." Interestingly enough, by January of 1994, my store and thousands of others closed their doors in the first round of closings before the historic chain closed all of its namesake stores.

In just 40 years, we went from the expectation of great service no matter what you pay, to no service and, ultimately, no customers at so-called self-serve, five-and-dime stores.

Where do you like to shop? What basic services do you require where you spend your money?

Almost *every* customer requires some basic level of service. Some stores and name plates are famous for their fantastic customer service and for their high prices. While going through the Dale Carnegie Sales Advantage™ training, I decided to test a theory on pricing structure. To the next person that brought up price, I would ask a pricing question. I had always hated pricing objections and had to try something new. I asked the gentleman what kind of car he drove. He proudly pointed to a new Mercedes-Benz® parked next to his office. I asked why that particular car was chosen as opposed to other brands. I was told that the dealership picks up his car every time he needs service. The man also mentioned the quality he perceived and the status symbol of the car. Consider the stores you visit, expecting to pay a higher price for outstanding customer service.

Clover's Collision and Mechanical Repair in Eastpointe, Michigan has a secret to gaining and keeping business. It is the customer service the small shop provides. Its oil changes and other services are priced about same as the competition. But the service is what differentiates it—every car is washed and vacuumed before delivery and company employees pick up and drop off cars for customers. Owners Diane and Mike believe a little service goes a long way.

Now, you may be thinking, "What in the world does any of this have to do with credit card processing or my business?"

The answer is simple. Consider how your business services customers and your pricing for what you offer. You do not ever claim to be the cheapest. Potential customers see the "cheapest" as no frills. They think you will not offer guarantees, back your work, or provide needed services. It is demonstrated time and again that customers want service and quality and are willing to pay more to get it. If your business competes solely on price, how do you defend yourself when a competitor undercuts your price? Everything else being equal, best price wins. A smart business owner provides services that her competitors cannot or will not, so price alone will not take the client from her.

The business owner needs to view her credit card processor in the same way. There are plenty of companies and agents who offer credit card processing. If the agent offers no special services, why do business at *any* cost? Basic services should mean lower cost. For a fair cost, expect good personal service from the agent. If paying a premium cost, expect premium personal service.

What services do you want from your processor? You need to know this before you even set up the appointment. This is why agent references are so important. The processing contract supersedes everything the sales agent says or puts into writing; so go with the agent that you know does what he says.

Services that good agents commonly offer merchants include first-line customer support (this means the merchant calls the agent first with questions on processing), tape for machines, monthly statement review, the agent's cell phone number and email address, complete training on processing (ask the agent if he has read the rules from the card brands), teaching the merchant how to read the statement, and making suggestions for the business.

Richard Pausch owns 12 Coffee News franchises in Oakland County, Michigan. I consult with him on a regular basis. I have had occasion to go to his home to help him and his wife Tammy set up recurring payments. As often as needed, I will continue to go until they are comfortable with the process. It was not pricing that got this account, although my pricing was lower. I got the account because I gave him tips to help his business, and I continue to assist him with his processing and PCI requirements.

## ADDITIONAL SALES

Why do so many merchants accept credit cards? To gain additional sales. Many customers look for the card brand logos on the door. If not there, they will shop elsewhere. Not only are sales increased by simply accepting credit cards, but impulse buying can drive sales even higher.

Consider a customer looking to buy a computer. Typically, if using cash or check, the computer purchased will be simple—only what is seen as being needed. If using a credit card, and especially a credit card with Rewards points, a customer will be more likely to look at computers with "more bells and whistles." He might still purchase on perceived needs alone, but he will more likely add on more RAM, a larger hard drive, a larger screen, and more years of coverage on the warranty. If not using a credit card, the customer still buys what he needs, but getting rewards through spending on a credit card will mean he might spend more money.

Business owners need to take a look at their total sales picture. If the business has a POS (Point of Sale) system, look up the higher-margin items to determine if customers used credit or cash (for a small business, this can be done by pulling up all tickets with a specific SKU). I recall a Visa survey a few years ago, which estimated that a merchant's overall sales are 56% higher when he accepts credit cards. Part of this may well be due to the ability to up-sell customers (MasterCard projects 20%–30% up-sell) to items with a higher margin and thus, more profit.

In negotiating the best rate for the best service in your merchant processing contract, it is important to remember that the fees you pay for processing are bringing you the opportunity to increase your sales and your gross margin. This can be done not only by adding those customers who prefer to use credit cards, but by the ability to up-sell those customers to what they want over just what they need.

## A LOAN

"What do you mean it's a loan?" Many business owners do not understand that the money being received is being loaned to them. Yes, it is a loan to the business. Even though the charge will appear on the consumers' statements and will add to the debt of the consumer (if not paid at month end), the card brands still consider the monies to be a loan to the merchant. When thinking about this, consider that a merchant must usually personally guarantee his account on the application with the processor, just like you would a personal loan. Further, consider that Chargebacks can occur when the product or service is not as the merchant promised. The fact that the processor demands a personal guarantee and has the ability to Chargeback shows that the merchant has responsibility for the money charged until the customer is satisfied with the transaction.

## A TRANSFER OF FUNDS

If simply moving money from point A to point B, Interchange rates would be much lower and thus so would the percentages being paid for credit card fees by the merchant. However, fees are at their current levels due to risk. There is the risk of the consumer not paying, and the risk of a business folding, leaving customers without a way to enforce guarantees.

Congress is considering tinkering with Interchange due to a mistaken belief that the card brands just move the money from the consumer's account to the merchant's account. But Congress fails to realize just what happens when the customer's card is swiped in the terminal. The amount available on a consumer's card is not available cash, but available credit. When the terminal batches, the card issuers are creating money and placing that money through a vast computer network into the merchant's checking account. It is not simply moving cash.

## FRAUD PREVENTION TOOLS

Interchange and Assessment fees charged on every credit card transaction also pay for the ever-expanding fraud prevention tools, which are necessary to keep up with changes in technology and to stay ahead of the criminal mind.

Take out a debit or a credit card and look at it. I will be referencing a MasterCard branded debit card issued by a bank or credit union. Current fraud detection tools on credit cards include: the hologram on the face of the card, the first four numbers on the front under the imprint, the logo of the card brand, and the appearance of how the numbers are laid out. This is just the front of the card. On the back of the card, there is the cardholder's signature (or section reading "void" if erased) with seven numbers in the field on the card I am referencing. The first four are the same as the last four numbers on the card. A security code of three numbers is behind it. This code is typed into the computer or terminal to prove that the person using the card had it in their possession.

Online tools such as Verified by Visa and MasterCard's Secure Code are easy to sign up for and more online businesses are accepting them. These tools provide the cardholder the ability to set a personalized password to use on an online site to verify his identity.

A common request when paying online or when keying into a terminal is AVS information. This information is the numbers of the street address and the zip code of the cardholder. The Address Verification System verifies that it is the correct billing address or authorized shipping location and thus it is safe to ship. This one system (AVS) makes online stores possible. Just shipping to wherever a caller or online shopper asks is a sure way to receive multiple Chargebacks for fraudulent use, likely shutting down a site.

# FOUR
# CARD BRAND RULES AND
# FRAUD AND ERROR PREVENTION

## VISA® POINT-OF-SALE RULES AND OTHER GUIDES

Visa offers a "Point-of-Sale Reminder Card" (Item Number VRM 09.08.07) for cashiers to use. This guide is simply a tri-fold brochure. It explains how to detect counterfeit cards. The rules of processing a sale are simple: swipe the card, enter the dollar amount, check the authorization response, and take appropriate action (as listed in the guide) comparing the signature on the card to the sales receipt (reference the guide for more information). The credit card is to be kept in the cashier's hand throughout the process. How many of you have seen this done properly? I rarely do.

The procedure I teach merchants who use terminals is based on the Visa guide. Swipe the card, key the last four numbers into the terminal at the prompt (your sales agent can set up a terminal to request this), key in the dollar amount, take just a few seconds to verify that the card is genuine using the Visa POS Guide (check the hologram, that there are evenly spaced and in-line numbers on the front of the card, a signature is on the back of card, the first number matches the brand, 3=AMEX, 4=Visa, 5=MasterCard, 6=Discover), and then when the receipt prints, compare the signature on the card against the signature on the receipt.

Many people do not want to sign their credit cards, believing that signing invites fraud. Ignorant of the rules, many merchants allow this. Do not be one of those merchants. If the card is unsigned, it is an ***invalid*** card as defined by the card brands. Accepting an invalid card can mean an automatic Chargeback and jeopardizes your ability to continue accepting cards. You, as a business owner, will say you do not want to lose business by enforcing this rule. However, if you are not requiring a *signed* credit card, you are potentially giving away merchandise. The next time a customer presents an unsigned card for payment, ask yourself if you are willing to simply give away the purchase to the customer; that may just be what you are doing.

The card brands prohibit requiring an ID to complete a sale, unless a card is unsigned and is being signed in your presence. If a card remains unsigned, it is not to be accepted. Requiring ID can be dangerous because cashiers have no training in spotting false IDs. If thieves are getting to the point of creating counterfeit credit cards with all of their security features, do you really think they cannot create a convincing driver's license? Cashiers simply give a glance—if the name on the card matches the name on the ID, it passes. But what if the man using the card does not fit same description on the ID or even resemble the picture? Cashiers simply do not have the expertise. Plus, lines would increase dramatically as cashiers take the time to review IDs properly.

Other helpful materials listed in the Visa USA Merchant Catalog (VRM 07.24.06) and available on the Visa website include:

- VRM 08.02.06 "Rules for Visa Merchants: Card Acceptance and Chargeback Management Guidelines"*;
- VRM 02.01.05 "What You Should Know About the Visa Cardholder Information Security Program (CISP)";
- VRM 06.02.06 "Better Signed than Sorry" (Pad of 50)*;
- VRM 05.03.05 "Improve Profitability: Eliminate Illegible Sales Drafts"*;
- VRM 10.02.05 "It Pays to Swipe the Stripe"*;

- VRM 06.04.05 "Five Simple Steps to Safer Key-Entered Transactions"*;

- VRM 08.17.06 "Card Acceptance and Fraud Awareness for Merchants: Fraud Factor," a DVD Training Video*; and

- VRM 09.08.05 "Merchant Fraud Awareness Training"*—a turnkey training CD to help train merchants and employees on fraud prevention, it features a PowerPoint® presentation and a Q&A guide.

These are only a few of the products Visa has to help train merchants. Items with an * have a cost and the merchant will need to pay for shipping for any of the items, whether they have a cost or not. Most of the materials are also available free of charge in PDF format at www.Visa.com/merchants.

## COMMON PROCESSING OR PROCEDURAL ERRORS

The following discussion addresses the top 25 processing or procedural errors that can cost business owners money, not just in processing fees, but in fines from the card brands and loss of customers.

1. *Accepting an unsigned credit card for payment.* Most businesses allow this as a part of their policy for customer satisfaction. Per the credit card companies (stated in writing on the back of every card), a credit card must be signed to be considered valid. Cardholders mistakenly believe that an unsigned card limits their liability if the card is stolen. If a stolen card is used and the Issuer can prove that the card was not signed, the cardholder may be responsible for all charges for not following the agreement with the credit card issuer. A prepaid legal services company had advised its customers not to sign their cards to prevent identity theft. This advice is ***wrong***. The limit of cardholder liability is $50 when the rules are followed and the card

is signed. However, if the card is unsigned, there is no limit to the liability of the cardholder.

Most people who do not sign their cards write "check ID" or "CID" or "See ID" in the signature field. This is not acceptable. Consider that most cashiers do not ask for ID, regardless of this instruction. The credit card brands prohibit merchants from checking IDs (see Visa's Card Acceptance Guide under the topic "Requesting Cardholder ID," and page 122 of MasterCard Rules, Entire Manual update of May 2008, section 5.6.3) as a condition of using their cards. The safeguard is to match the cardholder's signature on the card with the signature on the receipt.

If a man finds a credit card in the street, unsigned in the name of *John Q. Public*, all he needs to do is sign this name on the back of the card and bingo, the signatures will match every time.

Under the rules, when presented with an unsigned card, a cashier must: 1) Ask for positive ID; 2) Make sure the card is signed in front of the cashier; and 3) Verify that the signature matches the one on the ID presented.

Accepting an unsigned card violates your merchant processing contract. Before you think of allowing a customer to use an invalid card, consider these two things: 1) Would I be willing to give my product away plus $25 each time I do this? (A Chargeback takes away the charge and your processor bills you for each Chargeback request), and 2) If you had your ID and credit card stolen, wouldn't you want a store to do its due diligence to protect you?

2. *Failing to compare the signature on the back of the card with the signature on the receipt.* This is a simple, but often overlooked thing. It can be expensive to your business. Imagine going to a computer store to get a

new laptop. You decide to be cute at the checkout and sign *Ronald Duck* on the receipt. The cashier smiles and says, "Have a nice day." You get home and decide you do not want to pay for your purchase. You call your credit card company and contest the charge. The company pulls the receipt and since the cashier did not verify your signature, your reward is the laptop. Sound extreme? Unfortunately, this happens every day. Failure of your employees to verify signatures can cost you thousands.

Other things to verify are the name and initials on the card. Be sure your customer is the cardholder named on the card—not his child, sibling, spouse, or parent. Failure to verify is akin to literally giving away your product or service.

3. *Failing to imprint card. It is in your best interest to get an imprint of the credit card every time.* Some credit card processors may tell you that if you swipe a card, it is not necessary to get an imprint. Depending on the price of your product or service, the choice is yours.

   With the current technology of identity thieves, getting an imprint can prove that you saw the real card. There is technology in place that allows thieves to place stolen data in the magnetic stripe of another card. By getting an imprint, comparing signatures, and verifying that the embossed name matches the signature on the card and on the receipt, you can protect your company against staggering losses.

   Remember though, that you need to securely store the card imprints to remain in compliance with PCI-DSS (Payment Card Industry-Data Security Standards) regulations.

4. *Recording or circling anything on the credit card terminal receipt.* Most credit card terminal tapes are thermal, and they can fade with time. Since they need

to be photocopied and faxed for Chargeback requests, writing or circling anything can distort the original image and result in an unreadable receipt, which will cause you to lose the Chargeback. Further, receipts must be held for at least three years should the merchant be asked for documentation.

5., 6. *Recording the three-digit security code (at all) or the cardholder's address on the imprint.* You may key the code on phone sales, or collect it for online sales. However, you may not record this number. With this three-digit number, the credit card number, expiration date, and address, thieves have everything they need to steal an identity. Because of this, if any credit card company finds you have retained the security code or if you have written the cardholder's address on the imprint, it may fine you $100,000 per violation to a maximum of $500,000 for each type. This means that if you write the security code and the cardholder's address on the imprint, you may be fined $200,000 per slip up to a maximum of $1,000,000. Identity theft costs the credit card companies billions of dollars each year. They take the issue of security seriously, so should you.

7. *Failing to store customer information securely.* You need to limit access to your customers' information. If you release a customer's information (or if it is stolen from you), you can be liable in court for damages. Further, you may face PCI-DSS (Payment Card Industry-Data Security Standards) sanctions.

8. *Failing to verify the last four numbers on the credit card.* It is possible for thieves to reprogram the magnetic stripes on cards. Comparing the last four numbers is needed to verify that the swiped card information matches the imprinted information. Better yet, a business owner can have terminals programmed to require that these numbers are keyed in.

9. *Failing to review the expiration date on the credit card.* With current technology, there are only two common instances of finding issues with expiration dates. One is when the number is stored for recurring payments and the second is when the stripe has been reprogrammed. In the case of recurring payments, an incorrect expiration date will result in the card being declined and this situation needs to be corrected as soon as possible. If it is a stripe that has been reprogrammed, this will result in a loss prevention and fraud problem.

10. *Failing to verify shipping address.* The AVS (Address Verification System) is used to advise merchants whether the shipping address requested appears in the customer's file with the bank. If a merchant receives the message, "approved, no match," do not ship the product. This means that the card is approved but the address does not match. The best solution is to contact the cardholder and have him call his card issuer and add the shipping address to his record or verify that the address is the location where the credit card bill is sent each month. Shipping anyway is equivalent to giving away products for free.

11. *Failing to capture credit card information on a secure web page.* I was checking the web page of a potential client when I found there was no "padlock" image on the page to signify that it was a secured page. Upon further examination, I found a simple form that basically emailed the information to the owner who then hand-keyed it at the store. The store owner did not want to pay for the Secure Socket Layer (SSL) protection page or for the type of account that an online store needs.

Without the SSL, this florist store was open to massive losses because no security page means there is no protection of information. To make matters worse, she was receiving card numbers and customer information as email.

SSL and other forms of encryption can seem expensive. Broadcasting your customers' credit card numbers, addresses, and other personal information over the Internet is expensive in many ways. Releasing customer information can cost you your business; and if the business is not properly incorporated or insured, your home(s), car(s), and bank account(s) too.

12. *Setting a minimum purchase requirement to use a credit card.* Some party stores are really getting squeezed these days. To cut their credit card processing costs, many decide to set a minimum purchase level for customers to use a credit card. This is a bad idea.

If business owners think, "my store, my rules," they may be in for a nasty surprise. Every merchant processing contract states clearly that business owners must comply with the guidelines of MasterCard and Visa. They are even instructed in the contract where to find these guidelines. Credit card issuers tell their customers (the cardholders) that they can use their credit cards like cash. So, clearly stated in the guidelines of both companies, is the rule that there can be no minimum purchase requirement.

A complaint from a customer to their issuer will get the merchant a $25 Chargeback fee and possibly the return of the full amount of the purchase from the merchant's account. Fines by MasterCard and Visa for a first offense are up to $20,000 taken right from merchant's account without previous notice from their processor. The reason it is taken by the processor is that the card brands will automatically assign the fine to the processor, who then passes it on to the merchant. The merchant processing contract allows the processor to pass any fine due to the merchant's action onto the merchant.

Most businesses are simply trying to increase their profit margins. One suggestion is to look at the costs for a $1 transaction. With a decent processor, a $1 transaction will cost $0.22–$0.27 ($0.20–$0.25 transaction fee, plus $0.02 with a Qualified rate under 2%). If you pay more than that, get an evaluation of your statement. Another suggestion is to figure what percentage of your customers use credit cards and then create a calculation to build credit card fees into your prices like you do with other overhead. A simple example would be to calculate your effective rate (all costs on your statement divided by the Visa and MasterCard sales, then multiplied by 100), for example, 3.00%. Now, consider the percentage of people using credit cards, say this is one-third of all customers. Creating a simplified equation, 3% effective rate times 1/3 of customers, means you can raise your prices by 1% and you have built your credit card fees into your prices. One thing I recommend is to raise your prices across the board by 5%. This will allow the business to make more money, regardless of how the customer chooses to pay for his purchase. It is prudent to review your pricing structure at least yearly, taking into consideration all of your overhead costs, not just processing costs. For further questions on cost accounting, find a good accounting professional.

With Interchange Plus pricing, there are Interchange levels that deal with small ticket purchases at a lower rate. You can certainly post a sign that requests customers to use credit cards only for larger purchases. Most people will be accommodating. But if a jogger just wants a bottle of water, you cannot require a higher purchase amount.

13. *Setting a maximum purchase amount on a credit card.* Like minimum charges, maximums are also banned in the bank card guidelines.

Let's say you own an RV dealership. You add credit card processing to be used for your parts counter, but you do not restrict its usage to parts (perhaps by creating a separate company solely for parts). A rich man walks in and places his bank card on the table for a $200,000 motor home.

Just remember, any chance you have to limit the sales, if you wish to, depends on the business setup and the SIC codes listed on your credit card processing application. If your business is "John Smith RVs and Parts" and the business description says it is an RV dealership and also sells parts, you cannot limit the sale. But by the same token, if you limit the scope by stating that you will only sell RV parts and then you want to accept a card in bad times for an RV, you would be required to set up a second account or to redo the business set up and merchant processing account.

In this business climate, I would advise setting up as "Dealership and Parts," and be happy to pay up to $7,000 in fees for a $200,000 sale, depending, of course, on the margin.

14. *Adding a surcharge for credit card customers.* A surcharge is related to minimums and maximums, but it is slightly different. It is defined as adding a flat fee or a percentage of the sale for using a credit card. Some apartment complexes are trying it as well as auto repair and towing companies. Even gas stations are instituting surcharges now. The fee is a blatant attempt to discourage a cardholder from using his card because the merchant does not want to pay the fees for accepting the card.

In most cases, the merchant just needs to figure the charges into his pricing structure like everything else. Could you imagine having to pay your favorite big box retailer $5 when you walk in so that the manager will turn on the lights? Of course not! Companies have teams of accountants that build overhead into the price of each product.

According to Visa, accepting credit cards will help a company increase sales up to 56% on average over other companies who do not accept them. It helps to gain and keep customers by:

- showing customers that you are a reputable business;
- giving protections to customers that a "guarantee" cannot;
- giving customers a choice of payment types;
- allowing customers to make payments over time while giving the business owner all of the money now (minus processing fees); and
- for apartment complexes, it helps tenants pay on time, saving them late fees and increasing the percentage of on-time payments.

If you choose, the guidelines do allow businesses to offer cash discounts. The risk to businesses is figuring the correct amount of the discount. Suppose you raise your prices from $100 to $103 because you pay 3% in credit card processing fees. If you then offer 3% off for a cash purchase, you must remember that 3% off of $103 is only $99.91, so you would actually be losing money by offering a cash discount. Most businesses in this scenario could simply raise prices to $105 and not offer a cash discount at all. The cost of the card processing is now built into price, your profit margin increases, and customers are no longer annoyed at an extra fee.

Your customers do not see an itemized breakdown for other overhead. Just remember that the card logos on the door and in your ads are bringing in new business. Do not push customers away now by adding extra surcharges. People usually expect to pay more for quality and greater variety of options.

Consider home inspectors in the following example. In the Detroit area, their standard fee is $300. But if they accepted credit cards and advertised that fact to the lenders who use them and on their websites, they could now charge $325 to $350 because they are now unique in their market. It is estimated that fewer than 3% of home inspectors in this area take credit cards, but if they did, lenders could refer more people by offering the credit card option as payment. Further, the inspectors' websites could bring in calls (and purchases of their services) from out-of-state lenders requesting drive-by reports. Even if paying 5% in credit card processing fees, the inspectors would be increasing their profit margins by $10–$35 on each purchase. With the way gas is increasing in price, being able to dictate prices in a competitive market can greatly help the bottom line of a business.

15. *Improper tips processing.* If you own a beauty salon, each statement brings confusion. You signed up with a promise of 1.69%–1.84%, yet you see that most of your sales are being heavily surcharged with listings like EIRF on your statement, and some processors will not tell you the reason.

    EIRF stands for Electronic Interchange Reimbursement Fee and it likely means that the way you are processing your transactions is increasing your fraud risk. The most common cause is tips processing.

    Consider a good client who has a tab of $100. She hands you her card, you enter $100, and it is approved. She adds a $50 tip; after all, she loves your work. You file the receipt with the others and then move on to the next client. That night you are keying in the tips. That

$50 tip means you are processing the card for $150, not the $100 for which you received the authorization. Tip variances allowed by the card brands range from 15%–25%. A 50% tip triggers the transaction to downgrade from Qualified (swiped, and you followed the rules) to Non-Qualified (higher risk, potential fraudulent charge). This downgrade carries a surcharge of 1.25%–2.75% or more (depending on the processor), making that 1.69%–1.84% rate now 2.94%–4.59%.

The fix is easy. Newer Verifone® terminals print a cash receipt by pressing the #9 key and entering the sale amount. The customer fills in the tip and hands the slip and the card to the cashier who enters the sale and tip on separate prompts. Now, the authorization slip shows the purchase amount and the tip preprinted with the customer's signature. The authorization is for the complete price of $150. This eliminates the time-consuming process of manually entering tips. Further, it virtually eliminates Chargebacks that might occur from human error when the cardholder forgets to write in the tip on her copy of the receipt and later questions the difference on the credit card statement.

16. *Failing to watch for skimming devices.* Thieves pay some employees to carry and return to them tiny little devices called skimmers. Business owners, managers, and customers need to watch sales transactions. If a card is being swiped in two places to complete a sale, there is a skimmer likely in use.

   A skimmer is a handheld device that records the information on the magnetic stripe of the credit card. With the skimmer, the employee can copy the credit card information in the first swipe, then swipe again on the merchant's terminal to process the sale.

   A restaurant where the card leaves the sight of the cardholder is a risky scenario. This is why many restaurants are switching to handheld credit card terminals for the wait staff to carry to the table for authorizations.

The risk of not catching skimming devices is lost customer confidence and thus sales. Owners and managers who catch the use of skimmers and have the offending employees arrested before customers are hurt are much better off than when customers and the press bring proof to the business.

17. *Processing credit cards for a neighboring business.* Following are three examples of this and the problems that these transactions cause. Certainly, they can cost a business owner hard-earned profits through Chargebacks.

A. Two stores are near each other. Store one, ABC Co., does not accept credit cards. A customer walks in and wants to make a large purchase. The store owner goes to store two, XYZ Corp. and requests that the transaction be run through that store. He tells XYZ Corp. to just give him 90% of the sale price in cash and keep the rest to cover fees. XYZ Corp. processes the sale. The problem: the cardholder gets her statement and files a Chargeback request because she does not recognize the purchase. She has never been in XYZ Corp. Thus XYZ Corp. loses the sale and is assessed a Chargeback fee. Whether it is a legitimate sale or intentional fraud, ABC Co. has the cash. By processing a sale for another company, XYZ Corp. engaged in a process called *factoring* and loses the money paid to ABC. Factoring is defined as running another company's or individual's charges through your company's merchant processing account. If ABC intentionally defrauded its customer, the employee of XYZ Corp. who ran the sale could also face fraud charges, especially if he knew it was intentional fraud. The solution: never run a charge for any business except your own.

B. Jane Smith owns a hair salon. She decides to rent out space to a few independent hair stylists to bring more clientele to her location and possibly gain some product sales. The independent stylists retain their own "Doing Business As" (DBA) names. Jane allows them to use her processing account and pays them all receipts minus credit card charges, and rental fees and supplies. The problem: this is still factoring and Jane is still on the hook in the case of Chargebacks for up to three years from the date of the sale, whether she can recover from the independent stylist or not. The solution: most current terminals can hold up to ten (a few up to 20) separate merchant accounts. Each independent stylist and Jane just need to contract with the same provider where each independent stylist's sales will go into her own account. Not only is Jane now off the hook with the processor, but there is also proof that the independents are truly independent and thus there are no issues with the IRS or state regarding "wages, taxes, or withholding."

C. Dan Black owns five online sites. All five sites use the same merchant processing account. The names and scopes of the sites are different. The problem: this is still factoring. Yes, Dan owns all five sites. But the SIC codes of the primary business that is set up with the merchant processing account may not be the same and may cause issues. Plus, if one of the companies sells lingerie and the main company sells auto parts, there will be problems with Chargebacks. The solution: each business with a different SIC code (type of business) gets its own merchant services account.

18. *Processing a mistake as a return on the same day the mistake occurred.* A dental office in the Ann Arbor,

Michigan area is set up with two processing accounts on one terminal. The office uses two accounts so it can get both the 1.74% rate for Qualified (swiped) transactions and the 2.24% rate for hand-keyed processing of cardholders making payment by phone (instead of that processor's 1.26% surcharge, which would total 3% for the Mid-Qualified rate).

The clerk processes a $20,000 payment instead of $200. She realizes her mistake and processes a return for $20,000. On the next card processing statement, there are about $900 in charges for the error. The problem: the credit card terminals and computer systems, even in a bank, are stupid. A computer, no matter how good, can only process the information you key into it. In this case, the charges of $448.30 for both the sale and for the return were legitimate charges. Were the charges fair? No, but the fault was not with the processor. The fault was with the clerk in the dental office. Not having a brain or reason, the processor's computer could not see that there was an error in the process. If a person saw a $20,000 charge and a $20,000 return, they would cancel each other out. A computer does not double check; it is assumed that the customer intends to enter the transaction as she did. So, the bank transferred $20,000 to the dentist's account and then immediately back to customer's, just as the clerk told it to do. The solution: any error caught before the terminal batches needs to be voided, not returned.

Employees and business owners alike need to be aware that what you do not know can hurt you. Never make assumptions on how you think a problem can be solved. Always call your sales agent or processor's customer service department when you have any doubt on a transaction. By assuming she knew what she was doing, the clerk cost her employer $896.60 ($448.30 for both the sale and the refund). If she followed procedure and voided the transaction, the total cost would have been $0.60, the transaction fee for the sale and the void. By voiding the sale, there is no percentage of the sale charged because there is no money being moved.

19. *Using your own credit card in your store's terminal.* The effect of using your own credit card in your business terminal is a cash advance. Your credit card issuer permits cash advances under its own rules, including a 3%–5% surcharge. Although you are paying fees, the issuer would only receive the Interchange.

Issuers consider using your own card in your business terminals to be fraud. Credit card processing accounts also prohibit the practice.

In most cases, the issuer will know what you have done within moments of the transaction, but will wait until the next business day to notify you. You will have do a return and pay the fees on the return as well (not all processors charge a processing rate on returns).

Small amounts are permitted; for example, if you are using your credit card to test your store's equipment. It is best to keep the amount under $1.

20. *Failing to keep adequate records.* A Chargeback can be pursued up to three years after the transaction. You are on the clock from the moment the Chargeback is started. Reply late, fail to reply at all, or if you cannot provide the requested information, you will lose the sale.

Keep charge slips and receipts together in an envelope with the date written on the envelope. Use a larger envelope for months and a box or crate for the year. Keep the receipts in order as well as you can. A Chargeback request will list the date in question. Being organized will help you to find the receipt easily.

Important note: when you go to dispose of records in three to five years, hire a company to shred them on-site. Do not just place them in a dumpster.

21. *Failing to ensure that the name you process under is prominent on all receipts.* There are several companies that have created an innovative merchant processing product, a kind of "virtual" card terminal. These products allow multiple users, in multiple locations (even multiple states), to use a single merchant processing account provided that all funds are deposited in the same account and all companies/locations are the same business line (SIC code). The problem: if you have five different marketing websites, each with different names, you can run into the issues discussed earlier—factoring or risking Chargeback by using different names.

    The solution: in a prominent area near the checkout (shopping cart) of each website or on the store receipt, state clearly the name of the business that will appear on the cardholder's credit card statement. In the example, each website checkout page and every shipping receipt you send should show a statement like this, "Thank you for shopping at 120waystopromoteyourbiz.com. Our parent company, Promoting Your Biz, is the name that will show on your credit card statement." On a terminal receipt, the name of the business must match the name that will appear on the cardholder's credit card statement.

22. *Failing to secure a wireless network.* A processor I once worked with discussed the idea of being able to sit on your deck and process credit card numbers on your laptop using a wireless network. Having also worked in commercial computer sales and services with CompUSA®, this idea made me cringe. To see why, turn on your laptop and click on the option to find

all available wireless networks. On any given day, I can pick up 5–15 networks. Most home networks are not secure. I am an honest guy. If my DSL or cable is down, I might piggyback on another network to check my email. But I won't do it because entering their network means they can read my computer files and, if I knew how, I could read theirs.

A business needs to get an expert to set up its wireless network. An unsecure network is like broadcasting your customers' information and your business information to everyone within 300 feet or more.

WEP is used to secure most private party networks. (I switched to WPA in January of 2010.) But Master-Card's Security Rules book, section 10.23, states that WEP must not be the sole method of protection. It states WPA must be used, with a VPN (Virtual Private Network) highly recommended. The MasterCard guide shows what the acronyms mean. I choose to leave them vague. The reason for this is that I want readers with a wireless network to contact a professional security company. While my company, Merchant Processing Consulting and Training LLC, can show you effective solutions to pricing concerns, provide employee training, and guidance on compliance issues, wireless and other computer security needs require experts in those fields.

23. *Failing to promptly reply to Chargeback requests.* Under the Constitution of the United States, a defendant in criminal proceedings is to be considered innocent until proven guilty.

In Chargeback proceedings, it is almost as though the merchant is considered guilty until proven innocent. A Chargeback is initiated by a card issuer in response to a complaint or request for information from a cardholder. Once sent to the merchant, there is a tight deadline to produce the supporting documents requested to show that the product or service for which the card was used was delivered. Failure to reply within the deadline or replying with less than complete documentation will normally result is losing the case.

24. *Failing to specify the return policy on receipts, work orders, or websites.* If your store does not offer refunds or exchanges, state that clearly on every website checkout page, shipping receipt, and credit card receipt. If you fail to mention restrictions clearly, you will be assumed to not have mentioned them to the customer, and thus will lose in the case of a Chargeback.

25. *Failing to have a pre-agreed-to collection policy to protect the business in case of Chargeback.* Sometimes a business can do everything right and still lose a Chargeback case. But just because the card company charges a sale back does not mean you have to just accept it.

To protect your business, consult an attorney and place a variation of, "If I fail to pay as agreed (including a stop payment on a check or initiating a Chargeback with my credit card issuer), I agree to pay my balance owed plus reasonable collection or attorney fees. Further, I acknowledge my service provider may attach a lien against my home or property for work performed or for towing or impound fees."

A Chargeback is not the final word. The business did as it agreed; a Chargeback does not eliminate the cardholder's obligation.

# FIVE
# CREDIT CARD PROCESSING CONTRACTS

## WORDS OF CAUTION CONCERNING PROCESSING CONTRACTS

Before I start working with any processor, I take a look at their reputation from any source I can find. One source I commonly use when seeking the best partners is the RipOff Report®. It is a website created to allow customers who believe they were wronged to post the situation for all to see. The address of the site is www.ripoffreport.com. One common theme occurs in company rebuttals to complaints on this site—references to clauses in your processing contract.

Every merchant processing agreement consists of three to four pages concerning pricing and seven to 20 pages of terms, conditions, and other small print. Before you enter into a contract, you need make sure you get a full copy of it. Go over it in full before you sign anything. Many of the contract features are common on all merchant processing contracts, but some slightly differ from processor to processor. I will be going over a sample contract and what I believe to be the major points to consider (this has undergone an attorney review). However, I still believe it is in your best interest to have an attorney review your specific contract.

The processing company will refer to the contract any time there is a conflict. Shouldn't you know your obligations and rights before there is an issue?

## A TYPICAL CONTRACT OUTLINE

There are many reasons why merchants are suspicious of or downright do not like or trust merchant processing salespeople. Whether a sales agent is new to the industry and does not know any better or is intentionally deceitful means little to a merchant after he has locked himself into a contract where the cost is much higher than he expected it would be when he signed.

In the experience of the author to this date, no two processor contracts are exactly alike. Each has its own quirks, but there are common areas all merchants need to be familiar with.

Before outlining the pitfalls, the following discussion will cover the application portion of the contract.

The first section is normally titled "Business Information." This section contains basic information about the merchant's business—corporate and DBA names, addresses of DBA and home office, type of business structure, etc.

The "Merchandise or Service Sold" section requests information on what you sell. Selecting the right SIC (standard industrial classification) code or MCC (merchant classification code) as it is called by the credit card companies for your business is imperative to get the best Interchange level for which your business will qualify. In some industries, the right coding can make the difference in whether or not your business is able to take a particular card type. For example, pharmacies and medical supply stores that want to accept FSA (flexible spending account) or HSA (healthcare spending account) cards must have the proper MCC assigned to their businesses.

The information filled into the "Monthly Bank Card Sales" section needs to be the accurate current or estimated monthly usage to determine the proper underwriting. If you estimate too low a number, your business may be assigned a cap, limiting the amount of business you can do in a month (exceeding the cap will require you to contact underwriting). Estimate too high, and underwriting may decline your account.

"Average Ticket" is also important to fill in correctly. The average ticket (average amount of sale) is a critical focus of underwriting to determine the risk of your account. Assume that two companies average $100,000 per month; one averages $50 per sale, the other $1,000. The company with the $1,000 average sale has the higher risk because the loss for a single sale is 20 times higher.

"Highest Ticket" is to be treated like "Monthly Bank Card Sales." Setting the amount too low may cause declines and setting it too high can cause underwriting concerns.

"Percentage Swiped" is exactly that. A merchant needs to specify:

1. the percentage swiped,

2. the percentage keyed with imprint, and

3. the percentage keyed without imprint.

The total of all three needs to equal 100%. Swiping cards is the best way to process them. The Interchange rate is lower and so is the risk. If keyed in, and the merchant is in the presence of the card, the merchant must imprint the card to protect the business from Chargebacks. The percentage keyed in without capturing the imprint should only be comprised of telephone, mail, or Internet sales, assuming the use of proper fraud detection tools.

"Sales Method" helps underwriting determine risk by seeing how you process. When companies do equal amounts of swipe and keyed transactions, they typically have two accounts in a Tiered structure. With an Interchange Plus account, the merchant gets better overall pricing and needs only one account. This section should be filled out as accurately as possible.

The "Merchant Site Survey" is another critical area, but not for the merchant. The sales agent needs to complete this section properly to reduce the risk to his or her processor.

"Pricing Schedule" needs to be *completely* reviewed with your agent and, if you wish, your accountant. Do not focus solely on the "Qualified" rate. Pay attention to all of the numbers in this section. Although all processors use the terms Qualified, Mid-Qualified and Non-Qualified, these terms are made up, as each processor defines them differently. MasterCard and Visa have over 400 Interchange levels. Processors create the terms and then place the Interchange categories within the Tiered structure. The Pricing Schedule includes all methods of pricing that will be used for the contract. There are over 40 different items that can be priced, including the rates. The merchant needs to be aware to consider this section as a whole and not be misled by only paying attention to the one line (Qualified rate).

Signing up for the "Merchant Club" (supplies club) is often not a good investment. The paper might be free but the shipping is not. Your office supply store will carry the paper for most terminals. The exception to this is if you have a large store and you need terminal receipt tape by the case. For these businesses only, the Merchant Club might be a good idea.

"Cardholder Data Storage Compliance," a questionnaire, is now required for all merchant processing accounts. Some processors include this with the application. Others have it as a separate form and some have it online. The Self-Assessment Questionnaire (SAQ) is also available at www.pcisecuritystandards.org. Regardless of the method of completion, it does need to be filled in properly.

So, why am I going over the application before the contract? There are several important reasons:

- The application is part of the contract. In fact, many processors only require the application portion to be sent in since alterations to the contract are not permitted.

- The costs that you are committing to for the next three years are displayed here.

- The security features you are attesting to are part of the application.

- The small print in the contract states that by signing the contract, you are affirming that all parts of the contract are true. If the sales agent fills out the contract without verifying facts, you will be asking for trouble later when underwriting makes assumptions based on the agent's guessing.

The composite contract I am breaking down here was seven pages long in a small font. Once set to a normal typeface, these seven pages became 27. There are 31 sections in this sample contract (terms listed have been pulled from different contracts); I will be covering the details on each section.

The purpose of including an entire contract outline here is to drive home the point that a merchant really needs to review the contract before signing. There are multiple pitfalls that can occur if you do not read and understand what you are signing. Never sign any contract without reading it. The processor will hold you to the contract, so be aware of everything it can do. Any agent who wants to rush you into signing something does not have your best interests at heart. (The numbered items are typical clauses. The subordinated outline is the author's interpretation of the clauses.)

1. Introductions and definitions

    a. This explains that the merchant is bound by the rules of the processor and where those rules are located.

    b. Exclusive provider provision—this is where you agree to using only this processor (ABC Processor shall be the sole processor used by the merchant to process credit card transactions).

2. Service descriptions

    a. This is a list of the card brands.

    b. Debit card processors and networks are outlined.

    c. EBT card networks are described.

3. Procedures

    a. The merchant agrees to the rules of the processor and card brands. The processor is not liable to the merchant for fees assessed by the card brands.

    b. Lists the locations where the complete rules can be found:

        i. *Visa Card Acceptance Guide*,

        ii. MasterCard rules,

        iii. MasterCard/Maestro Worldwide,

        iv. Discover, and

        v. AMEX.

    c. PCI-DSS (Payment Card Industry-Data Security Standards)—although you are responsible for complying, the processing contract typically does not include much information on how to do so or where to find resources for help.

    d. Future rules from the card brands or PCI will be "Binding as soon as they are issued." This means that even though they may not be in the contract you signed, you are liable for compliance.

4. Marketing

    a. Merchant must use display marks (i.e., stickers on door or vehicles, logos in ads, etc.).

    b. A merchant must cease to use the marks when she stops accepting cards.

5. Payment, charges, and fees

    a. The merchant agrees to pay fees as owed.

b. The merchant agrees to pay fines, arbitration, penalties, etc., charged by the card brands.

c. Merchant agrees not to prevent, block, or preclude any debit by the processor whether directly or indirectly. This clause is basically telling the merchant that closing the checking account from which fees are withdrawn or blocking access will violate the agreement.

6. Equipment and supplies

a. This section is about any equipment (leased or loaned) or software used to transmit credit card data.

b. The only section I will cover is the obligation of the merchant to cooperate or participate in a dial-in download procedure, if required.

7. Financial information

a. The business owner agrees to furnish the processor with financial statements and information concerning himself, his co-owners, principals, and partners.

b. The processor may file a lawsuit if the merchant fails to produce financial statements upon request.

c. The processor states how long the merchant must retain copies of sales or credit receipts (usually 2–3 years).

8. With a change in the business, the business owner must give 60 days advance notice of...

a. transfer or sale of a substantial part (10%) of total stock, assets, or liquidation;

b. change in the basic nature of business; and/or

c. if all or part of the business is converted to mail order, phone, or internet sales.

9. Transferability

    a. The contract may be assigned to a new business owner, but the processor must approve the transfer.

10. Warranties and representations to processor

    a. A transaction represents a "bonafide" (actual) sale to a customer.

    b. The sales slip accurately describes the transaction.

    c. The merchant complies with all federal, state, and local laws, rules, and regulations.

    d. The merchant will fully complete his obligations to customers and will resolve disputes directly with cardholders.

    e. Signatures on receipts are genuine and authorized by the cardholders and not forged.

    f. The sales transaction and receipt are prepared in full compliance with the provisions of the Card Acceptance Guide and the operating rules of the applicable card association or network organization.

    g. None of the sales transactions come from telephone, mail, or the Internet or where the card was not physically swiped through the merchant's terminal unless specifically authorized in writing that such sales may be submitted. (This goes back to the question on the application about the percentage of sales expected through the Internet, mail, or phone).

    h. There will be no transactions for sales to any principal, partner, proprietor, or owner of the business. (In other words, do not run your own card through your credit card terminal for any purpose other than testing the machine with a transaction of $1 or less. Credit card issuers want cardholders to use proper methods for cash advances. Running sales through your own terminal will result in reversal of the charge, fees on both the sale and return, and possible loss of card processing ability.)

    i. Handling, retention, and storage of credit card receipts or card information comply with the rules of the card brands and PCI-DSS (Payment Card Industry-Data Security Standards).

    j. All information on the merchant application is complete and true. This is what is legally termed strict liability. That is, if one of these conditions is not met—for any reason whatsoever—liability for a breach of contract is established.

11. Indemnity

    a. Here, the merchant agrees to satisfy customer complaints and holds the processor harmless of liabilities, losses, etc. caused by any failure to resolve. Typically this would include that if the processor gets sued, the merchant will "indemnify" the processor for damages, fees, and costs, if any.

12. Limitation of liability

    a. The processor is not responsible for a merchant's inability to process for any of a long list of reasons, from power outages to "Acts of God." The maximum liability listed for most processors is one month's average fees charged over the last year.

13. Term and termination

    a. Most contracts are for three years and automatically renew each year thereafter unless notified in writing 60 days prior to the renewal date.

    b. Depending on the processor, Early Termination fees (ETFs) can range from the rare case of $0 to the average case of either $495 or the remaining months times the monthly minimum and statement fees, to the borderline ethical remaining months times the average profit lost (which can run several thousand dollars). Amounts are payable within 10 days of cancellation up to the dollar limit imposed for that state (some states have maximum limits placed on the amount of ETFs).

c. The processor has the right to cancel at any time, for any reason, without notification.

d. In the case of a breach of terms by the processor or Member (the Member Bank of the card brand that links the processor to the card brand), the merchant may, at his option, give written notice of termination within 30 days if the breach is not remedied.

14. Returned item/Chargeback

a. Chargeback is defined here. (Chargeback is the process of the card issuer taking money back from the merchant due to a customer dispute, fraud, or other cause).

b. Merchant is solely responsible for liability on Chargebacks.

c. Merchant understands that receiving an authorization is no guarantee of payment.

15. Reserve account

a. This is a special account containing a percentage of the sales kept by the processor to handle Chargebacks. (It may be used in cases where the merchant has a low credit score, the business carries higher than normal risk, or where the merchant has had previous Chargeback issues.)

16. Amendments

a. Amendments are made only in writing. They must be signed by the processor or Member and the merchant. This would occur before the original contract is signed. The card brands or the processor may change contract terms at any time with written notice to the merchant. Processors will list changes in a statement 30–60 days before it goes into effect. Changes will be considered accepted by the merchant when he processes a transaction after the change goes into effect.

17. Waiver

    a. No provision shall be deemed waived unless such waiver is in writing. (The agent is not authorized to make changes. A merchant must receive a signed waiver from the processor or Member bank listed on the contract.)

18. Exchange of information

    a. This provision basically states that the owner(s) who signed the contract may have his credit report run at any time.

19. General

    a. If any provision is found to be unenforceable, the rest of the contract survives.

20. Notices

    a. This explains how notices are sent and when they become effective.

21. Agreement

    a. This contract constitutes the entire agreement.

    b. This contract supersedes all prior memoranda agreements whether oral or in writing. (This catches many merchants and many inexperienced, well-meaning agents).

22. Choice of law/attorney's fees/venue/jury trial waiver

    a. Merchant waives a jury trial.

    b. This clause bans class-action lawsuits. (The Second Court of Appeals in New York declared that merchants could file class-action lawsuits in cases where legal fees could exceed the expected returns in an appeal regarding merchants vs. American Express in February, 2009).

c. The law of the specified state dictates the contract (the processor's home state, not the merchant's state).

d. Jurisdiction is granted to the home county of the processor. (This is designed to make it easier to defend in one court. This clause can be used by a crooked processor to deliberately make it hard to challenge parts of a contract.) A good example of a jurisdiction issue occurred with a processor based in Troy, Michigan. The contract's listed trial court was Oakland County, Michigan. The contract now lists the venue of Fulton County, Georgia due to its relationship with Global, a "super"-processor. (The problem I have with this is that the agent promotes the processor as being local to Michigan merchants, yet the contract stipulates filing action in Georgia, even though the agent, merchant, and processor are all Michigan based.)

23. Effective date

a. This is the date of acceptance by the processor and Member, not the date that the merchant signs.

24. Designation of depository

a. This is the bank to be used by the merchant for deposits from and payments to the processor.

25. Financial accommodation

a. The processor and Member are excused from the contract should the merchant go into bankruptcy. (Yet merchants cannot leave a contract because a processor enters bankruptcy or suffers a breach as a result of not being PCI compliant.)

26. Debit/ATM additional items

a. The processor is only responsible for access to the debit network.

b. The merchant is bound by the debit companies' rules.

27. Electronic benefit transaction (EBT)

    a. Merchants accepting EBT cards (food stamps) are bound by their state's rules.

    b. Merchants apply to accept EBT cards through their particular state; the processor only provides access to the network.

28. Marks

    a. This provides instructions on how to use logos and trademarks of the Discover card.

29. Mid-Qualified and Non-Qualified surcharges/Cross-Border Fees

    a. The listed rate is for Qualified transactions only.

    b. Transactions that do not clear as Qualified are subject to Mid-Qualified or Non-Qualified surcharges. (The issue here is that the processor decides what qualifies and what does not.)

    c. Cards from other countries may be assessed Cross-Border Fees.

30. Press release

    a. The processor has your permission to publicize its relationship with your business.

    b. The processor may allow the merchant to review the statement before it is released.

31. Employee actions

    a. The merchant is responsible for the actions of its employees. (It is interesting that the contract specifically states this, yet there is a clause that releases the processor's responsibility for the actions of its employees or independent contractor agents.)

## POTENTIAL PITFALLS OR TRAPS IN A CONTRACT

There are several clauses in most merchant processing contracts that I consider to be potential pitfalls or even traps for business owners. There are also other clauses that I find overly one sided.

The contract binds the small business owner to follow the rules of the card brands. Those rules are available from each of the brands' websites for download in Adobe® PDF format. MasterCard's *Entire Manual* is 353 pages, while its *World Wide Rules* is 749 pages. Both of these files are available from www.mastercard.com. Visa's *Card Acceptance Guide* is 141 pages and is available at www.Visa.com. Contracts once listed some of the major rules; now, with the Internet, they only list where to find the manuals. By signing the contract, the business owner is promising to abide by the rules and guidelines. You need to download and review these manuals or risk subjecting yourself to extensive fines. For example, if a merchant requires a minimum purchase or cardholder identification to use a credit card, that merchant may be fined $20,000 for the first offense of each circumstance. Following a complaint from the cardholder, the issuer will fine your processor, and your processor is allowed to fine you for any fees imposed by the card brands for your actions.

The PCI-DSS rules are also critical to follow. These Data Security Standards are not just guidelines but rules to safeguard your clients' private data. Losing private data will result in losing clients and potential bankruptcy of your business through fines imposed by your processor. But again, you are told to follow the rules but not given the materials. For more information, including finding the SAQs (Self-Assessment Questionnaires), go to the PCI website, www.pcisecuritystandards.org.

The Term and Terminations section is often a shock to merchants who do not review their contracts. Contract terms are set to be three years and can carry hefty early termination fees (ETFs). I think that ETFs are flat-out wrong. The largest ETFs seem to be assessed by the very companies that have convinced merchants that they can save them the most money. If the processor gets business owners to sign by promising them the best costs, logic follows that if it *is* the best cost, the merchants would never want to leave (except for service-related issues). But if the promises were only a ruse to get a merchant to sign, why reward the lying agent and processor by allowing substantial penalties for leaving the contract early?

I am including the agreement section into this pitfalls and traps discussion because processors use the following clauses to give their bad sales agents license to outright lie in some cases to get a merchant signed.

- The contract states that it constitutes the "entire agreement." Further, it "supersedes all prior agreements with the sales agent whether oral or in writing."

- Another clause states that only the "Member" (Member Bank contracting with the processor) may alter contracts.

Any sales agent who promises special treatment or lines out areas of the contract to obtain your signature will not be held responsible for any changes made because of these clauses. Simply put, agree or do not agree to your processing contract based on how it appears when first presented. Any line outs or changes will be ignored or not even known to the processor since most require only the pages filled out by the sales agent with signatures to be sent in for underwriting and approvals. I call this the "Dry Erase Board®️ effect" since, according to these clauses, any alterations to the contract are wiped away, as though by magic, once the contract is signed. However, one attorney has told me that, if documented, an agent may be pursued for fraud either in civil court or through criminal charges.

The final clause on most contracts addresses that the flat rate you were given (if a Tiered rate only) is the only rate applied if transactions are "Qualified." Thus it allows for surcharges for Mid-Qualified or Non-Qualified transactions. If you are given a single rate from any credit card processor (PayPal® uses a single rate, but technically it is a merchant), this clause will apply whether the surcharge rates are listed with the rates or buried in the small print. (This clause is not applicable to Interchange Plus pricing.)

There is a section called "financial accommodations" in most processor contracts. This section allows the processor and Member Bank to walk away from the contract if the merchant files bankruptcy. But what happens when the *processor* files bankruptcy? Nope, you are still locked in. It has been a rarity to see a processor in bankruptcy; nevertheless, the contract is one way. Cynergy filed bankruptcy and merchants are still locked into processing where their money can possibly disappear, depending on what the court decides.

And remember the *severe* penalties described for violations of PCI-DSS? Well, two processors were found to be noncompliant by Visa after breaches (release of credit card numbers), yet they were allowed to re-certify as though nothing had happened. RBS World Pay and Heartland escaped the death penalty that CardSystems suffered only a few years ago, on July 19, 2005, for what many speculated was a much smaller breach (40 million card numbers from CardSystems, while current projections place Heartland's breach at over 130 million). Merchants using these two processors should have been allowed to leave without penalty, in the opinion of the author. If it were the merchant with the breach, PCI would have lowered the boom and the merchant would be bankrupt and/or unable to process again.

# SIX
# WHAT CONGRESS OR STATE LEGISLATURES NEED TO FIX

## SUGGESTED LAW CHANGES

Many readers may expect a discussion on Interchange to appear in this chapter. Interchange will be discussed in its own chapter, but not here. There are many areas where processors are deceitful; Interchange is not one of them.

The following suggestions are in no specific order. Readers may decide which of the items need to be requested from their respective state legislatures. The state is the preferred venue. This is because some states have already passed laws on a few of these proposals and thus there are precedents already set at that level.

- *Require processors to identify the cause for downgrades.* Most processors use a "Tiered" pricing system. Merchants are signed based on the agreed upon "Qualified" rate, only to find that most transactions will downgrade to "Mid-Qualified" or "Non-Qualified" with much higher fees with little or no explanation. By not fully explaining the cause for downgrades or listing the specific Interchange category on the statement, the merchant cannot rectify possible errors or receive meaningful quotes from the processor's competitors. Even though most processors use the Tiered system, each defines it in a different way to intentionally make statements difficult to read.

- *Make leases cancellable.* Four states have laws specifying that leases for credit card terminals may be cancelled. Forty-six (46) states have merchants who are stuck for the full duration of their leasing contracts (typically 48 months) even when agents have lied or misrepresented the price or the need to lease a new terminal. For instance, a merchant may be told he is getting a "free" terminal but, in fact, the agent sneaks in a lease with the paperwork that the merchant is asked to sign. Some leasing companies pay agents up to $3,600 for a single four-year (48 month) lease of a terminal, which may retail for several hundred dollars. If leases were made cancellable, even conditionally, merchants would not be stuck in bad leases.

- *Limit or eliminate early termination fees (ETFs).* Most processors have ETFs buried in the small print; $50–$295 is typical and reasonable. Some ETFs are calculated as follows:

  *Remaining months of contract* × *(statement fee + monthly minimum),* or

  *remaining months* × *average monthly profit* (this can run into thousands of dollars)

  In looking at signed contracts, it seems as though the higher the ETF, the more the merchant has been lied to. Processors state that there are costs to board and remove accounts. This may well be the case. Nevertheless, I believe that if the agent promises lower costs and those lower costs are a mirage, the merchant should be free to leave without penalty. High ETFs are, in my opinion, simply a way to lock a merchant into a contract gained through deceit.

- *Mandate that the merchant's signature must appear on every page of contract, including the terms and conditions page(s).* Processors have attorneys draft the terms and conditions that are part of every processing contract. Most processors require agents to fax or otherwise submit only those pages that are filled out for or signed by the merchant. Some agents tell or show the merchant that areas within the terms and conditions can be lined out or changed. The problem is that if the agent only sends in the typically filled-in pages, the processor never knows that adjustments were made, and the merchant is held to the contract as though no adjustments were made.

- *Mandate that all contracts containing the clause that prohibits alterations and/or that the contract supersedes all promises made orally or in writing must appear in ALL CAPS and be initialed or signed by the merchant.* A contract states that it cannot be altered and that it overrules all agent promises. To protect merchants, placing this language in ALL CAPS and requiring it to be signed will reduce the chances of a corrupt agent being able to dupe a merchant into signing a contract that has been altered in violation of the clause.

- *Mandate that the merchant's statement must list all of the charges to the merchant.* Some processors list the charges on the monthly statement but may remove additional funds from the merchant's account without any explanation. An example of misleading charges is Enhanced Bill Back (EBB). This deceitful practice is the way processors add fees onto the current month's statement for processing that occurred the previous month. Some processors only list some charges on the statement while taking other charges directly out of the merchant's checking account without any notice. Each statement needs to have all of the costs incurred for the month itemized so that merchants know the true cost of processing and can properly account for all monies spent.

- *Mandate that all fees are listed on the merchant's statement in the month in which they occur.* This will prohibit EBB as discussed previously. Such deceptive methods make it appear that the merchant's processing cost is much lower than it truly is. Some processors recruit experienced industry professionals by allowing EBB and Enhanced Reduced Recover (ERR) because these are income producers for them. The author feels that agents who engage in this are dishonest. Once discovered, most merchants will change as quickly as possible to a new processor.

- *Prohibit processors from "locking" a merchant owned or leased terminal.* Processors *lock* a terminal by establishing a private password to prevent "unauthorized" changes, such as reprogramming by a new processor. This practice should be allowed *only* on processor-owned loaner or "free" terminals. Processors use locking to prevent merchants from leaving without giving the current processor a chance to retain the contract. This is another form of patronizing a merchant believed to be too stupid to determine his own best options. A suggested penalty would be to allow a merchant to recover triple the total cost of the terminal from the processor who places the lock or allowing the merchant to void the class-action clause to file legal action to recover damages.

- *Void the waiver of jury trial clause.* This waiver prevents a merchant from using a jury to decide contractual breaches. The processor has a staff of attorneys who write the contract. It is the opinion of the author that processors use this clause to cover for the actions of agents who induce merchants to sign unfair contracts. Voiding this waiver will give merchants the opportunity to ask a jury for fair compensation.

- *Void bans of class-action suits.* In 2009, the Second Circuit Court in New York addressed this issue, but did not go far enough. In a lawsuit of merchants suing AMEX, the court said that merchants could file a class-action suit, but only in cases where they would receive less than their individual court costs. The merchants lost the main intent of case. By removing the ban, a state could show processors that they cannot bully individual merchants by using their deeper pockets to swat aside viable suits. Even if there were conditions placed on voiding the ban, it could alleviate some of the bad contracts merchants are locked into.

- *Mandate that the specified state of the merchant is the venue of all court action and that the contract is dictated by that state.* When a Troy, Michigan merchant signs a contract with a Troy, Michigan based processor through an agent who lives in Troy, Michigan, why is it that the contract is dictated by the laws of Georgia and that all court action must be initiated in either the Fulton County, Georgia court or the Federal court based in Atlanta? Because this Troy, Michigan based processor is an Independent Sales Organization (ISO) for a processor who is based in, you guessed it, Fulton County, Georgia. The purpose for this is two-fold. First, so that the processor does not have to travel the country with its attorneys in tow. Secondly, and perhaps more importantly, it prevents merchants from filing justifiable actions because to do so would mean that most would need to travel hundreds or thousands of miles to fight in the home court of the processor. Why give a processor a free pass? The processor contracts with or hires the agent who approaches the merchant. The merchant signs based on the promises of the agent. Then when the merchant finds he has been taken advantage of, he has to close his store and go to the home court of the processor to file a complaint?

- *Hold processors responsible for the actions of their agents.* Under the Uniform Commercial Code (UCC), companies are responsible for the actions of their employees or agents under Agency Law. Since most processing sales agents are independent, this does not seem to apply. Merchants who dispute their contracts are simply told that they are bound to them as written, disregarding all changes and adjustments that were (mis)represented by their agents. If processors were held responsible for the actions of their agents, bad agents would be removed and blacklisted. Many agents on an industry forum hosted by an industry publication have been discussing bad agents and bad processors for months. Some think bad agents are caused by bad processors; others think bad agents just move from one processor to another. The card brands refuse to step up and regulate the industry. Holding processors liable for their agents is only fair.

# SEVEN
# WHY CONGRESS AND STATES
# NEED TO LEAVE INTERCHANGE ALONE

## CREDIT CARD PROCESSING FEES ARE COSTS OF DOING BUSINESS

Merchant associations like the National Association of Convenience Stores (NACS) want Congress to mandate controls on the Interchange rates set by the credit card brands to pay the issuers for the use of their cards by the merchants' customers.

I have yet to see the NACS campaign against electricity rates, landscaping costs, snow removal costs, accounting fees, storage costs, shipping costs, or anything else. I am sure business professionals who read this will laugh and say, "Of course not. These costs are the expected costs of doing business." Yes they are, but so is the cost of processing credit cards.

I have never been asked at a big-box retailer to place money in a jar or pay at the door to cover the cost of the lights, heating, or A/C. Yet I *do* pay my share of these costs. These companies have specialized cost accountants whose job it is to determine the optimal price point for each product. Product pricing takes into account the wholesale price, shipping, employee salary and benefits, and all other overhead pricing, which *includes* credit card processing costs.

So, for NACS to state that credit card processing fees are a hidden tax on consumers is no more valid than saying that the merchant's own employees are a hidden tax on consumers because the costs need to be included in the prices that the customer pays.

NACS is correct that there is a unique quality about credit card processing that stands out among other overhead costs. It is a completely *voluntary* cost. There is a very simple way in which NACS members and any other merchant can completely eliminate credit card processing fees. Stop accepting credit cards. Every other overhead cost has to be there. You can cut back in these areas but the cost cannot be eliminated totally whereas you can completely eliminate your entire credit card processing cost tomorrow.

Merchants *choose* to accept credit cards because their customers *want* to pay with credit cards. If the merchant does not accept credit cards, customers will pay by cash, but they will not return unless a specific item is needed that cannot be purchased elsewhere. Some customers might want to pay via check if not by credit card, but that will add risk for the merchant. Merchants accept credit cards to satisfy the demands of their customers. Common sense dictates that if no one wanted to use credit cards, merchants would never have to accept them. But customers *do* want to use their cards.

It is ironic to me that convenience stores are at the forefront of the Interchange battle. Convenience stores, including the large chain with the two odd numbers in its name, have the highest markups of any stores. The reason people shop there is that they only need to pick up a few items and it is more convenient (hence the term) to just pay more for the time savings. I can choose to go to the local grocery store and buy an eight pack of Pepsi® for just over $4.00, yet in the convenience store I am fine spending between $1.50 and $1.75 for a single bottle. Nice markup, seeing that the per bottle *retail* price was $0.50 at the grocery store and the same wholesale price prevails for either store. Bottle temperature may play role in my decision to pay the higher price, but even if I bought a warm Pepsi, the price would be the same.

If paying the cheapest price was the goal, I would stock up when the local grocery store had eight packs on sale for 4/$10 (32.5 cents per bottle) and put it in the refrigerator. I do not do this because even though I do like a Pepsi once in a while at home, I normally drink them when I am in between appointments.

Customers of a convenience store *know* they are paying a large markup on what they purchase. The NACS should not try to insult our intelligence by claiming that the 2–3% fees (depending on card type) are costing convenience stores so much when they are encouraging the use of cards to pack their stores and sell at their "enhanced" margins.

Merchants have three primary options in dealing with credit card processing fees and cost accounting:

1. To eliminate all processing fees, stop accepting credit cards. Never again will you need to be concerned with processing fees or how they are costing your business. The con side of this action is that your loyal customers who want to pay by credit card will move to a competitor who will allow them to pay as they choose. The American economy is based on choice. Accepting the cards, or not, is your choice. Whether they want to use the cards is the choice of customers. If they demand the convenience of using cards, your business will thrive or suffer based on your choice of whether or not to accept their preferred method of payment.

2. If your business overhead does not already account for credit card processing fees, this option will be worth reviewing with your accountant. Calculate the percentage of your sales that are from credit cards and the total percentage (effective rate) you are paying on the sales. If 50% of your customers use credit cards and your approximate effective rate is 2.5%, simply add 1.25% to the cost of your products. This calculation spreads the cost of card processing convenience over all customers

since contracts state that cardholders must not pay any additional cost for using cards.

3. The process I suggest for my clients is simpler. I advise them to raise all prices 5%. No matter how your customer pays, you will be getting a raise. Now, my clients balk at first. They say the economy is bad; they would not dare raise prices. But I ask them, and you, do you compete on the quality of your work (or products), or do you compete on price? None of my clients claim to be the least expensive option for their customers. They state that their work (or products) will exceed the expectations of their customers. If your only claim to get customers is the best price, what recourse do you have when a competitor undercuts your prices? And what about that 5% markup? If your service sells for $1,000, 5% is $50. If your service is a great value at $1,000, you can make the case that it is still a great value at $1,050. For those merchants who resell products, you can still make the case for value-added pricing. Nordstrom® sells the same products that others do, yet its customers prefer to shop there because its service is legendary.

If you sell on price alone, you are not in control of your business. As you have read in this chapter, people expect to pay more for quality, expertise, superior service, and convenience. Find the way to answer and exceed your customers' needs, and they will pay the price you set.

## SURCHARGE ON CASH OR CHECK CUSTOMERS

Many in the NACS and Congress point to raising your prices across the board for all customers as an example of unfairness because customers who do not use credit cards pay a portion of the fees for the customers that do.

The Americans with Disabilities Act of 1990 mandates that employers must provide reasonable accommodations to employees with disabilities. Further, the handicap accessibility laws require stores to be fully accessible to all customers, including the wheelchair bound. Stores have spent millions of dollars to become compliant with the laws. Who pays for these mandated changes? Every customer who buys from those stores pays the bill. If using the logic of the NACS and Congress, only those customers who benefit from the upgrades should be paying for them. Have you considered that blind shoppers pay for lights in the stores and deaf shoppers pay for sound systems used by stores? Although these examples may not seem to be politically correct, it would be hypocrisy not to include them. If people in wheelchairs were charged more for the items they purchase to pay for having wheelchair access, there would be news crews there in an instant. It seems as though making everyone pay the same costs is only okay when it is convenient for policy makers and politically correct commentators.

Here is a word of caution to those in Congress. There is a very large cash cow that you protect, even though many people who pay for it do not receive a bit of benefit from it. That cash cow, of course, is Social Security. Many people who are forced to contribute die before they can collect a dime, yet Congress has not lifted a finger to change the program.

If NACS really wanted to help its customers who do not pay by credit card, it could advise its members to create an automated discount percentage when customers pay with cash. However, it will not do this because it does *not* care about saving non-credit card users' money; the Interchange argument is about retaining more money to enhance store owners' profit.

## WHAT COULD HAPPEN IF MASTERCARD® AND VISA® STOP SETTING INTERCHANGE?

There are many lobbyists asking Congress why Master-Card and Visa get to set Interchange levels for credit card issuers. The reason is simply because the cards are Master-Card and Visa branded cards.

Visa has over 16,200 Member Banks; MasterCard claims 20,000 in its 2008 Annual Report. Interchange allows the card brands to set pricing for each card type issued by its Member Banks. It is not a violation of the Sherman or Clayton Acts (antitrust laws) because each card brand only sets Interchange pricing for its own brand.

If Congress or any court ever decides to strip pricing authority away from MasterCard and Visa, they will regret it. You see, Congress might try to justify stripping authority away from the card brands, but I cannot see any court in the country telling the Member Banks that they cannot set pricing on their own cards. Great, so now you have over 15,000 banks (from each brand) setting Interchange for each of 400 levels—6 million distinct Interchange levels (15,000 × 400). Can you imagine the size of those merchant statements each month?

## WHAT OTHER ITEMS MIGHT CONGRESS TRY TO SET PRICING FOR?

There are lobbyists telling Congress that Interchange must be controlled. In effect, they want Congress to tell someone how much they can charge for their own products; in other words, price controls.

Most economists will tell you that price controls are never a good thing. In a free economy, competition and choice must be allowed. Merchants *choose* whether or not to accept credit cards. Choosing to accept credit cards and then attempting to circumvent the pricing you agreed to by involving Congress and playing upon the "fear" of consumers is not the way to build trust.

Once you condition Congress to control Interchange because it "is in the best interest of consumers," what else might scream to be controlled? Food, fuel, and healthcare pricing will all come under scrutiny. All are far easier targets than Interchange, and they affect many more people.

Recently, I spent $2.68 a gallon for gas. Diesel is even more and used by millions of trucks each day to drive products across the country. Every penny increase in diesel leads to price changes or profit loss for companies that need to ship products. To date, I have yet to hear Congress talk about price controls on fuel. But once they decide to mess with Interchange, they will move to more popular targets. This is only one of two things that the lobbyists (who also have gas station members) have not taken into consideration. The other thing is that the card brands are not at fault for the high rates that some gas station owners pay. Merchant service providers and agents alike would love to provide low-cost processing for branded gas stations. They cannot. Branded gas stations are contractually obligated to purchase merchant processing from the fuel brand. They may sign with any vendor, but by doing so are stripped of the gas brand. When I offered Tiered pricing, my price for swiping a consumer card in the terminal was 1.69%. A friend's branded station was charged 2.5%. He hired me to set up a terminal for his service bays, but if he wanted to keep his gas brand, I could not touch his pumps.

Going after Interchange may seem like an easy fix for lobbyists and Congressmen who do not know any better. Not only is Interchange not the cause of higher gas costs, but once Congress gets involved with it, they will be flooded by people and lobbyists asking for price controls on other things.

Anyone recalling the gas policies of the 1970s knows what price controls will mean. Are we ready to see such lines for healthcare or food? Why legislate something that is completely a business owner's choice to pay when it may lead to rationalizing price controls on things we require to survive?

# EIGHT
## COMMON BUSINESS TYPES, PROCESSING NEEDS, AND SECURITY

### RETAILERS

Small retailers typically pay more for credit card processing than most other businesses that have face-to-face sales. This is because many card processing sales agents do not want smaller-volume locations. This chapter covers the typical needs of most retailers. It is important to find a good local sales agent with references who will deliver what they promise.

Most sales that retailers have will be exclusively face-to-face with customers. To accept cards, you will need a terminal for swiping the cards. Such a terminal should be capable of multiple programs, including check processing and gift cards. The Vx series by Verifone® is my personal favorite, but there are several other brands to choose from. The retail price range for these units is typically from $500–$700. There is a terminal called Orion™ by 4Access Communications that combines a check scanner with a terminal. It retails for under $900. As explained earlier, when evaluating terminals, do not accept a "free" one; you will wind up paying more in long run.

If your business is geographically distant from sales agents, some will charge you a much higher rate solely because they believe your options are limited. Michigan's Upper Peninsula has many isolated businesses in small towns along the main roads. One towing company was paying a swipe rate of over 3% because only one sales agent would drive out to his business to sign him up. Since most of his transactions were keyed in, the result was that he actually paid as much as 7% due to higher Mid-Qualified and Non-Qualified rates. Even in cases where your business is in a fairly isolated location, you *do* have options.

In the past, many small businesses kept credit card numbers on file so that regular customers could call in orders and not have to read their numbers to the clerk each time. I *highly* advise not to do this. Smaller businesses have a very high risk of security breaches because they tend to store credit card numbers with no security measures.

If you store card numbers in your business, you *must*:

- not place them in a computer that is used for e-mail or web browsing.
- have a secure firewall on your network.
- keep numbers and information in a locked cabinet or, better yet, in a safe.
- control access to areas where credit card numbers are stored.
- include security rules in your employee manual.

Visa® training materials can be obtained from www.Visa. com. Everyone who has exposure to cash registers should be trained on the proper procedures for handling customer information.

Many retailers mistakenly believe that the PCI-DSS (Payment Card Industry-Data Security Standards) do not affect them because they are not online. This belief is dangerous and can result in serious trouble for the small retailer. PCI-DSS rules are not only about securing websites, but securing credit card information from any unauthorized use. Employees of some small retailers and service companies have taken such information and used it for personal benefit. With PCI-

DSS rules, such a breach can now bring hefty fines that can bankrupt your business. The card brands are very serious about protecting your customers' credit card information. You should be too.

### Retail Sales with a Point-of-Sale (POS) System

Any retailer who can afford to, should look into having a POS system installed. POS systems offer many advantages. They can be used to track inventory, sales, and even employee time.

Before choosing a POS system, it is good to explore the many options, including pricing, early termination fees, rate structures, and reprogramming charges (converting the system to process with a new processor). You also need to verify that your new equipment only stores the information allowed by the credit card brands and local laws. You, as the business owner, are ultimately held responsible for any breaches of data. This discussion is not to advise you against processing credit cards, but to make known the precautions you need to take to protect yourself, your customers, and your business. Spanky's, a restaurant in Athens, Georgia, was featured in a two-part YouTube® video in July of 2007. It was uploaded there by the Retail Solutions Providers Association (RSPA) under the ID of pcirisk. The video clips discuss how the restaurant was fined after a breach through their POS system. It is wise to take precautions so that the same thing does not happen to you.

Investing in a POS system will help to streamline business processes and make it easier to order and track inventory. (There is a Bonus Chapter authored by Debbie Bone, a sales agent in North Carolina, who is an expert on POS and electronic cash registers [ECRs].)

## DELIVERY COMPANIES

Delivery companies have three major options for accepting credit cards.

1. Use a knuckle-buster (manual imprinter) in the field to imprint the card and then return to the sales office to key the number into a terminal or computer-based "virtual terminal." Knuckle-busters are difficult to handle. They also tend to turn off potential clients who are worried about security. The concerns are valid due to the risk of lost or stolen credit card slips. Also, if you choose to use an imprinter, do not write the customer's address or security code on the slip. Both are violations of the credit card brands' rules and can each subject your business to fines of $100,000 for every occurrence.

2. The virtual terminal is becoming much more popular these days. For instance, the eProcessing Network's (ePN) virtual terminal can be used on any computer with Internet access. The sales scenario might work something like this. The delivery company's home location or store would take the customer's call. The clerk would gather the credit card number and security number and input them into the virtual terminal. Once authorized, a receipt would print so that the delivery person could use it to obtain a signature at the delivery location. The ePN virtual terminal also can be used with Blackberry® or other selected cell phones to key in or swipe cards and transmit using the data plan on the phone. With ePN, there is a one-time setup fee for each cell phone, in addition to optional equipment.

3. Another option is a wireless terminal. Swiping is almost always less expensive than keying transactions, and far more safe than carrying imprinter slips. But there are costs to consider with a wireless option. Wireless terminals are fairly expensive, ranging from $700–$1,200 each. They also require a wireless access fee per unit of up to $35 per month and an additional fee of $0.10 per transaction. Most businesses will only need $3,000–$5,000 in sales per terminal per month to cover the access fee

per terminal considering the savings of swiping cards vs. keying them in. Because Interchange Plus pricing makes keyed transactions only marginally more expensive than swiped (approximately $0.25 for every $100 processed), businesses that have this structure will need sales of up to $14,000 per terminal per month to justify the cost. In other words, if you are only saving $0.25 for each $100 you process with Interchange Plus pricing, you will need $14,000 in sales per unit to cover the $35.00 access fee. If the fee is only $25 per month, then a business would need $10,000 in sales.

Fleets with high-dollar-per-terminal sales are the only businesses, other than those needing POS systems, for which I would recommend leasing. If the business uses Blackberry® phones, the ePN option would be much less expensive over time since there are no additional wireless access fees.

You may notice that I failed to mention a process called "Store and Forward" (S&F) in the options, which allows a delivery driver or crafter to swipe cards into the terminal and then transmit the data when it finds a signal or when it is plugged into a phone line. Omission was intentional. S&F works by recording full swipe data and transmitting it later. Under my interpretation of PCI-DSS rules, S&F is in violation because the process retains full swipe data. Admittedly, my interpretation may be a bit narrower than PCI intended. But I would much rather err on the side of caution. An S&F terminal stolen before the data is transmitted would not only mean lost sales for the merchant, but may allow a thief to steal the full swipe data, which can result in fines.

## ARTISTS, CRAFTERS, AND AUTHORS

### Artists and Crafters

Artists and crafters typically have higher costs than other merchants for credit card processing, but this does not need to be the case. If you have an online store and use a terminal that works via phone line, you need different merchant processing accounts for each. Most artists and crafters use both sales methods, thus there is higher cost because you need two accounts.

One common solution is a merchant account using a gateway. My preferred vendor is eProcessing Network (ePN). I offer the ePN solution exclusively because its wholesale costs are lower (retail cost depends on the sales agent). The customer service team at ePN is very knowledgeable and the product links to third-party shopping carts easily. You can find out more about ePN at www.eprocessingnetwork.com.

The gateway is a great solution for artists and craft show owners because it can include (if using ePN):

- a "virtual terminal" using an Internet connection;
- a swiper that can be plugged into the USB port of a computer;
- a wireless swiper using a Bluetooth® connection to a Blackberry® phone or other select cell phone;
- easy linking to shopping carts and websites; and/or
- a Mobilescape® 3000 or 5000 wireless unit (the 5000 can also swipe checks to transmit money directly into your account). These units also may be used solely as wireless terminals. More information can be found at www.mobilescape.com.

Using a gateway for credit card processing means the business owner only needs one merchant account. When using gateways to both swipe and key information, the best pricing structure is Interchange Plus. This is because the business will be paying costs based on how each card is processed. If pricing were set as Tiered keyed, then the business would pay a premium of about 80 basis points (2.50% instead of the customary 1.70% swipe rate), resulting in the website and keyed processing costing close to 3.50% or more. With Interchange Plus pricing, the business pays the true cost of processing plus a small consistent percentage for processor profit (for all types of cards, whether or not they are swiped or keyed).

Table 8-1 lists processing options with their expected pricing variables (each $ represents up to $200) and PCI-DSS risks (! is lower risk, !!!!! is higher). The last column indicates whether the card number is keyed (K) or swiped (S).

The table sums up the following facts when it comes to processing options:

- Businesses that rely on manual imprinters have lower setup costs, but they tend to also have the highest security risk because of using credit card slips and lacking methods to secure the data.

Table 8-1. Comparing processing options, cost, and risk

| Options | Equipment Needs | Startup Cost | PCI-DSS Risk | K/S |
|---|---|---|---|---|
| Keyed later | Terminal, imprinter | $$–$$$$ | !!!!! | K |
| Keyed entry | Virtual terminal, imprinter | $ | !!!!! | K |
| Keyed entry, website gateway | Virtual terminal, imprinter | $ | !!!!! | K |
| Website gateway | Virtual terminal | $ | !!! | K |
| Website gateway, mobile | Virtual terminal, mobile application, imprinter | $ | !!!!! | K |
| Website gateway, mobile application, Bluetooth® wireless | Virtual terminal, mobile application, Bluetooth unit | $$$ | !!! | K/S |
| Website gateway, USB swiper | Virtual terminal, USB swiper | $ | !!! | K/S |
| Website gateway, Mobilescape® | Virtual terminal, Mobilescape | $$$–$$$$$ | !!! | K/S |
| Wireless swipe only | Mobilescape | $$$–$$$$$ | ! | S |
| Wireless swipe only | Virtual terminal, mobile application, Bluetooth unit or USB | $–$$$ | ! | S |
| Wireless swipe only | Other wireless terminal | $$$$–$$$$$ | ! | S |

- Businesses that use a website gateway, with or without swiping ability, can experience setup costs close to that for a virtual terminal and imprinter. If not swiping a card, using an imprinter is recommended (it can mean winning or losing a Chargeback). However, the use of an imprinter causes higher PCI-DSS compliance risks. The gateway carries moderate risk, depending on the security features in place and whether scanning is used.

- Swiping alone carries the lowest risk of not complying with PCI-DSS provided that the equipment does not store the security code or other identifiers. Startup costs will vary from $200 to over $1,000, depending on the method chosen.

While the startup cost is around $200 for using a computer with a USB swiper, you will need to have a laptop card for secure Internet access, which can vary from $20–$60 per month. Virgin Mobile® now offers Broadband 2Go™, a card that costs $100 with service as low as $20 per month with no commitment for occasional use only (if you are using it on a more frequent basis or if you need more bandwidth, get a contract and pay the $60 monthly with a national carrier). *Never* use a public "hot spot" or you risk transmitting card numbers where they can be recorded. You can typically tell if your network is not secure if you do not need any kind of password to access it.

There are several items to consider when deciding the method of processing. Among the most common include PCI-DSS security risk, speed of transaction, knowing immediately if a card is approved or declined, paperwork or receipt ability, setup cost, and monthly fees.

The best solution will vary depending on the individual needs of the merchant. Table 8-1 only shows the most common variables. The business owner needs to sit down and answer some questions before speaking with a sales agent.

If a business owner does not state his needs clearly, he opens the door for the agent to sell what the agent thinks the business owner needs. Unfortunately, most salespeople fail to ask questions to determine the needs of the client.

The following questions will help you to clarify your needs:

- Will I be using a website?
- When I am at a show, how important is an instant answer as to whether a card is approved?
- What is the average amount of a sale?
- How busy will the event be? Will there be long or short lines of customers waiting to pay?
- If I use a manual imprinter, can I safely and securely store the sale slips?
- Will I have assistants or employees at all events? (This question may rule out computer-based solutions due to theft possibility.)
- How much am I willing to spend up front? Each month?
- What carries the most importance to me?
- Are there other pertinent questions I need to answer?

### Authors

There is a variable with authors that I believe make them slightly different from artists or crafters.

The variable is book signings. Book signings typically take place at seminars or bookstores. Since bookstores already have the facility to sell books, we will look at seminars at which the author is facilitating or is a guest speaker. At such events, lines would be long and need to move quickly. Since it would make sense that the author would have an assistant to allow her to handle signings, the best option would be a wireless solution with a gateway. The assistant would key in the dollar amounts and supporting information on the computer, cell phone, or wireless terminal, obtain signatures, and then file the receipts.

If using a USB swiper with a computer, the author would have the option to email the receipts to customers if they provide their addresses. Even though a card is swiped, I would recommend using an imprinter slip or preprinted receipt (in sequential order) to list the purchase and obtain the customer's signature. This will offer some protection for the author in cases of Chargeback along with the ability to record sales. Sequential numbers can be used as the invoice numbers in the gateway so you can quickly find a particular sale if needed.

Using a Bluetooth® option with a Blackberry® or computer will still require recording sales information manually since there is no way to input this onto any wireless device. The customer is required to sign the receipt that prints from the wireless terminal, if so equipped.

A processing industry magazine, *The Green Sheet*, in its December 28, 2009 edition, states that, "Beginning with the 2010 calendar year, merchant acquirers, processors, and ISOs must report to the IRS the transaction volumes of the merchants in their portfolios. Said data must be submitted early in 2011." This mandate will ensure that businesses report all card processing receipts. Business owners need to ensure that they have a way to record all sales data. Consult your CPA or state to determine if you need to collect sales taxes.

## PHONE SALES

Some business owners only want to process transactions over the phone. Before you apply for such an account, you need to be straight with the processor and sales agent on the nature of your business. If telemarketing is present, it needs to be inbound only. The credit score of the person(s) who signs the contract (the guarantor[s]) will be scrutinized as well as the business type. If the business type is determined to be high risk, the business, if approved, may be required to establish a reserve account. If the processor, Member Bank, or card brands find that the business owner (or the sales agent) lied about the nature of the business, the account may be closed and the merchant may lose any funds held or in reserve.

The best processing option for phone sales is using a virtual terminal with the AVS (address verification system) turned on.

Using a virtual terminal, the merchant's employee can key the information requested right into the computer. Whether a call center has one operator or 100, one virtual terminal can be set up using passwords and IDs for each employee. If using a normal terminal, operators would need to write down all of the information (including security numbers), and then enter it into a single terminal, which would kill productivity. Common call center accounts include ticket centers, insurance offices, and theaters.

While medical billers can use credit card processing, collection agencies cannot, since credit cards should not be accepted for third-party debts.

If a merchant wishes to add Internet processing to a current setup, the only additional costs will be for the website and shopping cart (if needed).

## MAIL ORDER & INTERNET SALES

### Mail Order

Mail order companies are fading with the Internet's increasing popularity, but such businesses would use a virtual terminal. Employees open mail and key in numbers and orders, so AVS is critical as are fraud prevention features. Mail order companies have a high risk for PCI-DSS compliance issues because of the written credit card numbers and codes.

### Internet

With website processing, the customer inputs his own credit card number and security code. The merchant can also tweak the gateway protocols for tighter or looser restrictions on card acceptance. Tighter restrictions can mean lost sales on good cards, while looser restrictions can result in more sales, but higher incidents of fraud and Chargeback problems. Since the card numbers are not written, the risk of PCI-DSS issues is greatly reduced over mail order ***provided*** that full numbers or security codes are not retained and the network is completely secure. Gateway providers, like ePN, can store numbers on their servers if certified by the card brands to do so. When users, even management, review transactions, they can only see the last four numbers of the credit card.

If you are setting up your online site with a third-party shopping cart, review the website of that provider to find the list of compatible gateway providers. If the gateway is compatible with the third-party shopping cart, the method of linking them will be typically easy.

### PAYPAL®

A discussion on Internet processing would not be complete without mentioning PayPal. Many merchants believe that using PayPal to accept credit cards is like using other processors, but it is not. Strictly speaking, PayPal engages in *factoring,* a practice that is prohibited by the card brands for other businesses. Factoring is the act of accepting a credit card payment for another merchant. This is one reason that PayPal has a return policy that many users feel is "anti-seller"; PayPal needs to control Chargeback issues too, or risk losing the ability to process credit cards.

PayPal uses three rate levels, just like most processors. The difference is that the rate is a flat rate for all transactions. The rate is dependent on the sustained minimum volume (three straight months and then constant after) for the merchant each month. The rate can be as low as 1.99% + $0.35 and as high as 2.99% + $0.35. It takes high volume to get the lowest rate and it is a rate that no processor can touch because Interchange is much higher in some cases than 1.99% + $0.35. How can PayPal offer rates this low? Because while processors process credit and debit cards only, PayPal allows buyers to pay from their accounts, a linked bank account, or credit card. No matter how the customer pays, the merchant pays the set rate on all transactions. Payments from PayPal accounts have no cost to PayPal, thus PayPal uses them to subsidize credit card processing costs (and still makes a good profit).

Low-volume merchants (under $10,000/month) will pay 2.99% + $0.35 for PayPal. Many startups turn to PayPal because there is no up-front cost, no statement fees, and no contract. Most merchants will reduce their costs by switching to a conventional processor once the business is established.

I had to set up a PayPal account to receive affiliate payments from a few of my business partners. I would prefer another method, but I had no choice. Customer service is important to me as is personal service. Calling the call center, wading through menus, and waiting to speak to a real person are not fun to me.

There are a few conditions where I would recommend using PayPal to accept credit cards online:

- you have a new online business and are not sure of its viability,
- you have very low volume and wish to pay no set monthly fees,
- you do not need personalized service or a direct number to a dedicated agent, and/or
- your market is aimed at 18–35 year olds.

People over 35, myself included, tend not to like or trust PayPal. It is uncomfortable listing a credit card or linking a bank account with a system that you know is a target to hackers worldwide because of its sheer size.

Most businesses would actually benefit from using both PayPal and a credit card processing company. The more payment options you offer your customers, the better off your business will be.

Before you sign up to process credit cards with PayPal, or *any processor*, get references. If you cannot find local merchants who use PayPal, search for "PayPal" in your preferred search engine to find a user site.

## REAL ESTATE

Talking about real estate in the same sentence as credit card processing makes some people very nervous. They say that the economy is in the shape it is in because of people spending above their means using credit cards. First of all, it is not up to merchants to help control the spending habits of people. More importantly, I am not advocating accepting credit cards from renters who are more likely to have tight budgets and who tend to abuse credit cards and wind up over-extending themselves. If rents exceed $1,000 a month, then the property owner should consider credit card processing as renters who can afford this amount tend to be better credit risks. Many people place all expenses on their credit cards to gain the rewards. Then each month, they pay off their bills in full so that they are not carrying a balance or paying interest on purchases.

There are four categories to discuss under the topic of real estate: commercial properties, apartments, homes, and ReMax® offices (and similar situations).

### Commercial Properties

Commercial real estate consists of offices or buildings used for business. Owners of commercial properties could streamline their billing departments by allowing or mandating electronic payments. Easy to set up, such processing would require the property owner to set up a gateway online and enter all of the customers' information one time with an automatically recurring payment made monthly. Now, the property management company can receive all payments on time.

This opportunity should not be overlooked because of the need to pay up to 3.5% of the money you take in for accepting credit cards. Think of the savings in labor and postage you will enjoy by not having to chase down renters who become past due.

### Apartments

Apartment management companies need to consider accepting credit cards for their apartments where the average rent exceeds $1,000. Why $1,000? Well, admittedly the number is arbitrary. Setting the point too low may allow too many renters to place the rent on their credit cards and carry the balance, while spending money elsewhere. The $1,000 is a point where credit ratings are likely to be higher; thus the renter is more likely to use a Rewards card for purchases and pay it off at the end of every month.

The purpose of accepting credit cards is to get closer to 100% of payments on time. Most apartment complexes receive only 80–90% of payments on time. So, if a complex has 1,000 apartments, this means that 100–200 tenants are not paying on time; at $1,000 per month, this could mean up to $200,000 in late rental payments. Since apartment complexes still need to pay their bills on time, that $200,000 is off the profit of the complex. You might think, so what? It is only late, and the complex will recover most of it. The property owners are not putting that money in a private vault; they are placing it in a bank, making investments or property upgrades. That money belongs to the property owner and it has attached cost, not only for manpower and postage to collect, but in lost interest.

With Interchange Plus pricing, Rewards cards will only cost 2.5% (assuming a 50-basis point markup). If apartment complex owners raised rents 5% across the board, then they would be earning more money, regardless of how renters pay.

A word of caution is in order. Under card brand rules, if you offer the option of credit card payments to anyone in a complex, it must be offered to everyone in a complex. You do have the choice of accepting either credit cards or debit cards (taking money straight from a checking account). But if you accept credit cards for your complex, *all* renters can pay via credit. Luxury apartments can offer electronic payments without much concern. Other complexes need to decide on a case-by-case basis whether each complex is right for card acceptance. Even if your complex chooses not to accept credit cards, you can still opt for accepting debit cards or using a lower-cost ACH payment setup. Such setups use the renter's checking account on the same virtual terminal/gateway that would be used for credit card processing.

## Homes

Homes are a different matter than apartment complexes or commercial renters. Property managers or owners would need to own several homes to justify accepting credit cards. As with apartment complexes though, I advise setting a minimum rent level to set up a credit card processing program. Accepting credit cards for rent will ensure on-time payments. Although a business owner is not responsible for customers who over-extend themselves on credit cards, property managers who set the bar too low for payments will find renters who wind up having to leave the property because of financial issues. Use the renter's credit score and the amount of rent to determine whether or not to accept credit cards.

## ReMax® Offices (and Similar Situations)

"ReMax, why would ReMax want credit card processing? Why would you want credit card processing for real estate deposits?" These are the most common questions when people hear ReMax and credit card processing in the same sentence. I know; that was my response to a ReMax office asking me about getting a card processing terminal.

I learned that ReMax offices are independently owned and that the agents lease office space from the broker. The fees can range a bit depending on the location, amenities, number of listings and other variables; but agent fees at the offices I have visited average about $1,000 per month.

When first asked, I did not have a solution I was comfortable with. The broker would have needed to maintain a spreadsheet of the agents' credit card numbers, names, and codes. I advised against this because it was too high a risk and would expose the broker to liability if the credit card numbers were stolen. It was a bad idea then and still is.

Now, there is a great solution for ReMax brokers and other business owners who lease space to independent agents. A virtual terminal/gateway, like the one I offer through ePN, uses a recurring payments module and an optional USB swiper. The agents' information can be stored on ePN's Visa certified servers and is processed automatically on a set day of each month. Any time an agent's information is brought up on ePN, only the last four numbers of his credit card will be seen.

The ReMax brokers and other companies that house independent agents are in a different situation from many businesses. The processing environment is closed; no one is coming in off the street—all cards are from the people working in the office. If agents are responsible for a share of all fees or obligations of the office in which they work, then the broker is not on the hook for credit card processing fees. The fees would be split up among all agents, whether they use a credit card or not for payment of office fees.

With a recurring payment set up in a ReMax environment, there could be two payments each month. These consist of the routine, unchanging base charge and an additional charge a few days later to recover any additional fees depending on listings advertised and office incidentals. With a virtual terminal from ePN, the additional fee is transacted very easily using its "sale" button on the list of recurring charges within ePN.

Broker acceptance of credit cards for agent fees will reduce the time and effort of chasing late payments and will increase cash flow.

## REMAX AGENTS, INDEPENDENT AGENTS, AND BUSINESS OWNERS

This discussion is not about accepting credit cards—it is about using them.

It is advisable for independent agents, business owners, and ReMax agents to find *one* credit card to use for *all* business expenditures. The moment you receive the statement, pay it off. So long as the balance is paid in full each month, the rate will not be a factor in deciding on the brand of card.

I recommend using a Rewards card. If you do not currently have one, check out your favorite airline, gas brand, or product for offerings. If unsuccessful, www.creditcards.com allows you to select a rewards, airline miles, or cash-back credit card and apply for it right there. I have not researched the site personally, so should you find a card you like but are uncomfortable with applying there, you can approach the issuer directly. Do not apply for any card online unless you are comfortable that the site is safe. (Look for safety and lock icons, and "https" in the URL name.)

Once you find the right card, use it *exclusively* for all of your business expenses. Each quarter, just take your credit card statements and income statements, along with your appointment book and other items requested, to your CPA to figure your quarterly tax payment.

## CHURCHES AND NONPROFIT ORGANIZATIONS

To some church-goers, the idea of churches accepting credit cards brings mental images of Christ chasing the money changers from the temple. I admit to having made the same connection when I heard of Catholic churches in California placing credit card terminals in their vestibules to encourage parishioners to swipe their credit cards to donate to the church.

While I believe that accepting credit cards can help churches of all denominations, I would suggest a less intrusive or offensive way—the virtual terminal and gateway solution. Make the announcement that credit cards are accepted and offer several ways to set up donations.

1. Keep a USB swiper in the church office for congregation members to swipe their cards.

2. Members could complete a form with their card information and turn it in the collection plate. However, there are potential PCI risks with this scenario.

3. Offer a web option for church members. They enter their own credit card information and choose one-time, weekly, or monthly recurring payments. This is likely to be the most popular option because no one would see the card numbers.

Churches and nonprofit organizations would likely receive lower rates than the average business, especially if a member of the organization sells card processing services.

The benefit of accepting credit card or ACH payments is a steady flow of donations. In Michigan, many residents move to Florida or Arizona while the snow flies. With a recurring payment plan in place, the church collects contributions from members no matter where they are located or whether or not they attend services.

# NINE
# HOW TO CHOOSE A SALES AGENT

## TWELVE COMMON DECEPTIVE PRACTICES

Salespeople use a variety of methods to get before a prospect. Unfortunately, some credit card processing agents use deceptive means to get a merchant to sign on with them. In the credit card processing industry (also referred to as merchant services), signing with a deceptive processor can be a very expensive endeavor. The merchant will be locked into a three-year contract and likely pay a lot more than he or she was promised.

There are a number ways to be deceptive in the sale of credit card processing services. The following is a list of the 12 most common.

1. *Leasing terminals.* This involves paying a set monthly fee (plus tax and insurance) for a terminal for a set number of months. For some businesses, leasing makes sense. When abused, leasing is extremely expensive for the merchant. Some agents make several thousand dollars on a single 48-month lease of a terminal at $119/month. The reason is that most terminals have a cost price of up to $500 and retail for up to $700. At $119/month, a merchant will pay over $5,700 over four years and cannot cancel the agreement early.

   If you choose to lease, look for a monthly payment of $29 but no more than $49. Leasing can get you the newest equipment for a low monthly payment, but a better option might be to buy the terminal at full retail price on your credit card and pay on it until it is paid off. If leasing, remember to cancel the lease at termination. There are many merchants still paying leases signed 20 years ago because they never were cancelled at contract end.

2. *There are over 40 types of fees.* Do not judge solely on the main rate quoted to determine the best processor. It is like telling a car salesman that you can afford $X a month for a new car and you walk out paying $X + $50 to $100 per month. Keeping your eyes on the rate alone is an invitation for the processing agent to pad your bill with a variety of other fees. The rate you actually pay is always higher than contracted. This is the "effective rate," which takes into consideration all of the fees paid. To find your "effective rate," add all of the fees from your monthly statement, divide this amount by the credit card net sales from the statement, and then multiply by 100.

3. *"Your equipment is not PCI-DSS compliant."* This is something many merchants are hearing these days. PCI refers to Payment Card Industry and DSS to Data Security Standards. Rules are being continually updated to ensure that the information used to process credit cards does not wind up helping criminals defraud credit cardholders. When buying a terminal, always buy the latest equipment and beware of purchasing anything used. If you have an existing terminal that you are being pressured to replace, verify that it indeed needs replacement. Refuse to deal with pressure from salespeople.

4. *"Free" terminals.* Although it sounds like a great deal, in truth, the offer of a "free" terminal is a reason to be cautious. A terminal is not free for a business owner; it

is actually a loaner for as long as you remain with the processor. If not returned promptly (within 10 days) and in great condition after switching to a new processor, the merchant's checking account will be debited the full amount specified on the terminal agreement form. Such terminals cannot even be described as "free use" as there are normally minimum requirements on rates, monthly fees, monthly minimums, and other fees assessed to obtain a "free" terminal.

5. *Changes to contract.* A deceptive sales agent will happily make any changes you would like to a contract. There are several problems with this for the merchant. First, the contract typically prohibits changing it. A deceptive agent will simply transmit the parts of contract completed and signed (since changes to the body are not permitted); thus the merchant processing company will not be aware of changes elsewhere. Secondly, in such a scenario, since most sales agents are independent, the processor will claim no responsibility. Do not accept line outs in the contract body as a commitment of change. If you are a victim of such an occurrence, contact an attorney and ask if you can pursue the processor under the Agency Law section of the UCC (Uniform Commercial Code), which states that a company is responsible for the actions of its employees or agents.

6. *"This is your processor and we need..."* Merchants that hear this on phone calls are being scammed. The caller is fishing for information to use on a new processing contract. This works because most merchants do not *know* who their processor is and will volunteer information not seeing it as being dangerous. Just remember, your processor will have any information needed. And, if other information is needed, most will contact the agent you signed with and have them contact you.

7. *"If I cannot save you any money, I'll give you $500."* This is a scam used by a deceptive agent to get a look at your merchant statement. It is a scam, because no matter what you are paying, this person can beat it on paper. Since there are many fees that can be used in addition to rates, it is guaranteed that this agent can save you somewhere. Why is this listed as a scam? It is deceitful. The merchant sees it as way to collect if he or she is happy with the current provider, but it is a sucker bet to even entertain such an offer. Even if this agent pitches the best program, his ploy will show savings of only a few dollars a month. This may or may not be enough to get the contract, but it is enough for the agent to avoid paying the $500. At worst, he will omit data (such as not including downgrades or hidden fees) or not verify whether you are currently under contract and whether you will owe an Early Termination Fee (ETF) if you terminate early.

8. *You are given a lower rate than what you are qualified to receive.* This scam is actually initiated by the merchant. A merchant asks a deceitful agent, "What is the lowest rate I can get?" This common question sets the wheels in motion for the scam. The problem is that some agents will quote 0% or 1.39%. A 0% rate is an outright lie. There is no way to get 0% on any transaction. A personal identification number (PIN) debit might have a markup of $0.35–$0.75, but Interchange still will be over 0% (Interchange on PIN debit cards is increasing up to 0.95% + $0.20 on several networks). The 1.39% rate is a common debit card rate, but only swiped debit cards will qualify for it. The fact is that most cards taken by businesses will not qualify for these rates; thus transactions will actually default to a much higher rate.

9. *"We are one of the top processors in the USA."* What this agent does not mention is that he represents

an Independent Sales Office (ISO) of a top processor. Some of the top processors are First Data, NPC,
Bank of America Merchant Services, and TSYS.
Thousands of ISOs utilize the front- or back-end of
these companies to transmit data. A good analogy
is a small reseller for Xerox® claiming to be one of
the top sellers of printers and copiers in the country because it uses its partner's sales. Ask the sales
agent about the services he provides to customers,
not the companies he represents. One way to verify
this claim is to ask for a blank contract; the contract
will list the registered processor at the top.

10. *"We work directly for MasterCard and Visa."* If you
hear this, you know this agent is among the worst
scammers in the industry. MasterCard and Visa are
separate companies. MasterCard and Visa do not issue cards; nor do they process cards. Member Banks
are the only ones these two entities directly communicate with and only they can issue or process credit
cards. Every processor needs to register with the
card brands *and* be sponsored by a Member Bank.
Control of the processing is through the Member
Bank. Independent Sales Offices (ISOs) and Independent Sales Agents (ISAs) must work through
registered processors until they pay registration
fees and get sponsored by a Member Bank. All registered processors pay the same Interchange fees and
Assessments. The registered processors then set
pricing based on these costs to their ISOs and ISAs.
Some pass along the true cost; some pass along fees
for risk or Bank Identification Numbers (BINs). You
will get different quotes from different processors,
but agents who state they work directly for Master-
Card or Visa are lying or too inexperienced to know
any better. Neither should be trusted with your processing needs.

11. *"We offer a low flat rate for all transactions."* This is exactly what business owners want to hear. The fact is this creates the most expensive scam for business owners. The merchant hears a "flat rate" of 0.75% to 1.69% and will sign immediately. What the merchant is actually signing is an Interchange Plus contract with a profit margin up to **eight** times higher than the typical retail Interchange Plus contract. A common retail "Plus" markup is 20 to 35 basis points. The markup of 1.69% is equal to 169 basis points. The agent, if called out, will tell you he meant the flat rate over Interchange. What the agent says means nothing. Read the contract and review the agent's local references.

12. *"Just sign this blank contract and I will put in the numbers we discussed later."* This is plain fraud and, believe it or not, it happens. Once you sign, the agent or processor is free to put any amount into the contract and hold you to that number. If anyone suggests that you sign a blank contract, do not sign it. Show this agent the door as he is trying to commit fraud against your business.

Here are a few quick tips for dealing with credit card processing agents.

- Do not discuss credit card processing with people who call you uninvited.

- Ask friends for referrals to find an agent who is recommended highly by those who use his service.

- Ask for local references from the agent.

- If currently under contract, find out if there is a cancellation fee for leaving your current processor.

- *Do not* sign based solely on rate; find out the complete cost and commensurate service provided.

- Determine whether the sales agent will personally provide installation and customer service or whether you will be required to phone a support person.

- Read the FULL contract before signing it. If you are not sure of any clause, present it to your attorney for review. If you do not have an attorney, you may ask your local chamber of commerce or bar association for a referral.

- Make sure you receive a full copy of the contract before the agent leaves.

## CHURNING

*Churning* is the practice of a sales agent signing up the same merchants every time the agent changes processors. Some processors give up-front bonus payments to agents for bringing them processing contracts. Some agents will move from processor to processor and re-sign merchants they have signed with a previous processor.

Churning is an expensive practice for processors **and** for the merchants they sign.

Processors who offer bonus payments (which can range from $200–$1,000 depending on the volume of the business signed) depend on retaining the account for at least the three-year term of the contract. All processors have explicit contracts with sales agents that forbid them from interfering with any contract they placed with the processor for a minimum amount of time (usually three to five years). Business owners may contact the agent on their own, but the agent may not initiate contact.

Business owners are told stories by their agents to get them to sign the new contracts. The merchants sign to stay with someone familiar, but the "familiar" friendly agent they like is placing the merchant in an awful bind. By signing the new contract, the merchant will trigger Early Termination

Fees (ETFs) from his current processor. In many cases, the sales agent either lined out the ETF on the current contract or promised to waive the ETF for the merchant even though he knew he could not legally do either one. If still bound by an existing contract, the end result to the business owner will be paying the ETF when convinced to change to a new processor. A sales agent in Texas reported on an industry forum (owned by industry magazine, *The Green Sheet*) in March of 2010 that one merchant he encountered had over 12 accounts at once! The agent who signed her up each time promised that he cancelled the previous one. Her ETFs were estimated to be over $12,000. This merchant may have been the victim of fraud (the agent may have forged her name on new contracts). Please, watch your bank statements for evidence that your account has been churned if you have been signed up more than once by your agent. If you suspect fraud, contact the local authorities.

How is re-signing a merchant with a new processor "interfering" with a contract that the agent originally signed the merchant to? As I mentioned in the contracts section, the sales agent has no ability to alter a contract or change its terms either up front or when he changes processors because he is not a party to the contract. The business owner is one party and the Member Bank is the other party. The processor acts for the Member Bank and the sales agent signs the merchants. The sales agent either prices exactly as the processor directs or has a "buy-in" cost that he can start from. As stated before, the sales agent can only fill in selected areas of the contract; he cannot line out anything in the language or make any alterations.

Sales agents who practice churning should be banned from processing; nevertheless, they will always find new processors for which to write business. After all, they will bring in new accounts. Then next year, the new processor will have the business taken away when the agent moves to yet another processor.

It is in the business owner's best interest to stay clear of agents who want to move you to their new processor. Even if you like the agent, having him come to you every time he changes processors will cost you money in the end. Think about it; if he disregards his contract with his processor, what makes you think he cares about your contractual obligations when he is not even a party?

## MAKING THE CREDIT CARD PROCESSING DECISION

### Banks

Business owners often turn to their bank when they want credit card processing. Most banks want merchants taking loans from them to process credit cards through them, although forcing them to do so might be a violation of Federal law (section 106 of The Bank Holding Company Act of 1956 concerning "Tying Arrangements"). Merchants believe that all processors are the same and that their bank will treat them better. Banks want the merchant relationship for two primary reasons: belief that the more services used will keep customers from leaving the bank (making it more difficult to sever ties) and because they can charge higher rates and fees for the convenience.

Thirty years ago, banks gave away toasters to get new customers. Now, it seems they compete to see who can create the highest nonsensical fee. Just a few years ago, one of the national banks tried to charge a $3 fee to use a teller instead of using an ATM.

Few banks own their own processing company (most that do are actually owned and run separately by the same bank's holding company). Most banks and, I believe, all credit unions that offer credit card processing use third parties even if it is branded under the bank or credit union name.

In cases where the bank does control the processing company, the sales agents are typically salaried employees. To recoup the salaries, the sales agents are often assigned quotas on the business they bring in—up-front fees, number of accounts, etc.—and they are given little to no leeway on negotiating fees with customers. While with AAMS (ABN AMRO Merchant Services), a joint venture controlled by LaSalle Bank, the pricing I could offer was dictated and depended on several factors. Application fees were required and I was only permitted to offer Tiered pricing.

Banks and credit unions that use third-party processors use their relationship with the merchant to get the merchant's account. Like the "bank-owned" processors, third-party processors allow banks and credit unions to offer additional services to make it a harder decision to pull your money from the bank. A difference is that with third-party processors, the banks and credit unions receive commissions on the referrals and, in some cases, a percentage of the volume each month.

If you like and trust your banker, go ahead and use your bank to process credit cards. Just know that you will typically pay more, sometimes a lot more, for the privilege of using your bank. Most banks are publically owned, for-profit, corporations. With lending restrictions tightened, they need to build profit somewhere. I believe that is the reason why some banks are now heavily advertising credit card processing services to business customers.

### Big Name Providers

Most merchants really do not know the big-name merchant services companies by name. These include First Data®, Bank of America Merchant Services®, Chase-Paymentech®, Global®, and a few others. Another big name is Heartland Payment Systems®; most have heard of this name, but not for the right reasons. I encourage readers to enter the company name in the Google® or Yahoo® search engine. A blog at securosis.com dated January 20, 2009 and Heartland's recent court cases against Verifone®, a major terminal manufacturer, leave concerns in the opinion of the author.

Big-name providers may not be in the merchants' best interests in the long term. When you buy a car, you go to a dealership to pick it up, and when it needs service or you have questions, you go back to your salesperson. Large processors typically want their sales agents to sell and customer service to service the account and answer questions. Name recognition is nice, but knowing you can count on your agent to be there when you need him is preferred by most when given the choice.

## Small Companies and Independent Contractors

As I stated at the beginning of the book, I am an independent contractor. As such, I can write processing contracts for the different credit card processors who I represent. I like being able to use different processors as some companies specialize in different areas. This makes it possible for me to customize solutions for my customers.

The merchants I have signed are with me because I promised fair rates and great service. They have remained with me because I have delivered on my promise and I am the primary contact for customer service. My merchants' job is to take care of their customers; my job is to help them and be available when needed. When an issue or question arises, they call me on my cell phone. If I can give a quick answer or suggestion, I do so. If a call to the processor's help desk is required, I arrange to be there to place the call and resolve the issue.

Many sales agents claim, "The time I spend on customer service is time I am not selling." But as you will read in Kathy Koze's Bonus Chapter, it is thought to be six to seven times more expensive to gain new customers than it is to retain existing ones. Retaining and servicing existing clients will actually help increase your customer base through referrals and references, and at the same time reduce attrition.

Independent contractors will typically give better service and more reasonable costs than either banks or big-name companies. They have little overhead and their customer service is often much more personal.

## Making the Decision

Merchants need to evaluate the sales agent who comes to see them. It is not about where you bank or the size of the company he or she represents. If you do not believe the agent will be there for you, do not sign with that agent.

## IF AN AGENT WILL NOT COME TO SIGN YOU...

It amazes me how many sales agents succeed in gaining new processing accounts without ever meeting the merchants. It further shocks me that business owners who sign up with processors by phone or online are upset when they cannot get assistance in person. If a sales agent will not come to your business to sign you up in person, what makes you think she will come see you in person afterward?

Merchant processing accounts need to be set up in person. With all of the scams on the market today, the business owner should not disclose such confidential information as his bank account numbers and Social Security number to someone he does not know over the phone. Further, how can someone get to know you or how you want to process credit cards without taking the time to meet you in person? Niles Crum, a friend in the industry in the Chicagoland area, offered the only exceptions I can accept to using non-local agents. The exceptions are using an industry specialist that is known by you or a referral from someone you know and trust.

Even when the agent comes to you, you need to be cautious. Only sign with an agent you trust, and then, only after you check the agent's local references. The agent must agree to what you want and need in exchange for the rate and fees you are agreeing to pay. Verifying references will determine if the agent has done as he agreed to with those merchants.

Be advised, there is no guarantee that he will live up to his promises to you, even with verifiable references. This is why I recommend that you request only local references and exercise due caution.

## BAD AGENTS BEWARE

There are thousands of bad processing agents across the country. They mislead merchants and are not held accountable by the card brands or the processing companies they represent. Merchants are locked into contracts that they never would have signed without the misleading statements.

The processors have protected themselves. Their contracts specifically state that they cannot be altered by sales agents. Further, the contract states that it is the only agreement, and supersedes anything the agent says or does. I would think that Agency Law under the Uniform Commercial Code would force a processor to honor its agent's promises; but to my knowledge, the law has not been applied.

Once a merchant realizes that he has been had, he protests to the agent and the processor. The practice of redlining the contract typically works because the alterations are only on the merchant's copy of the contract. Even if both copies have been altered, the processor will only key in the sections that the agent is permitted to complete. Everything else is ignored. The processing company needs only to point to the contract to absolve itself of responsibility. The agent who signs the merchant is not a party to the contract and it would be difficult to pursue action against him or her. The best defense against this type of fraud is to have an attorney review the contract.

I will suggest a way to determine the honesty of an agent. Visit my website, www.creditcardprocessingbook.com, for a form that you can adapt to your needs by working with an attorney in your state so that it reflects the local laws. Use it anytime a processing agent approaches with a contract and ask him to sign it. The form will have check-offs that reflect the promises or statements most agents make. There are also several blanks to be used for adding other statements that the agent makes. Be sure that all of the agent's promises and statements are documented:

☐ You will save $____ per month.

☐ Your terminal, _____, is non-compliant.

☐ You need to lease a new terminal.

☐ The terminal is yours with no strings attached.

☐ And so on.

Now comes the moment of truth. Ask the agent for his driver's license and record the license number, his complete name and address, and have him sign the form. This *must* be done *before* you sign the processing contract. This will give written, actionable documentation of what the agent promised. Now, if the agent fails to provide as he promised, or the merchant discovers she was lied to in order to get a signature on the contract, she can take legal action against the agent (including criminal charges) to recover any cancellation fees levied by the processor or leasing company.

Most agents will balk when first requested to sign the document and provide identification. Once reminded that they ask you for identification, your Social Security number, and other information, many will see that you are trying to protect yourself and will sign the form. I would interpret any further resistance to signing the agreement (that they will live up to their promises or actions) as an indication that the agent might be trying to pull something and should be shown the door.

Is it possible that an honest agent would be shown the door in this situation? Of course, it is. But any agent who knows his stuff and is being straightforward with you will have no trouble signing except to question where you might keep his personal information.

As an honest agent, I am tired of seeing liars promise the world to merchants and not deliver. People ask me all of the time why the contract they signed with a competitor is more expensive than they expected. Processors cannot weed out bad agents unless there is written documentation. Further, once they remove bad agents, other companies still hire them on (until the card brands or regulation penalizes them). There are also bad companies that have supervisors who tell new agents to make alterations to the contract, knowing that their employer (the processor) will not honor the alterations.

Until the card brands, honest processors, and honest agents can find ways to clean up our industry, we will suffer a bad reputation and invite regulation.

Since no one has stepped forward to protect merchants, the merchants need to protect themselves. By having the agent sign the document, you are in effect creating a contract between yourself and the agent. The agent is therefore held accountable for his promises.

## SERVICE VERSUS COST

Like everyone else, a business owner wants the best product and service for the lowest price. And as with everything else, each person needs to decide the exact point where he feels the best value is gained. Just as you will refuse to sign if you believe the cost is too high for the service you need, a sales agent will walk away if he does not receive the amount he wants in profit for the amount of service you want.

Be careful in cases where the service and pricing seem to be a great bargain. You may be dealing with a new agent who cannot deliver on what he is promising you. If you wanted to buy a new Rolex® watch that retailed for $11,825, a reasonable bargain to you might be $10,000 if you found it at a reputable jeweler. However, if you found it for $2,000 anywhere, you would know you were not getting what you wanted.

Hopefully this book has helped to inform you of the options available for pricing and service. You just need to decide on the level of service you desire for the fees you are willing to pay (see Figure 9-1).

## YOU ARE IN BUSINESS TO TURN A PROFIT, SO AM I

Why are you in business? Of course, you are in business to make money. Many people, myself included, need to enjoy what we do and feel a sense of helping others. I have two companies: one for credit card processing, consulting and training; the other is a publishing company that I created to produce this book and others in a series to better realize my dream of helping others. Both of the companies are for-profit.

There are many steps and costs involved in becoming a registered credit card processor: Member Bank sponsorship, registration fees, financial backing, a relationship with a major player like First Data, Global, or TSYS, plus more if handling your own credit risk decisions. The expenses

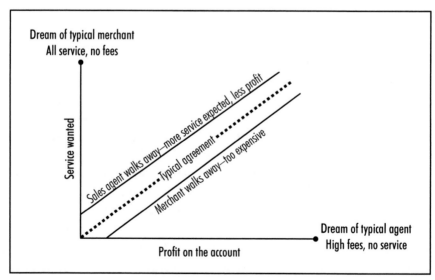

Figure 9-1. Fees versus service.

involved do not include computer security, customer service, technical support, office space, utilities, or other expenses. Credit card processing companies invest all of their money with the expectation of making money. They will price competitively; but they do need to earn money.

Most processors use independent contractors for the following reasons:

- no salaries or wages, production-based compensation only;
- no Social Security, unemployment expenses, or fringes;
- no taxes withheld from compensation;
- all expenses to sign merchants are borne by the sales agents.

Sales agents like being independent because there is no cap on what they can earn and they are their own bosses. But sales agents do work very hard for what they make. They travel to meet new prospects, set up equipment, and train new customers, all while being on call and keeping up with existing customers. And now, we also need to help all clients become and remain PCI-DSS compliant.

While I do understand business owners' concern over pricing, they need to understand that my experience adds value for which I do need to be compensated.

## HOW SALES AGENTS MAKE MONEY

Sales agents make money in several ways. Their primary compensation comes from up-front costs to merchants, rates, Statement fees, other fees, and other services.

Sales agents can make money up front on equipment sales, by reprogramming existing equipment, and from application fees, lease proceeds, and up-front contract bonuses (not all processors offer this, mostly processors with inexperienced agents). Equipment includes Internet gateways, terminals, wireless equipment, and POS systems.

Processors offer independent sales agents several options on buy rates. With Tiered setups, there are two possibilities. One is where the processor sets a base rate and the processor and agent split profits. The other has a higher base rate and the agent keeps everything over it. With Interchange Plus pricing, agents are offered true Interchange and, in some cases, a few other fees like BIN fees that make up our wholesale cost. The "Plus" that agents add is the total profit, which is split between the processor and the agent. Referral fees are typically paid by the agent when a third party introduces the agent to the business owner (like business associations).

Common Statement fees are $10 to $15 per month. Lower Statement fees are typically a sign of a new agent or an agent who will low-ball on Statement fees and rates. Such agents will more than make up for low Statement fees in areas where the customer will not look (Mid-Qualified and Non-Qualified surcharges and other less obvious fees).

There are a number of other fees that can be added onto the contract. Most honest agents will limit these to their actual cost or add only a modest profit. Some agents will bury most of their profit in other fees while listing the rates and statement fees well below most other agents.

Independent processing agents will commonly offer other services in addition to credit card processing. Check processing, gift cards, phone cards, and ATM machines are common services. Consulting and other products also may be offered.

Once you find an agent who you like and trust, ask him about the other services he offers. Buying more than one service can bring better overall pricing. Agents want to sell more than one service because it makes it more difficult for customers to leave.

Why should you care how agents earn money? Because knowing can help you negotiate for better pricing and service. Once you are comfortable with an agent and his references and that he will do what he says he will, you need to be willing to find an agreeable arrangement. Buying equipment and other services from your agent or paying an Application fee or Annual fee will give the agent up-front income and your rates should be more flexible. Negotiation is give and take; listen to your agent's offer and then ask if up-front payments might lower your rates and fees.

# EPILOGUE

I have considered writing this book for some time. I knew I had information to share but thought that my writing skills were not good enough to be a writer. This year I had five things occur that together inspired me to write this book: 1) I found a great editor, 2) I was interviewed for a national industry magazine based on my writings on its forum, 3) I acknowledged my dyslexia and ADD, 4) I took the Dale Carnegie Sales Advantage Training™, and 5) I worked with Business Coach and Author, Minesh Baxi.

I fight with my editor every day, but she takes my industry knowledge and makes it readable. The sales training motivated me to start writing down ideas, which became enough for a book, and Minesh suggested using the book as a marketing tool. A chance meeting put me in front of investors who encouraged me to take the book national.

The credit card processing industry is filled with a lot of honest companies and agents. But there are also vipers and companies that thrive by hiring agents who do not understand the industry. Agents are openly taught underhanded ways of landing contracts.

This book was written to give both new and existing business owners an idea of how the industry works and its pricing and profit structures. The good and the bad are covered. There are also ideas of what I believe an agent should provide a merchant—great value for a fair cost. Both the value given and the cost received need to be negotiated.

The agreement (PDF posted on my website, creditcard-processingbook.com) I am recommending that merchants complete and have agents sign is important for one reason— to bind the agent in a contract with the merchant.

There is one important thing that this book is *not*; it is not a marketing tool to make merchants want to sign with me from across the country. I emphasize in the book how important it is to have a local agent. While I might be willing to consult, I am not looking for credit card processing accounts on a nationwide basis. At present, I cannot give a business owner in Seattle, Washington or Newark, New Jersey the same personal customer service that I am accustomed to providing business owners in metropolitan Detroit. The book's purpose is to give business owners details on the industry and to show them how to find good agents local to them.

I have added 22 "Bonus Chapters," which are authored by experts in their fields. These are to help entrepreneurs with great ideas get from the drawing board to thriving businesses. By hiring experts, a business owner can focus on what she knows best.

Business profits can be increased in three ways: by reducing overhead, increasing productivity or increasing sales. I believe business owners reading this book will find ways to accomplish all three.

## ABOUT MY WEBSITE

I am creating a database on my website, www.creditcard-processingbook.com, for the purpose of matching experts and business owners across the country. The listings will be fee-based, but low cost. The listing will show a company's name, address, contact information and an offer to get business owners to contact them (if desired).

The one industry that will not be charged for listings is credit card processing agents and those will be by invitation only. Only those agents or companies that I believe truly have the merchant's best interest in mind will be listed if they request it. They will not be charged so I can easily remove them if I choose.

The database will initially be set up to find experts listed in a given state. As the database grows, it will be changed to reflect local zip codes.

If the reader would like to find out more about placing listings, I can be reached at bill@creditcardprocessingbook.com.

The author, Bill Pirtle, and MPCT Publishing Company accept no responsibility for actions of anyone found in the listings. Business owners should interview all vendors personally and fully read any contracts before signing. Businesses listed in the database are expected to conduct themselves properly. Unresolved customer complaints may result in removal from the database with no refund.

In addition to the form and database, I am also planning to periodically add resources or links to resources on creditcardprocessingbook.com. Among them:

- The Better Business Bureau and Visa have partnered to create an extensive report on PCI compliance. This 29-page PDF includes checklists and clickable links to other resources. The report can be found at www.bbb. org/data-security/becoming-pci-compliant/overview.

- I will be seeking input and whitepapers from experts in check processing, gift card processing, bill payment, and ATM placements for the website.

- I am planning a blog and encourage readers to email me questions.

- I am also asking readers to sign up for my mailing list. Newsletters and information will be sent out periodically (you will have the option to unsubscribe if you so wish).

# BONUS CHAPTERS

# USING SOCIAL MEDIA IN YOUR BUSINESS

### By Al Crawford, The Crawford Connection

"Who is your customer?" seems like a reasonable question, right? Little did I know that it would be a question that would change my life as January 2009 marked the one-year anniversary of my leaving a 23-year career in the mortgage industry.

Now working for a company selling copiers and having no customer base to work from, my goal is to contact 50 people a day and visit 10 businesses a day. My territory is southern Oakland County. The business district has been hit hard by the economy and it is not unusual for me to go into an office building where half of the space is vacant. I do as I am told, making the calls and the visits, but without much luck.

Basically, I have three ways of generating sales.

1. *Cold call.* This means wandering in and out of businesses praying someone needs to buy a copier and that I am able to sell it.

2. *Telemarketing.* Working in the mortgage industry for quite some time, I did my share of calls and closed millions of dollars in mortgages. But now instead of calling homes, I am calling businesses. They have many layers of people to speak to before you have a chance to talk to the decision maker. Needless to say, trying to speak to the decision maker is next to impossible.

3. *Networking groups.* This seemed easy. Show up; shake a hand; hand out your business card, and then what?

I did not know. But here was the issue. Most networking groups meet two times a month, some once a week. How could I make this work for me?

I joined a networking group, the Local Business Network (LBN), and listened to everybody talk about what they were selling. I did the same. This seemed to make sense. I could do this without a problem.

LBN had 40 chapters and I had no competition, so I could visit as many as I could find time for. I joined a chamber of commerce and two other networking groups. Before I knew it, I was attending 22 networking functions a month! I found myself coming face to face with over 250 people a week who were all looking to generate sales. When you network, you quickly learn that you must give to receive. Needless to say, I had a lot of mouths to feed within all of my networking groups.

I collected a gigantic stack of business cards, which I tried to organize alphabetically—not a chance! I tried putting them in clear sleeves—also a bad idea. How was I going to be able to remember all of these people and what they sold?

## DISCOVERY OF SOCIAL MEDIA

Frustrated with the usual sales methods, I was willing to try anything. So, I attended a class on social media.

The concept of social media was amazing and I was hooked. Now the real problem, how do you use it? The people teaching the class said it was up to me to figure this out.

### Digital vs. Social Strategy

According to a recent blog, BNETinsight (blogs.bnet. com), which explores the views of Harvard Business School, a business owner needs to know the difference between a digital strategy and a social strategy when it comes to using networking sites.

"Want to build a *social networking strategy* with your customers and partners? Here's one piece of advice: Twitter™ is not going to help you. Facebook, yes. Twitter, no."

According to Harvard Business School professor Mikolaj Piskorski, who is doing research on how people use social sites, there is a difference between developing a digital strategy and a social strategy. The best social strategy, he says, is one that helps your customers connect with other customers:

"With Twitter, a company can talk to customers or potentials, and it is two-way communication. This is a great example of a digital strategy that you use as a cheap platform to communicate with your audience. It is a fantastic idea, particularly because it's free! ..."

But using Twitter alone is not a social strategy. According to Piskorski:

"This is not social strategy yet, because it does not allow two people in the audience to be better friends or to meet new friends. It does not allow people to improve their friendships in the same way that Facebook does. And so it does not build the same level of engagement. Note that you can have just a digital strategy, and that's perfectly fine. But you will be missing out on huge opportunities to connect customers to each other. This is where you can really generate huge engagement."

### LinkedIn®, Facebook, and Twitter™

My first learning hurdle was LinkedIn, which is an amazing tool, but one that is misunderstood and misused by most people. I spent about three months researching it and became a huge fan.

Part of networking is doing what is called one-on-one meetings with fellow group members. Usually about an hour in length, you discuss your respective businesses and learn more about one another. I began discussing LinkedIn with people and realized that many of them were signed up on the site but had no idea how to use it. I found myself spending more and more time during my one-on-one meetings teaching people how to use it.

"Who is your customer?" This is the most important thing to keep in mind in any networking situation whether it is in a group or online. I was horrified to find that most people I talked to did not know the answer to this question. In the past, they just put an ad in the phone book and waited for a customer to call. Those days are gone and they had no clue where they went. This prompted me to ask this very question of each person I did a one-on-one with, ultimately helping many business owners define their customer audiences.

A unique feature of LinkedIn is that you have the ability to join 50 of its groups and to define who you are in each one along with the business you are in. For instance, there was one insurance agent who joined five insurance groups. Where were his customers?

## USING SOCIAL NETWORKS TO IMPROVE YOUR BUSINESS

I quit the copier company, finding my niche teaching people how to use LinkedIn (and other social media) to improve their businesses. Many experience immediate sales from the new contacts within the groups they join. Two people actually landed the largest contracts of their careers through the groups I advised them to join. I have helped more than 300 people learn about social media and the results are mind numbing.

Many people think they need to have a presence on all three sites, LinkedIn, Facebook, and Twitter, but have no idea how to do it, how to manage it, etc. What I have come to realize is that every business does not need all three and some may need only one. The decision is based on who the customer is, and how much time the business owner has to spend on doing it. Based on customer audience, I can advise business owners on which social media site they should learn about first, second, etc. It is impossible to tackle all three at once. I spent three months on LinkedIn before I joined Facebook, and it was another two months before I joined Twitter.

I now have a network on LinkedIn of more than 12.5 million people and over 2,600 first-level connections. My number of Facebook friends grew to more than 1,600 in less than nine months. This means that I touch more than 4,000 people per day with information about my company. It takes me less than 40 minutes a day to manage it and, best of all, it is free!

So which site should you tackle first? I guess that depends on who your customer is.

LinkedIn is for any business owner who wants to network with peers (and groups), other business owners, and decision makers. There you can join industry groups (or start your own), find and network with colleagues, and keep up on current trends and news within your industry.

Facebook is the next conquest. Much like the White Pages™, on Facebook you have the ability to search for people in many ways, by name, the schools they attended, region, etc. You have the ability to find people from your past that you never dreamed of finding again. I have found people from my past that I had not heard from in over 30 years. Do you think you are too old for this? I graduated almost 30 years ago and found 175 people from my high school class there.

What does this mean for your business? Remember, people want to deal with people they know, like, and trust. People from your past or present are those people. Use Facebook to teach people you know about what you do for a living. You will be amazed at how many will want your products or services. You have the ability to create what is called a "fan page," a forum that allows you to place a so-called "commercial" for your business on your profile. In this way, your connections can express interest by attaching themselves as a "fan," without feeling like they are being sold to. You can also create a group for your company, allowing you to post events, meetings, etc., along with photos, video, etc. If you have a business that has a local presence, Facebook is a must to reach your customers.

As for Twitter, it is the one that needs the most attention. Over 50 million people "tweet" now, but the number of active "tweeters" is actually much lower. Tweeting is really more like "texting" than anything else. A "tweet" is a short phrase or statement about anything you wish to convey and can include a hot link . . . news of a new product, a helpful tip, etc. You need to post around 10 times per day to be seen and gain followers. Major corporations actually hire full-time people to tweet all day long. People who follow you are also following many other people and companies. This means that you need to be posting something—all the time. If you have a younger clientele, this may be where you need to focus your time.

I see in some situations that someone will use a tool like Tweetdeck™, which allows you to post on all three networking sites at the same time. Although it may seem to make the job of posting easier, using such tools creates some issues. For instance, you would never speak the same way to someone on LinkedIn as you would on Twitter. Your audiences are different, and thus the messages you post should be targeted to your specific "customers."

The bottom line for any business is that social networking is where marketing has gone. If you think you can survive without using it, you are wrong. It can take as little as 40 minutes a day for you to maintain a successful presence on LinkedIn and Facebook. A little more time would be needed to do the same on Twitter. But it is not impossible. If you do not have time to manage it, hire someone.

There is nothing evil, scary, or dangerous about these forums. You share only the information you want to make public. Facebook has just added more security features that make it that much more safe for the small business owner. If you have used the Yellow Pages® online to your advantage—you must look at LinkedIn—it is the new Yellow Pages on steroids.

Using social networking sites has changed my life and the lives of those whom I have trained. The author of this book was such a huge fan of social media after receiving my training that he asked me to write this chapter.

## USING SOCIAL MEDIA TO FIND JOB CANDIDATES

I was asked to conduct a series of social media classes for people who are "in transition" (we are no longer allowed to say "unemployed" as it is not politically correct). What I heard from human resources people, hiring managers, and recruiters was, "If you are 'in transition' and don't have a presence on LinkedIn and Facebook, you are not employable." Why?

Employers do not only get a single resume for an open position. Many are submitted. So, to weed people out, they search online for information about potential candidates. If an individual is not on LinkedIn and Facebook, they are inclined to pass. Here is why. As an employer, you need to get a truer picture of the person, which is not available from just a resume. Before spending time and money, you look on LinkedIn to see a candidate's employment past, recommendations from former employers, the positions listed, etc., allowing you to compare the information posted to the resume in hand. In the tight labor market, many employers have found former upper-level managers "dumbing up" their resumes to get lower-level positions.

Okay, but why look on Facebook? You want to see who the "social" person is, the groups he belongs to, what he is saying about people, and the places he has worked. For potential candidates, this may seem like having a big brother. You bet, and it is for real. If a candidate protects his profile from being viewed, your next question is, "What are you hiding?"

Another useful tool that LinkedIn offers is the ability to post job openings—another way to get the word out.

\*\*\*

Give these amazing tools a try. If you are looking to link with your peers and customers, the time you spend on social media will be the best 40 minutes you spend each day.

\*\*\*

Al Crawford is a regional manager with the Local Business Network. His consultancy, the Crawford Connection, specializes in training business owners on the use of social media. He can be reached by email or phone, alcrawford@thecrawfordconnection.net, 586-883-5838.

# THE IMPORTANCE OF QUALITY PHOTOGRAPHY IN YOUR BUSINESS

*Bob DiTommaso, www.GetShotByBob.com*

We have all heard the advice that "You only get one chance to make a first impression." In actuality you may not even get that one chance. In today's world of websites and social media, your electronic communications are often your real first impression. Electronic media can go a long way toward endearing potential customers to you and your brand; but if not done well, it can disappoint them to the point that you may never even hear from them.

I often listen to self-help programs. Several that I have refer to the fact that we think in pictures. If someone asked you to think of your house, an image of your house becomes clearly visible in your mind. When you think of friends or business associates, you can formulate a picture of them in your mind as well. If you have never met someone and they are seeing your picture for the first time, that picture has to speak on your behalf. Your headshot should clearly convey who you are. For many it will be their introduction to you; as such, it should give the viewer some insight into what you are about. I believe the photo of me at the beginning of this chapter tells you that I have an air of adventure in the way that I approach life, and that I enjoy what I do.

## CRITICAL ELEMENTS OF A GOOD HEADSHOT

We all do business with others when we feel as though we know them; we like what we see and we trust them. Does your head shot help potential customers to get a sense of who you are? Does it instill a sense of trust? Does it make you happy when you see it? It should do all of these things. The simple act of viewing your photograph should allow potential customers to feel as though you are there connecting with them. Assuming you agree, and you should, what elements are critical to a good head shot?

1. You should be clear and prominent in the image. You should not be competing with any other element in the image. Studio photos accomplish this by placing you in front of a pleasing background without any other elements in the photo. As my headshot shows, this also can be accomplished outside the studio. By employing proper composition and making appropriate use of the camera controls, my image manages to isolate me from the background while still clearly showing that I am out in nature.

2. Do not try to isolate yourself from a group picture and make it your headshot. This ties in closely with rule number one. There should be no distractions within the image to make the viewer wonder who got chopped off.

3. Use an image that is appropriate for the space allotted. I had sufficient space at the beginning of this chapter to include a fair amount of background in my image. When possible, I prefer to show the background

because it helps to give a greater sense of who I am. However, when space is limited, crop, crop, crop. LinkedIn® offers one of the smallest profile pictures of all the social media sites. I would not use the full frame image shown at the beginning of this chapter for my LinkedIn profile. It requires cropping to be viewable and as effective as possible on a site such as LinkedIn.

4. Do everything in your power to look your best. If you look at my picture, you will notice there are no dark shadows or bright highlights obscuring my face. Natural light, if done properly, is wonderful. A professional photographer will pay close attention to the quality of the light falling on your face, either indoors or out.

5. Give potential customers the opportunity to connect with you. You should be looking into the camera, but not leering or staring. Glasses are fine if you wear them all the time, but definitely not sunglasses. Eye contact is a key part of how we connect with each other, either in person or via a well-executed photograph.

6. Do not be afraid to reveal who you are—be real. I love being outdoors, and my picture unequivocally conveys my ease at being in nature. As a professional photographer, prospective clients seek my services because they are looking for someone artistic to execute a project on their behalf. My headshot is appropriate for who I am and what I do. If you are an information technology (IT) specialist who happens to love hunting, I would not recommend that you be photographed in the woods with your rifle; but I might suggest that you sit on the edge of a desk with a computer out of focus in the background. While a studio image is always a safe choice, an image with you in your "environment" is often much more telling.

7. Lastly, be yourself; we all have an innate sense of what is real and what is fake. If you do not typically wear a suit and tie everyday, then I would not encourage you to do so for your headshot. I often advise my clients to wear clothes that make them happy. If they act confused, I say, "What outfit would you reach for if you could wear anything in your closet?"

## WEBSITE IMAGE QUALITY

Great, now you understand that you need to update that headshot photo ASAP. But what about updating the rest of your website? If you feature images of your work there, are you proud of those images? All of the arguments given to this point about your head shot also apply to all of the images on your website. You want potential as well as current customers to come away from visiting your website with the unmistakable conclusion that you are a professional.

I was recently asked to consult with an architect regarding his website. While the work he did was clearly first rate, the images on his website failed to communicate the breadth and quality of his talent. The pictures were poorly composed and often overexposed. There was no detail in large areas of one image because it was taken in bright sunlight and the glare off the windows caused much of the picture to be so bright you could not see the underlying design.

My professional assessment included a recommendation to re-shoot the images either early in the day or late in the evening when the light would be much more diffused as it neared the horizon. By altering the camera placement and using an appropriate selection of lenses, I was able to show the unique characteristics of his design that had initially captivated his customer and led to his being awarded the project.

I see similar instances of poorly executed product photography as well, such as florists websites featuring bouquets of flowers photographed against stark white backgrounds. People buy flowers for their beauty, and the images on a floral website need to speak to that beauty. Anyone can go to a grocery store to buy plain ugly flowers. If you are a professional florist, prospects seek you out for your experience, knowledge, and creativity. Your website needs to demonstrate all of those things, and beautiful images speak volumes on all three accounts.

***

No matter what your business, there are creative ways to capture your unique approach and convey what makes you special via photographs. The use of professional photography will improve your website and printed advertising materials. Step back and take an objective look at your imagery and decide if your business is in need of a photographic facelift.

***

A skilled and creative professional, Bob DiTommaso will work with you to craft images that meet your specific needs. Bob can capture your professional headshot, product display, real estate/interior design, or other commercial entity. Some of Bob's clients include Chrysler/Mopar, Ford, and SCAM/KH Homes.

Bob also shares his decades of photography experience with photo enthusiasts through his workshops, which include classroom technical training as well as hands-on field work.

You can contact Bob by phone: 248-608-8563, cell: 248-941-4859, email: Bob@GetShotByBob.com; or website: GetShotByBob.com.

# DATABASES— ORGANIZING INFORMATION AND MAKING IT USEFUL

## By Michele Robinson, Office Productivity Consultants

## WHAT IS A DATABASE?

In one of my children's videos, Pooh Bear calls an empty honey pot a "useful pot for putting things in." A database is also a useful pot for putting things in—those "things" being bits of data—while the "pot" is a virtual container on the computer.

The database itself is an empty pot—actually a series of empty pots—where you can put data to organize it, label it, and make it easy to find when you need it. But a computerized database can do much more. It allows those "pots" to be *related* (or *linked*) to each other. Databases are designed to easily sort, process, and analyze your information, providing useful reports and summaries to you, often at the click of a button.

People use various databases every day. The simplest ones store your basic contact information—names, addresses, phone numbers, and email addresses of your friends, family, and business associates. You look up "Smith" (you know you will find it under "S") and see the phone number you need to call John Smith.

Examples of more complex databases are those used for online shopping. At Amazon.com®, you can search under "jewelry" for "pearl necklaces" and you quickly get a list of all the currently available pearl necklaces listed in Amazon's products-for-sale database. If items are added or removed from the database tonight, the list you get tomorrow will reflect those changes.

Databases provide up-to-the-minute information, fast. Returning to the Amazon example, product managers and marketers can also get reports from the database showing how many of each item are in stock, what else customers bought in the same order with a specific item, and how advertising campaigns are affecting the sales of items. This kind of information helps them run their business, and target their marketing efforts to increase sales.

## WHY EVERY BUSINESS NEEDS DATABASES

Every business collects information and must have a place to put it—a system that will make it easy to store and retrieve it. The information can be as simple as lists of customers and basic things the business needs to know about them—names, addresses, phone numbers, etc.—or as sophisticated as including buying habits, history, demographics, etc. Information can be stored in many ways, among them being on a cell phone (it has a database for that), in a spreadsheet, in an email program like Microsoft Outlook® (a database itself), or in a customer relationship management (CRM) software package (a database).

Depending on the business, there is also other information that needs to be "put" somewhere. This can include data on products and services, price lists, suppliers, raw materials and supplies, and production and maintenance records, to name a few. This data may or may not have a place to fit in the same system the business uses to track basic customer information. If not, there is a need for another, more comprehensive system to store it.

The kind of information you have and the volume will help you determine the best type of system for your business. If you provide two kinds of service and have ten customers, you can keep your customer and sales information on paper in file folders, or in a simple spreadsheet on the computer. You can probably find any information you need, and make any calculations you might want in a few minutes. But if you grow to offer ten services and sell to 200 customers, it can be harder to keep everything organized, and take longer to find information. For instance, if you want to determine which customers have (or have not) purchased services in the last three months, or which services are most popular in a particular city, it could take hours (or days!) to review all of the files and "mine" for the data you need. A computerized database system is capable of providing these types of summaries in seconds.

If you expect to have large amounts of information, complex information, or want to be able to *efficiently* analyze, summarize, and report based on certain criteria (that is, actually use it to help your business), you need some sort of database system.

## COMMERCIALLY AVAILABLE VS. CUSTOM DATABASES

There are many commercially available software packages that can be used for your business. ACT® or Gold Mine® is designed to track contact people. Quickbooks® can help you track your finances, payroll, and invoices. Specialty medical and dental offices can buy software designed for their type of business, which will track appointments, patient history, and insurance payments. These types of software are readily available and usually a reasonable cost option, since their development cost is spread over hundreds or thousands of users. Such off-the-shelf systems not only offer convenience, but cost much less to buy than what it would cost to create a customized system from scratch.

What if there is no commercially available software designed to fit the specific needs of your business? You can try to use something that "sort of" fits, and live with its limitations, or you can look into custom options.

## IF YOU HAVE CUSTOM NEEDS, HOW DO YOU HANDLE THEM?

Wanting to save money, "custom" options often start with a staff member or relative who "knows computers" designing spreadsheets or even basic databases for the business. This can work for awhile or, if the person is actually knowledgeable and experienced, it can result in a seemingly good solution for the company. But there are a number of potential pitfalls that should be considered, including:

1. The person designing the system may move on to a new job elsewhere, or become too busy doing their "regular" job to be available to update the system as the business needs and technology changes over time.

2. The system, unfortunately, is most often only a partial solution, poorly structured, and does not take full advantage of the features and options that a well-designed database can offer to help a business grow.

The other option is to have a database custom designed to work for the business. Everyone knows that "custom" is not synonymous with "cheap." A custom-designed database, built by knowledgeable experts, certainly will not be free. It has the potential, however, to be the most cost-effective option for your business.

## BENEFITS OF A WELL-DESIGNED DATABASE

A well-designed database can help a business owner save time (and money) by making it fast and easy to find information and answer questions about business performance, customers, products, and more. For instance:

- A national union can quickly locate information about locals and the companies it serves, as well as contract expiration dates, pay increases, and other provisions— all in one spot, rather than spread among dozens of people across the country. There is only one central, shared database that gets updated.

- A company providing maintenance for a hospital system's test equipment (x-rays, scanning equipment, etc.) can instantly identify and eliminate duplicate billings for expensive parts from suppliers. In the old system, duplicates were missed during manual reviews of hundreds of invoices, resulting in money lost paying for the same items twice.

For marketing and advertising purposes, a custom database can "mine" the information needed to target customers and prospects for special offers, brochures, catalogs, announcements, etc. For example:

- To recruit young actors for a play, a theater group can easily send out casting call notices only to group members with children, rather than to *every* member of the group (saving postage, paper, and processing time). The same theater group also can easily send invitations for a special event to high-level donors and season-ticket holders.

- An industry membership organization can send invoices to its members via email (generated automatically by its database), with links to pay online. Reminder emails can be later sent out to those who have not yet paid. Thus the entire paper mailing time and cost are eliminated.

## YOUR DATABASE IS A BUSINESS ANALYSIS TOOL

A good database can help you build your business and make more money by making it easy to summarize and analyze information for selected groups of customers, products, time periods, etc. For example,

- Are certain products more popular in one geographic area than another?

- Tracking sales of items, or groups of items, over weeks, months, quarters, or years—how are they changing? Do you need to change something?

- Identify slow-moving items for possible additional marketing efforts.

- Identify fast-moving items to avoid out-of-stock situations.

Compiling statistics over time can help you track performance, as well as target ways to grow your business. You may want to determine:

- How often do customers reorder specific products? Can you create subscription and automatic shipment programs to service them better (and help encourage them to stay loyal to your business)? Can you send reminders to other customers of those items to make them into repeat customers too?

- Which of your marketing people is responsible for maintaining relationships with which customers? Who have they not contacted in the last 30, 60, or 90 days? How about generating a report on Monday that tells sales people which customers they should call this week, along with a summary for each one (purchase history, notes from previous conversations, and information about their businesses and needs)?

A well-designed database system, customized to work with your business, can be worth many times its initial cost.

## WHAT DO YOU NEED TO LOOK FOR IN CHOOSING A DATABASE DESIGN EXPERT?

The main qualities you should look for are:

1. Someone who is an experienced and trained expert, capable of creating a properly designed database and

a user-friendly interface (the screens that the users actually see).

2. Someone who is capable of understanding *your* business—what you do, how you do it, and where you want to go with it.

3. Someone skilled at process design and detecting inefficiencies.

The first is almost self-evident. You need to hire someone who is technically capable of doing the job. What kind of education and experience does he have? How long has he been doing this kind of work? What kinds of databases, and how many has he created for other companies? Can he show you samples of his work? Can you contact other customers for references, or does he have testimonials from other customers?

Number two is just as important. If you are paying to have something custom-built for your business, the designer(s) need to understand how your business processes work, how you prefer to work, and your ultimate goals. Only then will they be capable of creating a system that works with you, complements your business, and helps you grow. If they do not understand your business, then they may create a system that is great—but for someone else. A tech-geek (or company) with little business knowledge or experience may be a big disappointment in the long run. Again, you need to ask the right questions. Has he done work for companies in different kinds of businesses, or all the same kind? Can he listen to you describe your business, and then ask questions and discuss it in a way that makes you comfortable that he understands what you are talking about? What do his other customers say about him in this regard?

The third quality is especially important since your database application will automate your current business activities. You want a consultant who can spot waste in your current business practices so that it is not carried over into your brand new system. This helps improve the productivity of your system and, more importantly, your staff.

Another thing to keep in mind is communication. There needs to be lots of communication to ensure that the designer(s) understands all of the needs of the business. Also, when automating a process that is currently in place, the people actually working within that process should be consulted, not just their managers. They can provide information about the normal flow of the process. More importantly, they can explain any special cases they run into, and the challenges associated with them. Designing with these in mind eliminates, "Oh, no —what do we do now!" crises later.

*\*\*\**

Databases are used every day by most people. They not only provide a way to store, organize, and retrieve information, but also have features to make that information more useful and valuable to a business. A good database can be the difference between a business that just hangs on, and one that grows and thrives.

*\*\*\**

Michele Robinson has a B.A. in Mechanical Engineering from the General Motors Institute of Technology (now Kettering University) and an MBA from the University of Michigan. In business for 20 years, her company, Office Productivity Consultants, specializes in software solutions for companies. She can be reached at 248-553-8000, email: mrobinson@opcinc.com, website: www.opcinc.com.

# EFFECTIVE BUSINESS PLANNING

## by Joan Florian, TTX Ingenuity, LLC

The primary job of a business owner is to manage and run a business, and to do this effectively, a plan is needed. The term *manage* implies the task of planning and execution. Without a plan, it is not clear what to execute and success is tough to monitor.

Business plans are commonly an entry-level requirement to getting government money, investor capital, or bank loans. They are also used to define the actions associated with growing or transitioning a business. As such, they are often referred to by business owners to make sure that actions and decision-making are in step with the plan. Further, key elements of the plan should be reviewed and discussed in a yearly strategic planning event.

### THE BENEFITS OF BUSINESS PLANNING

The process of business planning helps reduce risks and guides the company through execution. Typical business plans project one year, five years, and ten years into the future state of the business. Thus a business plan is needed regardless of whether a company is an existing business or a start-up. The benefits include:

- Basic business planning is a systematic methodology for reducing risk and enhancing success for any type of business operation.

- It is the framework in which to structure concepts and information about the business or a project within that business.
- The business plan organizes, directs, coordinates, controls, and facilitates the development of a project from its inception to its completion.
- It communicates in writing the strategic and tactical direction for the company.
- The plan refines the product offerings and compares them against the competitive landscape.
- It highlights product/service strengths and exposes weaknesses or barriers to entry into particular markets.
- It ensures the company's position in the marketplace (there is proof that entry into a new market and/or current position is sustainable).
- The business plan provides a powerful tool for acquiring investors and company participation as it provides the information needed by others to evaluate a venture, especially if seeking outside financing.
- The process of business planning forces the team to truly assess feasibility.
- It clarifies the financial requirements for delivery and provides the reality check for business viability.

## BUSINESS PLAN CONTENTS

The key contents of a business plan are included in the following sections, in the context of a start-up business. Existing companies should use the elements as a guide for yearly strategic planning.

### Executive Summary/Concept

The Executive Summary includes an overview of the business plan. Even though it will be at the beginning of the plan, write it after the rest of the plan is completed. It brings together the significant points of the plan and should convey excitement in a thoughtful and clear way.

Remember that the summary, which starts your plan, is the single most important part. Many people will not read past the summary. Whether the company is a start-up or existing business, this section is critical for external use with investors; thus it needs to be written clearly.

The Executive Summary contains a succinct description of the company's product(s) or service(s) with its unique selling proposition; the business model for making money; the market penetration plan with the target market; and closes by talking about the management team's demonstrated experience to inspire confidence and ensure the plan's delivery.

### General Description

The General Description explains the type of company and the industry it serves. If it is an existing business, a history is given. If it is a new start-up business, some of the qualifications to start the business are noted. It is also important to be clear in explaining why the business is needed and its chance for success.

### Management Team and Organizational Plan

The Management Team and Organizational Plan section identifies the people who will be active in the business and the key positions they hold. Skills, experience levels, and credentials are described. Team advisors, additional members needed to round out experience for required growth, or those individuals who are critical to success are also included.

### Marketing Plan

The Marketing Plan identifies the company's target market. There should be specific target markets that will need the company's products or services and be willing to pay for them. Analysis is given of the industry size and potential, trends, financial profitability, and distribution channels.

The types of customers are defined and whether or not they have a direct or indirect need for the company's particular product or service.

With a firm understanding of the customer, a marketing strategy is derived—one that will draw customers to the company rather than the competition. The primary competitors are listed along with an honest appraisal of their strengths and weaknesses and how your business will compete successfully against them.

In the initial phases it will be a challenge to be exact. Nevertheless, the focus should be directionally correct, especially if there are many competitors in the company's market.

For an existing business, the examination of the market forces, trends, and dynamics needs to consider the question of what happens with a product or service if the market moves. Do you move with it (revise/repackage the product offering) or move away from it and reposition in a new market? The impacts of these decisions dramatically affect both revenue opportunities and expenses, so look at the return on investment of your decisions.

There are many sites to use to investigate industry and other demographics. Listed below are a few:

- U.S. Census Bureau—Business and Industry, http://www.census.gov/econ/
- North American Industry Classification System (NAICS), http://www.census.gov/eos/www/naics/
- Michigan elibrary databases, http://www.mel.org

### Product/Service Plan

The Product/Service Plan section describes the product and/or service sufficiently so that business people without specific product background can determine what kind of product is being sold and what problem it will solve. People buy products and services, not technologies; technologies are only enablers.

Define the unique features of the product or service and explain why customers will come to this business. Communicating this effectively requires refinement and skill, but the easier it is to understand, the more people will be interested.

### Financial Plan

A big part of the job is to build and manage the financial position of the company.

This effort for many is daunting and in some cases terrifying. Take a deep breath, as there are many resources available to help you. It is always good to seek counsel from CPAs and accountants. However, to minimize expense, it is worth educating yourself first and saving the main expense for clarifying critical questions or direction. Taking an accounting class or doing some Internet research will help.

If you are just getting started, you need to gather some key information on expenses in two categories, both start-up and operating expenses.

State the company's financial requirements and where these funds will come from: project revenues, costs, and profits. Your efforts in developing the financial statements will help you understand the cash flow of your business, your breakeven point, where profitability is achieved. and the sensitivity of your business to fluctuations associated with market and business factors.

### Start-up Costs

Start-up costs are usually one-time expenses associated with registering your business with federal, state, or local municipalities; setup costs, down payments or deposits on utilities, equipment, rent, or land; permits, licenses, and fees to join regulatory bodies; inventory; and other like expenses.

### What are Operating Expenses?

The cost of the day-to-day operations of a business once it is up and running are considered operating expenses. Most expenses paid monthly for the duration of the business' life cycle are probably operating expenses. Below is a list of standard operating expenses:

- wages and salaries;
- rent/mortgage/lease and utilities;
- bank and loan fees;
- advertising, marketing, and promotions;
- office supplies;
- storage and distribution;
- association dues and fees;
- training and education; and
- maintenance.

To estimate what is needed to start a business, add the list of operating expenses and multiply that monthly number by six to get a full six months' worth of operating costs and then add the total start-up costs.

The next step in creating a financial plan is to create the three financial tables included in the business plan: the income statement, balance sheet, and cash-flow statement.

**Income statement**. This provides a look at how the business is faring from a profit standpoint, using a very simple equation: revenue minus expenses equals either profit or loss.

The document serves as a report card that tells whether the company's strategies are working. It is largely a tax document developed in accordance with IRS regulations.

In managing a business, it is important to assess the expenses incurred to deliver the revenues; adjusting actions on both is essential to long-term success.

**Balance sheet**. The balance sheet component of the business plan takes information from the income statement and cash flow projection and compiles the data into one, easy-to-read document.

The income statement only shows a portion of the financial picture of the business, company profitability, while the balance sheet describes what the company owns, who owes the company money, and who the company owes money to, such as banks or other creditors or investors.

The other financial statements do not give a good enough view to a bank manager or loan company as to just how solvent a company is; for instance, are there assets to liquidate that could potentially pay off the company's debt?

**Cash-flow statement.** Two critical objectives of the company are financial profitability and cash flow.

The cash-flow statement shows the money flowing in and out of the company on a monthly basis.

While the income statement reports sales, the cash flow statement reports revenue in time. The income statement will report sales, but yet the cash is not yet received. Frequently, expenses incurred in month one may not be covered by receipts in the same month as a result of established terms and conditions and, in many cases, customers who do not pay on a timely basis.

Also, the income statement may not show significant outflow of cash; for example, inventory or payments to owners or in-flow for items such as borrowing cash from a bank. Therefore, the cash-flow statement becomes one of the most important supporting documents because it shows the ability of the company to meet its financial obligations.

Once the company is operational, the cash-flow statement becomes one of the primary management tools that the team needs to run the business. The company should acquire competent financial advisors, analysts, and accountants to facilitate effective business and operational decisions, as well as to keep the company federally compliant.

### Operations

The Operations section explains any systems or processes that will be used. It defines the facilities, if any, and what supplies will be needed and where can they be obtained.

In most cases, the original plan may presume a simpler process, where product is produced in small batches and the location may be part of a dwelling. Then as customers and revenue increase, there is a need for buildings and more employees. All of these can and should be projected in the plan.

Also describe the labor plan (full-time, contract, part-time) and how it will be accessed. What are the hours of operation of the business? Are the products and services acquired only through a representative, an online site, or a mixture of these and a store front?

### Legal

The Legal section describes how the business is registered legally—sole proprietorship, partnership, "S" corporation, limited liability company, or corporation. If patents or trademarks are involved, they should be listed here too.

## THE MANTRA FOR SUCCESS: EDUCATE, EXPERIENCE, AND EXECUTE!

The key to success is to plan your way to it. Don't let life or business just happen. Many small business owners treat their company in the same way they do their personal life, only doing things because they have to. They do not possess large amounts of staff yet need to accomplish the required tasks efficiently. How do they accomplish this? The answer is to connect with professionals in their industry through associations, trade shows, and journals. These avenues facilitate hiring a consultant, who is best located by a referral, and whose expertise is specific to the company's need. CPAs/CFOs, lawyers, and marketing experts with industry experience also should be consulted as needed.

Mentors are available through local small business efforts such as SCORE, http://www.score.org/findscore/index.html. Michigan also has SMARTZONES, which are business incubating centers. Located around the state, they offer mentors and consultants to assist business owners in their efforts (more information is available at www.michiganadvantage.org).

It is also important to research the following journals and other sources, which are available at your local library:

- Financial data supplied by Risk Management Associates' member institutions are included in the *RMA Annual Statement Studies*. It is organized by NAICS or standard industry classification (SIC) code and contains 19 widely used financial ratios. Make sure you have the correct industry code number before using the book. It provides benchmark industry ratios for large, medium, and small-sized firms. You can also look on-line at www.SECFilings.com.

- Dun and Bradstreet provide data on industry norms and other key business ratios.

- Small Business Administration assistance is available through federal, state, or local sites. In Michigan, there are two sites: www.michiganadvantage.org and www.michigan.gov/business.

Whatever path is chosen, owning and managing your own business can be both rewarding and challenging. Take heart in the thought that your efforts are critical to economic rebirth.

\*\*\*

A Kettering University graduate, Joan Florian has 20 years experience in the areas of product development, program management, and manufacturing operations. She has led teams, successfully integrating unique disciplines and diverse backgrounds, while developing strategic plans and leveraging product knowledge to engineer and produce new and exciting products. Her analytical skills and ability to understand the customer and the competitive battleground have facilitated her efforts to grow businesses and improve margins through best practices, product leadership, and innovation. Joan can be contacted via her website, www.ttxingenuity.com.

# FINDING THE BEST PROMOTIONAL PRODUCTS CONSULTANT

## by Tim Somers, Bizarre Promotions, Inc.

Although it may seem that all promotional products companies offer the same merchandise, they are not created equal. Some companies are nothing more than order takers, filling the needs of clients who know what they want. Most are ill equipped to advise clients on what they need in regard to using promotional products in their marketing plans.

There are well over 750,000 items available on which you can custom print a logo or message, and the possibilities are endless. Many end users do not put much thought into purchasing promotional products. They are told to give something away at a trade show booth or to include something in a direct mail piece that has no relevance to the campaign's theme. This is where a well-qualified promotional products consultant (PPC) comes into play.

If you have a need for a promotional item and you have a pretty good idea of what you want, do not share that information with your PPC. Tell the PPC all about your event or campaign and, most importantly, tell him about your goals. A well-seasoned PPC will then put his game face on and come up with an action plan on how to achieve the outcome you desire. If the PPC is really good, you will get more than one option to choose from.

In searching for a perfect promotional products consultant, you should use the following checklist to evaluate a company prior to a personal meeting.

1. Does the PPC have a website and is it current and professional looking? If it is not well designed, chances are that the company operates in a similar manner. Further, if a company is not good at branding on its website, how on earth would you expect it to provide you with meaningful recommendations? Even worse, if a company has no web presence at all, it is defiantly not up on current industry trends and should not even be considered to represent you and your company.

2. How long has the promotional products company been in business? Shady companies come and go; you want to make sure the company you choose has been in business at least 10 years. This will give you a sense of experience and reliability, and you will want to continue working with a company that will be around for the long haul.

3. Is it a brick-and-mortar store or a part-time home business? Many promotional products distributors are work-from-home, part-timers. While many may be qualified to offer you brilliant marketing ideas using promotional products, others are simply not committed nor do they have the training and experience that a full-service, brick-and-mortar PPC offers.

4. Google® the company. If it has any web presence, you can use the Internet to see what customers are saying about it. You should also check out the Better Business Bureau; search its online database to see if the company has complaints against it. You can quickly see if a company ignores their complaints or handles them swiftly and to the satisfaction of customers.

5. Get a referral. You can turn to your network of business connections and find a company that has a proven track record with your inner circle. Or, if you happen to see an intriguing campaign that used a promotional product,

contact the company that sent it. Ask its marketing manager who he procured the promotional product from.

Once you have selected a promotional products company to interview personally, you should ask its representative to bring in several examples and case studies that his company has implemented and executed. Seeing what is brought to the meeting will determine the length of the meeting—lame and weak promotion examples or none at all can speed along the meeting so you can move on to another firm. But if there are quality examples and you think the PPC will provide superior results, you can confidently tell him what you want to achieve. However, keep in mind that this meeting is still just an interview—make no promises; you may wish to interview several companies before you decide to choose one to handle your account.

There are approximately 20,000 promotional product distributors in the United States—all offering the same 750,000 plus items. You can easily get overwhelmed in sifting through them to find one you are comfortable with. Choose a promotional products consultant who asks about your business goals and is knowledgeable about the products he offers and how he can customize them to meet your needs. Only then will you be sure to get targeted solutions that will give you the maximum return on your investment. Do your homework; make sure that the company has good business practices and prompt customer service. In the end, the company should deliver the right product, when promised, and at the price you agreed upon.

\*\*\*

Tim Somers is president and founder of Bizarre Promotions, Inc. His company has been in business for over 20 years, helping all types of companies grow through the power of promotional products. His innovative marketing strategies have gained the trust and loyalty of countless clients from small businesses to Fortune 500 companies.

Tim can be reached by phone: 734-782-9600 or 888-675-7883, website: www.promostuff4u.com.

# BUYING TECHNOLOGY: WHAT THE SALESMAN HOPES YOU DON'T KNOW AND WON'T ASK

### by Mike Whelan,
### YourPCpitstop.com and PCbuyersAgent.com

Like the credit card processing business, the computer industry has its secrets. Some of them are one-time opportunities to be victimized; others will haunt your business with every passing day, bleeding away productivity, patience, and time with every mouse click. Early intervention is the key to preventing long-term suffering. It is my hope to save you some misery by revealing some of the pitfalls of buying new technology.

## START WITH THE RIGHT EXPECTATIONS

You use technology because it saves time and manpower, and therefore money. It is important to understand that the savings is in the process, not the equipment. Trying to save money when buying your computer does not work; it only postpones the expense, giving it time to compound. Buy a cheap computer and it will fail sooner and perform slower; both effects decrease the benefit gained by applying technology to the problem. The same is true of expertise applied to your computer. After 17 years focusing on small business networks, I can verify that the clients who pay the most are those with a "clever" nephew or brother-in-law who knows just enough to be dangerous.

## KNOW THE PLAYERS

You may think of your business as being one-of-a-kind, intricate, nuanced, and difficult to understand; but this is nothing compared to the landscape of technology. It is likely that your business needs are 90% the same as most others. Most of your technology needs will be met with one or more of thousands of existing products. But if you are convinced that you will never find the solution off the shelf, you can re-sign yourself to calling a tech recruiter about the manpower you will need to customize a solution.

If you lack a full-time information technology (IT) em-ployee, the hard part about buying new technology is wad-ing through all the wanna-be-best software companies to find the right combination of capability, compatibility, and support to fulfill your business needs. This may become the job of companies that manage your technology, collectively known as *systems integrators*.

### Everybody Does "All You Need"

Here is the model of solutions companies and systems integrators that do it all:

- they invest in the business relationship by gathering information;
- they invoice you for the system (vendors pay them commissions);
- they help you finance the system (finance company pays them a residual commission, even nicer); and
- they perform the configuration and provide monthly maintenance (you pay regularly and predictably).

Many people in the computer field are trustworthy and transparent; but companies have no soul. In some companies, seemingly trustworthy individuals can still bureaucratically (but honestly) participate in an untrustworthy process strategized by the director who was promoted away soon after creating the sales system. Processes and procedures are constructed every day to slice and dice areas of responsibility to eliminate counter-productive practices—like transparency.

I recently walked past the front desk of one systems integration company to service a client 25 feet away. The client had naively overpaid the integration company for an under-configured system. The result was a system that needed constant maintenance, tuning, and management, thus ensuring the integrator's income stream. Sharing office space, my client eventually heard enough to seek help elsewhere. I spent two hours tweaking some settings and teaching the client all he needed to know to maintain the system for a year.

Even with the negatives involved, do not eliminate the possibility of using a solutions company; just change the rules. There can be much value in having a single throat within arm's reach when something goes wrong.

### If You are Confused, You Lose . . .

Fear, uncertainty, and doubt (FUD) surround any decision. Movie buffs first saw it on screen when Dorothy quaked in the presence of the all-knowing Oz. The apex of FUD's evolution was reached by certain sales staffs in the 1970s and 1980s. Several big-name technology companies with inferior products out-survived their superior competitors only because of their sales force's ability to befuddle decision makers.

Many practitioners in the computer industry have adopted the same tactics, seeking similarly excessive profits and delivering inferior service just because the buyer does not know any better. Any good systems integrator should be able to speak in words you will understand, transcending the deceptive "Trust me, you can't understand" practices.

## Short Circuit the Potential for Abuse

The power of the sales system (and its possible abuse) is built on an imbalance of information—about the hardware, the purchase process and maintenance, and the technology cycle. There are two ways to balance the scales: by retaining control of a key part of the purchase process, or by hiring a watchdog.

1.  You may be able to regain partial control of the hardware sales process by purchasing directly from the hardware vendor (possibly via an independent consultant) or through a buyer's agent. (Search the Internet for "PC buyer's agent.") The sticking point is that only your solutions provider can correctly specify what you need from the hardware manufacturer. If the configuration is simple enough, the purchase can be made in the vendor's online shopping cart in just an hour. It is probably worth paying a solutions provider an hourly fee to configure your order before you make the purchase. The fee will be substantially less than what his normal mark-up would be, and it removes the motivation to over-sell you (to get a higher commission). However, the greater the system complexity, the less likely this will be a reasonable approach.

2.  Hire a technical advisor. You will need someone you can count on so that when something fails, as it most assuredly will, you will know who to call. Just as you should have an attorney review your contracts, your technical advisor can learn your business needs in a couple of hours and readily represent you through the research and sales processes for new technology. This can improve your likelihood of success a thousand-fold.

## You Need an Expert on Your Side

The occasional presence of your consultant acts to keep a solutions company honest. A good consultant's technical proficiency is massive, sifting away 95% of the trivial details by asking fewer questions to get to the important answers (from you and from vendors or integrators). Consider a solo consultant, who sells only advice, to be your designated project manager or cost analyst. He has no reason to limit the scope of his answers or to over-configure the solution. His expertise in cross-checking competitive quotes will keep the margins reasonable.

If you know a business similar to your own that is satisfied with a consultant, who has references you trust, start there. If you can not get a referral easily, contact your local networking organizations or chambers of commerce. You will want to hire a consultant who is able to interface with people, not just machines. Those without people skills avoid networking, so existing social structures can help you weed out inappropriate candidates. Look for someone who has 15 or more years of experience.

### Picking a Consultant is Easier if You Already Know the Answers

You may need to develop the technique of asking questions you already know the answer to. What follows is a discussion of several critical components of your technology strategy. Each point includes enough detail to help you pose questions to weed out the imposters from the real professionals. When interviewing prospective consultants, resist the temptation to show off what you know. Instead, get to the answers they propose.

## PAY FOR SUPPORT AND THE EXTENDED WARRANTEE

Things go wrong. One or two hours on the bench of a broadly skilled technician (after he clears his backlog) is more expensive than the cost of the extended warrantee. The vendor can dispatch a narrowly trained parts replacement specialist the next day with exactly the right parts. But this is only if you buy the service plan. Consider it a form of *cost-effective* insurance. If you do not pay for the service, you will end up listening to your consultant spelling phonetically for three hours only to find out that the first-level support cookbook is not good enough. He will then leave a message for second-level support. They will call back five minutes after you both go home for the day; and your problem will go to the back of the queue as retribution for wasting their valuable time.

Even systems integrators who have partnerships with their vendors have no way of getting parts and repairs faster or cheaper than the vendors' own warrantee extensions.

## SECURITY COMES FIRST

Business owners often think: "Who would want to hack my network?" "I am isolated, no one can find me." "My data is not valuable enough." Or, even worse, "Now that it works, we will come back next month to adjust security."

Here are three facts you should know:

1. College students are being assigned homework: "To learn about wireless security, download the sniffer software and camp in a coffee shop until you crack into five people's sessions."

2. Distance is no obstacle: search the Internet on "cantenna" for instructions to turn a Pringles® can into a directional antenna capable of isolating wireless signals way beyond the expected range.

3. Your credit card number and enough personal information to use it is only worth $1.50 on the black market. What really raises the stakes is insurance policy numbers. Forget the urban myths about ice-filled bathtubs and surprise kidney donors. The truth is people *are* unwillingly donating their insurance payments for thieves to get medical care. Because of the localized nature of medicine, your local hospital, when

fooled, creates records with your name and the thief's data. You may clear up the insurance records. Hopefully the hospital gets every database record fixed so that a doctor does not "think" he already knows your blood type.

If your computer will ever have medical records of any type, the Health Insurance Portability and Accountability Act of 1996 (HIPAA) requires stringent security precautions. Do not mention the fact that you handle such information when interviewing; let the technical resource bring up the topic of security. If he does not, he is unqualified. The same goes for the topic of disaster recovery. In both cases, once he begins talking, let him see that you have made some notes already on each subject.

A lack of security in a product, or lack of careful attention from a technical or even sales professional is reason for immediate dismissal. Interview tip: ask the technical professional to show you and explain the difference between the inferior wired equivalent privacy (WEP) encryption, and today's standard wi-fi protected access (WPA) encryption for wireless connections. If he does not mention that WEP can be cracked in 15 minutes, he does not qualify to service you.

## DISASTER RECOVERY

Disaster recovery is another area to watch. The traditional approach has always been to save data to tape. The cartridges, the drive, and the software have always been huge margin products due to gross overpricing. When disk space was expensive, there was not much choice. Now, a disk drive that stores more, copies faster, and costs less than a tape drive often makes more sense. "Backup to the cloud" or copying to an Internet archive is mature enough for day-to-day incremental backups, but not yet to the point where you can trust it with your only "archive" copy.

A couple of providers have gone bankrupt overnight, without warning, taking all data with them. Be sure to have a local, off-site, disk copy of data you might need in the long term. An encrypted backup disk in the supervisor's glove box is usually far enough off-site and close enough to make the monthly backup cycle convenient.

Another underused disaster recovery tactic is duplicated equipment. Having a spare identical computer is sometimes less expensive than what it would cost for a couple of days of downtime. I have seen crisis orders being "hand-walked" through incur three weeks delay.

## SERVERS AND CERTIFICATIONS

Before there were servers, Windows® was able to share printers and files across a small number of personal computers. Your consultant should be experienced enough to discuss whether this approach makes sense for your business. Some applications require secure access to a heavyweight database, which requires server-level software. If it is possible to avoid a server, you will cut your IT support bill in half each year. If you do need a server, you need "certified" technical talent (more expensive). The greater complexity decreases your ability to troubleshoot any problem, though it tends to make the (more expensive) application more reliable.

*** 

Mike Whelan has been a computer professional since 1984, and an independent consultant since 1993. During his career, he has been contracted by leading-edge integrators to manage networks and IT projects for the world's largest companies in multiple industries. Mike's career started with programming a computer-aided design system that is still in use after 26 years, and managing e-mail servers for GM in the 1980s. Since 1992 he has concentrated his efforts on technical, marketing, and management consulting for startup companies, non-profits, and small businesses.

Over the last seven years, Mike has built YourPCpitstop. com and PCbuyersAgent.com companies, both focused on helping businesses and families get more mileage from their existing computers and avoid spending more than wholesale when buying new systems. He can be reached by phone: 248-557-1001 or email: Mike@PCbuyersAgent.com.

# HOW TO CHOOSE
# THE RIGHT NETWORKING GROUP

## by Charles G. Gifford, Local Business Network

Given the extraordinary number of networking groups available today, how do you go about selecting the group or groups that will be best for your business? Answer: select the group(s) that provides the greatest opportunity to achieve your business goals cost effectively. Although there are many types of networking available to businesses, this chapter explores one of the most important—networking groups that meet in person.

## BUSINESS NETWORKING GOALS

Before evaluating networking groups, you should clearly define your business networking goals. Most would agree that the following six goals are typically the most important to businesses.

1. *Institutional advertising or creating brand awareness.* Business owners use networking to maintain a presence in front of peers and potential customers, making others aware of new products, services, and business offerings.

2. *Sales and marketing.* For many business owners, the primary goal of networking is to find prospects for their products or services.

3. *Referral and strategic partners.* Building relationships and alliances with others is important to receiving

referrals on a regular basis. Strategic partners are individuals who offer a product or service that complements the business owner's own, so both can be offered as a package.

4. *Resource development.* Networking frequently leads business owners to those who offer products or services that they themselves, or those they know, need.

5. *Master-mind group development.* Many network to find individuals who can help them solve problems or deal with common issues. For example, a younger person might seek a mentor.

6. *Career advancement.* Networking activities offer the opportunity for business owners to broaden their exposure to influential people, not only in their own industry, but others as well. Further, business owners gain knowledge that can help them perform better in their professions.

It is important for you to identify which of these goals are most important to you, so you can select the networking group or groups most likely to help you. You may, of course, have more than one goal and choose different groups to achieve a specific goal.

### Types of Groups and a Search Process

There are many types of networking groups ranging from informal to formal, from eclectic to industry specific, from marketing oriented to educational, from gender, age-defined or ethnocentric to all inclusive, from local to national, etc. Some encourage marketing, others discourage it. Each group has its own focus, its own value proposition, and its own cost.

To narrow your search, the following process is recommended:

1. Clearly identify your goals.
2. Define the geography within which you want to work.

3. Preliminarily select two or three groups that serve the geographic area you have chosen.
4. Research the offerings and cost of each group. Do not just look at cost; do your best to weigh the cost versus the benefits. "Free" may be too expensive when you consider the ineffectiveness of a group. Your time is valuable.
5. Visit and evaluate the specific group or chapter you will be joining. Gather information on both the parent organization and the local group.
6. Select an organization, participate and evaluate your results.

### Meeting Goals

Most individuals who join a structured networking or business referral group are primarily interested in receiving referrals. Others are looking for a support group of other business professionals who can help them deal with problems or aid in career advancement. Some structured networking groups provide excellent training in basic marketing, basic networking, and referral-based networking, and many people seek these organizations to benefit from that training. These groups, by their nature, also provide participants with a team of referral partners. For the purposes of the following discussion, assume that the business owner is seeking the right structured networking group to meet all four of these objectives, but referral generation is the primary goal.

### Local Chapter Assessment

When visiting a structured networking group, a prospective member should evaluate the following factors.

- *Convenience.* It is important that you select a group that will be convenient for you. If it is not, you will have a difficult time fulfilling your responsibility to attend meetings regularly.

1. Is the meeting location within a reasonable drive time from your home or business? If you have to drive too far, you might find that it is not worth the effort or the sacrifice of time.

2. Will the frequency, start time and length of meetings be compatible with your schedule? Some groups meet every week, others just once or twice a month. Morning meetings are sometimes inconvenient for those who have children to get to school or other early morning commitments. Evening meetings seem to work best if they are right after work, rather than later in the evening. Although many people have good intentions regarding lunchtime meetings, it can be difficult for members to participate regularly. They get embroiled in events at work and cannot always break away.

3. Does the group meet in an area where you know enough people to be able to generate referrals for others in the group? The number of referrals you give will determine the number you receive, so if you cannot give referrals, you will fail.

4. Is it reasonable to assume that people in the area where the meeting is held, and presumably where most of the members are located, will do business with you? If you are in a convenience business and the meeting location is 15 miles away, residents and/or businesses there will be more likely to patronize a local provider of your products or services.

- *Warmth, friendliness, camaraderie.* Obviously, you want to join a group in which you feel comfortable. Therefore, how you are treated as a guest is important.

1. When you make initial contact, are your questions and concerns addressed properly? Are you connected with someone who will be at the meeting to greet you and make you feel welcome?

2. When you arrive, is there a greeter, someone who welcomes you and gives you information about what will happen at the meeting, and who introduces you to others in the room? Is the person with whom you spoke previously there to greet you?

3. How do the members treat each other? Is there obvious familiarity, camaraderie, mutual respect? Are some of the conversations before the meeting begins about ways in which they are helping each other? Do there seem to be cliques or competing groups?

4. When the meeting starts, are you acknowledged, given the opportunity to speak about your business, and made to feel welcome?

5. At the end of the meeting, do members thank you for visiting? Does your sponsor, the host, or an officer of the chapter offer to answer your questions and provide direction if you want to apply for membership?

6. Are the attempts to recruit you overly aggressive and discomforting?

- *Compatibility of the members.* The most important element of any referral-based networking group is its membership. You need to assess whether this group of people is the right fit for you and your business.

  1. Are the members of the group credible, honest business professionals who seem to be experienced in their respective fields? Would you be comfortable sending them referrals? No group is perfect, but you should have affinity with the majority of members.

2. Do the members of the group seem to share your ethical standards, way of doing business, and way of dealing with customers?

3. Are at least some of the business owners in the group possible referral partners for you (they are in related businesses where they deal with the same target market you serve)?

4. If you are seeking a support group, are the professions you need represented in the group by individuals you feel could be good advisors, mentors, etc.?

5. Do you like the people? Over the years, these people could become your best friends and cohorts. Can you see a few of them as future "best friends?"

- Meeting effectiveness. If you are serious about networking and referral generation, you want to see a professionally run meeting, not a social event.

1. Is the meeting location appropriate for a business meeting?

2. Does the meeting start on time? Your time is as valuable as other people's time at the meeting. Is your time respected? If there are 60-second presentations by those at the meeting, is this time limit enforced? Does the meeting end on time?

3. Is there an agenda followed, or does the meeting just wander along? Are those who run the meeting trained to run it properly?

4. Are side conversations and interruptions kept to a minimum?

5. Are the members respectful of the leaders and their fellow members?

6. Is the meeting fun? Do the members seem to enjoy each other's company?

7. Are you made to feel a part of the group?

8. Is the overall length of the meeting reasonable for you?

9. Is there an opportunity to network before and after the meeting? Networking groups work best when members have an opportunity to spend time with each other.

- *Referrals.* Since the primary reason for joining a networking group is to give and get referrals, it is important to see that referrals are being passed. Most groups devote time at the end of meetings so that members can share what they have accomplished. Pay close attention to what is said. Typically, members will be asked to either share information about the referrals they have generated or give a testimonial for another member. In some cases, members are told to thank other members of the chapter for past referrals if they have nothing that day. In some cases, members submit slips for actions that are not true referrals. Listen carefully to distinguish between qualified current referrals that will actually generate income and testimonials, past referrals, or other recognized activities. You might want to keep track by marking down referrals, testimonials, past referrals, and other activities as each member reports. Sometimes a chapter officer will total the referrals submitted and report the results at the end of the meeting.

  1. The vast majority of members should have at least one current referral.

  2. At least half of all reported actions should be dollar-generating referrals.

  3. Total the referrals given and divide by the number of members present to calculate referrals per member, a statistic that can be compared across groups to determine the one that is most productive. Note

that there can be wide swings in the number of referrals reported from meeting to meeting, so you should ask if the number reported that day was typical.

4. Sometimes members of a referral group manufacture or make up referrals. If a friend has invited you, ask if that happens often in the group.

### Parent Organization

The effectiveness of an individual networking chapter is significantly impacted by the policies and procedures, business philosophy, training, and ancillary services of the parent organization. Services provided by the parent organization can also significantly impact the value of the membership. Following are some of the critical issues to ask about.

- *Business philosophy.* Some structured networking groups are specifically designed to benefit the owners, managers, or creators of the organization, while others are truly dedicated to serving their members. Ask members:

  1. Have they truly benefited from their participation?
  2. Are all members treated equally and fairly?
  3. Are members required to work primarily for the benefit of the organization or its leaders, rather than themselves?
  4. Is the organization truly dedicated to helping members or is it primarily focused on filling its own coffers?

- *Exclusivity.* Many structured networking groups allow only one person in each business category. This exclusivity, however, is not always honored. It is important to make sure you understand how your business category will be defined before you complete your application. You should also check with the person who invited you to determine if exclusivity agreements are honored. Organizations that continually reduce business categories are more interested in the revenues derived from bringing in new members rather than in the welfare of their members.

- *Training.* Proper training of all members can double, triple or even quadruple the number of referrals members receive. Properly trained members become productive members, contributing thousands or even tens of thousands of dollars of referrals annually. Those who do not receive proper training often drop out. Members must at a minimum be taught:

1. what structured networking is and how it differs from traditional one-on-one networking;

2. how to be an effective referral generator;

3. how to build effective referral partner relationships;

4. how to train and motivate fellow members to promote their businesses; and

5. about the opportunities offered by the organization and how to be a successful member.

   In the Local Business Network (LBN), new members are provided portfolios that contain training materials. Each member is assigned a mentor, attends a free 2-1/2-hour training session, and is given access to additional free training materials on the LBN members-only website. Chapter officers also receive free training on how to effectively manage their chapters and their members.

- *Accountability.* The success of a structured networking group depends upon the active participation of its members. Members are the ones who generate referrals. They are the ones who maintain or expand the chapter's membership. And, they are the ones who run the local chapter meetings and take the time to meet individually to learn how they can help one another. Unfortunately, some members do not take their responsibilities seriously. Some are there simply to take advantage of the system, to get referrals without giving them. Therefore, it is necessary to tell members what is expected of them, to hold them accountable for meeting those expectations, and to have a process for removing those who fail to meet their obligations. If non-performers are allowed to remain, they destroy all discipline in the organization and discourage those who are living up to their obligations.

Typically, there should be expectations that members will attend meetings regularly, learn about fellow members and support them by bringing referrals, help to recruit new members, and uphold standards of ethical treatment both with respect to fellow members and those referred.

When evaluating a structured networking group, ask about the existence of policies and procedures regarding accountability in these areas and the existence and use of processes for enforcement.

- *Cross-chapter networking*. Some businesses, simply because of their nature, are unable to derive enough referrals from a local networking chapter to justify their participation. To be successful in a networking group, they must be able to network with members of other chapters. In the Local Business Network, nearly half of all referrals are either from or to members of other chapters. In other words, cross-chapter networking nearly doubles referrals and, for some, the ratio is much higher. Ask if some of the following cross-chapter networking opportunities exist:

1. Is there an internet site where members of all chapters can share information?

2. Is there the option to visit any chapter where there is no direct competitor?

3. Do they hold regional events that bring members together from all chapters? For instance, LBN sponsors regional mixers (an expo type of event) three times a year, industry exchanges that bring together people in related business categories to form referral partner relationships, and speed networking and training events attracting regional participation.

- *Relief from administrative tasks.* One reason people turn to and pay for participation in a chapter is that administrative tasks such as billing and collections, ordering, preparation of training programs and materials, preparation of marketing materials, communications with members, public relations, database management, website development and maintenance, management of cross-chapter events, etc., are assumed by the parent organization. This leaves chapter officers and members free to concentrate on referrals, recruiting, and conducting effective meetings. Ask whether most administrative tasks are handled by parent organization staff and if officers can fulfill their obligations in just a few hours a month.

- *Chapter support.* In addition to providing administrative support, a good networking organization will have staff to support each local chapter. In LBN, these are the regional directors. They help chapters develop, make sure members are properly trained, and then monitor and support the chapter officers. Officers are volunteers who receive a few hours of training, yet they manage chapters capable of generating millions of dollars in referrals. They need the support of professionals in the business of referral-based networking to help them maximize the return for their members.

- *Cost.* The final factor to consider when evaluating a structured networking organization is cost. Saved for last, it is the least important factor when considering a structured networking group. Far more important are the benefits, because they should outweigh the cost by a factor of ten to one, or even one hundred to one in some cases. Sure, it is important to ask about the cost, particularly to uncover hidden fees. For instance, some organizations charge a meeting fee, which can double the cost of participation.

Some structured networking groups are free, but these groups typically do not provide training, support, cross-chapter networking opportunities, or other features that can double, triple, or quadruple the volume of referrals you receive. Which deal is better, a free group that generates $500 a year in referrals, or one that charges $35 a month and produces $100,000 in referrals?

## WHAT DIFFERENCE DOES IT MAKE?

Is there truly a difference between structured networking groups? Is it really necessary to go through an analysis before joining a group? The following example will help you understand the importance of selecting the right group for your business—think referrals, referrals, referrals!

Jane became a regional director of LBN after having been an officer of a chapter of another structured networking organization. While with that former organization, she recruited a flooring specialist. During her years with that group, the referrals she received were negligible despite the fact that she more than doubled the size of her chapter. Her friend was equally unsuccessful.

When Jane joined LBN, her business tripled in the first year. It is many times larger now and over 50% of her business still comes from LBN referrals. When she recruited her friend to LBN and showed him how to use all that it offers, he generated over $100,000 in business within his first six months and then repeated that rate of business generation for three consecutive six-month periods.

***

President of Local Business Network, Chuck Gifford also founded the ten-year-old business referral organization, now with 40 chapters and over 600 members in the state of Michigan. Called the "power networking organization," it is recognized as one of the most effective structured networking organization in its market area.

Chuck is co-author of *Network Your Way to $100,000 and Beyond!* (Minesh Baxi & Associates 2007). He also offers consulting services to individuals and businesses interested in significantly increasing their business through business referral relationships. Chuck can be reached at 248-620-6320 or cgifford@locbusnet.com.

# CLIENT RETENTION—GO THE EXTRA MILE

*by Kathy J. Koze, SendOutCards*

When it comes to client retention, if you have been doing the same things as you were in the past, it is time do more. It is not enough to continue doing the same things, expecting bigger and better results. Competition is heating up and today's client has more options besides your products or services. Customers will purchase from a competitor on an impulse even if you provide a great product or service. This shows the importance of staying fresh in your clients' minds.

According to a study by the American Society for Quality, on average, American businesses are losing 20% of their customers per year, resulting in a complete turnover of their customer base every 5 years. The cost of replacing a single customer can be six to seven times more expensive than the cost of retaining a customer who already knows and values your product or service. Thus it is wiser to spend money on customer retention than on new customer acquisition. Savvy business owners are aggressive in their approach to retaining clients. They know there are plenty of competitors who will be the ones capturing their client's attention if they become complacent.

One reason for a customer leaving is that he or she simply forgets about the product or service. For every month that a business owner does not contact or communicate with his clients, it is estimated that 10% of his influence is lost . . . so, if 10 months go by without communication, then virtually 100% of his influence is lost!

Studies show that the average person will not take action until they have heard or seen a message at least seven times. This is why it is vital to business success to have a systematic way for keeping in touch. Just saying thank you (do not try to sell) to your clients, particularly new ones, will increase business.

Here is another staggering statistic. According to research, of all the leads generated at trade shows and expos, 67% of them are never followed up with. These potential customers are waiting for contact that never comes. Who do you think they will choose to deal with . . . you or your competition? Considering the cost of exhibiting at a trade show or expo (time, cost to rent the space, cost for booth display materials, etc.), the lack of follow-up can cost more than just the missed opportunity to connect.

## RELATIONSHIP BUILDING

In approaching customers, when you act first as a business partner and then a friend, you will be more likely to become a trusted source. In turn, you will more easily convert your prospects into clients. This is true relationship building. When people feel appreciated, they will remember you for a long time, if not forever! Think of how you respond to someone who makes you feel appreciated and valued. What would it be worth to you and your business if you were to make each of your customers and prospects feel the same way?

Most business owners are missing a big opportunity. The easiest and least expensive customers to keep are referrals and repeat business, but many business owners do not stop to think about this. They spend most of their time cold-calling to attract new clients.

If you are a business owner or a sales or service professional, you know that people do business with people they know, like, and trust, and *remember*. When someone is ready to make a buying decision or give a referral, it does not matter how much you are liked and respected if they do not remember you.

Customers need to feel appreciated and acknowledged. One of the reasons why they fail to continue doing business is *perceived* indifference. When you communicate effectively with your customers, building relationships and loyalty, your clients will give you repeat business and referrals. They will gladly serve as references for you.

## CREATE A DATABASE

Can you name the people who have had the greatest impact on your business? Do you know the companies they represent? Do you know their birthdays or anniversaries? What do you know about their families? Do you know the names of their spouses or significant others? Do they have children or pets?

Creating a system to keep this information is well worth the effort and will pay dividends over and over. Keeping track of the people in your network is necessary to conducing business successfully. Such a database could be as simple as an old-fashioned rolodex or as sophisticated as a computer database or contact manager.

It is just as important to maintain the contact information on your clients and prospects. Your database should have the most up-to-date information on all of the communication or interaction you have had with them. Note when and where you met, and any information they share with you that you may want to recall at a later date. Make sure to include any information that will give you a reason to connect with them again.

## EXPRESS GRATITUDE AND GIVE THANKS

*"People will forget what you said; people will forget what you did; but people will never forget how you made them feel."—Maya Angelou*

Gratitude is sorely lacking in today's business world. Expressing gratitude to associates and clients is vital to the cultivation of fruitful business relationships. People like to refer others to business professionals who go above and beyond their expectations. Thanking others at every opportunity will help you stand out from the crowd.

Expressing sincere gratitude to the people who will be there to help you is not just a courtesy; it's the right thing to do. Let clients know that you appreciate their business and you will be long remembered and appreciated too.

Make a difference in the lives of others and watch what happens in yours. Acknowledging something small or profound, like saying "thank you for meeting me for coffee," or "thank you for being a positive influence in my business," can be very powerful.

One of the most effective ways to build strong relationships and appreciate others is by sending personal greeting cards. A good way to do this is to have a box of cards for all occasions and write them out with an ink pen. However, if you are too busy to do it this way, there are systems out there that are automated and make expressing appreciation simple.

Only 3% of our mail is personal. How do you feel when you open your mailbox and see a personal card addressed to you? Your clients and prospects are no different.

Sending cards and notes to clients may increase the number of referrals they send to you, but it can be time-consuming and expensive. You go to the store and wade through thousands of cards to find one that suits your needs. It has to have the right sentiment but not be too personal to use for business contacts. Then, you have to decide whether to print labels or hand-write the addresses. Or, you buy a box of blank cards. Then, you go blank wondering about what to say to your clients.

What would happen if you sent one card every other month to your top 60 clients (a birthday card, "thank you" card, a "thinking of you" card, holiday card, etc.)? How many more clients might that generate for you? What is a client worth over the course of time?

*"The best and most beautiful things in the world cannot be seen or even touched. They must be felt with the heart."— Helen Keller*

If you are taking money from your clients for your products or service, you should be thanking them. Realtors, business owners, loan officers, consultants, and sales professionals can use a simple system to increase their business in one year simply by making their clients feel special and cared for. Send out a card each day and watch your business transform! Sending cards is a powerful sales tool.

Go the extra mile. A simple "thank you" card may not sound like going the extra mile, but it truly is. The old-fashioned, personalized handwritten card has been largely replaced by e-mail. When was the last time you received a handwritten "thank you" card? What was your reaction?

A "thank you" note might consist of three sentences. Sign your name, put the card in the envelope, put a stamp on it, address it, and get it in the mail. It will be on its way to making someone's day.

When someone goes the extra mile for you, send them a card and let them know how much you appreciate them. This is true relationship building—not selling your business. It is an expression of gratitude and it's *not* all about you or your products and services.

Doing what others do not do gives you the edge. It can position you head and shoulders above your competition. You will stand out in a positive way. People will be attracted to you and to your business.

\*\*\*

After more than 30 years in human resources leadership positions, Kathy Koze is now a senior manager with Send-OutCards, a company that offers an automated system for sending printed greeting cards. SendOutCards can be personalized in less than 60 seconds and the printing and mailing are done for you. With this incredible tool, not only can you remember people and share appreciation, but you can motivate, uplift, encourage, and truly make a difference. Business is built on relationships and SendOutCards is a tool that can help you do that.

Kathy is member of the following organizations: Southern Wayne County Regional Chamber; the Downriver and Detroit Business Association (DADBA); Women In Networking (WIN); and the Downriver Networking Group (DNG). She can be contacted by phone: 734-676-1541, email: kkoze@msn.com, or website: www.sendoutcards.com/9766.

# HOW TO CHOOSE A CPA FIRM

### by Dennis Glasson,
### Tobias, Vandeputte & Skulsky, P. C.

Choosing the right certified public accounting (CPA) firm or the right accountant for you or your business is not easy. It is one of the most personal decisions you will make and one of the most crucial. You need advisors who will not only stay on top of tax and accounting matters, but who really take the time to understand the unique characteristics of your business and circumstances.

When choosing a CPA firm for your business, always start by considering your needs. Not all firms will provide the same range of services. Some may offer a general variety of services and others may be highly specialized. A CPA should be aware of your needs and ensure that he can meet them not only now, but also in the future. When you enter into a relationship with a CPA firm, you should expect that relationship to grow and adjust over time.

## WHAT SERVICES DO YOU NEED?

Obviously, tax preparation is a must, but you also should have the proper tax planning to avoid penalties and unexpected cash flow needs. Besides taxes, you may need help with bookkeeping, accounting systems, and business plans. Do you need financial statements prepared for your business? Must those statements be audited or reviewed? Can your CPA firm assist you personally with estate planning, trust services, and personal financial planning?

## SELECTION CRITERIA

Once you have created your list of needs, you can begin the selection process. Experience, integrity, and qualifications are a few things to look for when interviewing a CPA firm. A good way to begin your search is to seek recommendations. Talk to relatives and friends, colleagues, and business contacts such as attorneys, bankers, and insurance agents. They can possibly refer you to a few reputable CPA firms.

When you examine your options, you will have an idea of some key questions to ask. Does the firm have the expertise and industry knowledge of your business? Many CPA firms have websites where you can find background information and a list of services offered. What types of qualifications does the firm have? Accounting firms who have the CPA designation must adhere to certain accounting standards. Also check for membership with the American Institute of Certified Public Accountants (AICPA) and local associations. CPAs who are members of national and local associations acknowledge that they not only represent themselves, but the profession as a whole. Most CPA firms are required to frequently undergo a review of their accounting and auditing practices. The peer review is designated to ensure that firms have adequate quality control systems. You can ask to see the last peer review report. The apparent savings in fees of doing business with an unqualified firm could prove costly in the long-term.

## THE BUSINESS RELATIONSHIP

When you hire a CPA firm, you should receive an engagement letter that will clarify the business relationship. Before any work is done by the CPA firm, it is important to know specifically who will be performing the work, the level of services to be provided, and the cost of the services. Most firms will typically charge their clients an hourly rate that differs between members of the firm based on their expertise. Bring your records to the interview and the prospective CPA firm may be able to give you an estimate as to what a particular service will cost. To save you unnecessary fees, keep good records and avoid using your accountant's professional time for routine work.

Once you establish a relationship, be prepared to keep the firm aware of your plans and objectives as well as any changes in your professional and personal life. CPA firms can most effectively advise you when they understand your situations and goals. You should always receive prompt responses to your requests, and projects should always be completed timely. Your CPA should be committed to keeping you informed of any updates and changes that could affect you or your business. Overall, an informed decision will ultimately lead to a good decision when choosing a CPA firm.

***

Dennis Glasson holds a BBA in Accountancy from Western Michigan University. He has over nine years of public accounting experience and joined Tobias, Vandeputte & Skulsky in 2006. His areas of expertise include accounting, tax planning, individual and business taxes, trust administration, audits, and financial reviews. He has worked with an array of industries including real estate, construction, nonprofit, legal, services, and healthcare. You can reach Dennis by phone: (248) 641-8400, Fax (248) 641-5001, or email: dglasson@tobiascpa.com.

# THE REMARKABLE ADVANTAGE OF VISUAL BRANDING

### by Bill Kleist, Identity Graphic Design

In the business world, *brand* and *branding* have become very popular terms. Still, there is much confusion about what they really mean. A common definition of *brand* may be, "A trademark or distinctive name identifying a product or manufacturer," but the term has come to mean so much more.

Today, having a professional visual brand will mean the difference between competing at the top of your game and just getting by. If every startup business would budget a portion of its initial capital to building a visual brand, many new businesses would be off to a much better start. Too many business owners do not make this investment because they do not realize how critical a dynamic visual brand presence is to positioning a new company as a serious and competitive player in its respective industry.

## THE BRAND, THE LOGO, AND VISUAL BRANDING

One way to describe a brand is first to identify what it is *not*. A brand is not a logo. It is true that for thousands of years farmers, out of the need to identify their property, "branded" their livestock with unique shapes and letterforms to confirm ownership. These symbols have been used throughout history to not only identify "who owns this," but also "who made this," and for persons of significance, "who is this." However, the term *brand* is no longer used to merely describe the symbols or icons that label. Simply put, a brand is not the *surface perception* the seller presents to the buyer, but the *internal perception* the buyer has of that seller.

- *Surface perception*: a symbol or wordmark with the intent to identify and distinguish—a logo.
- *Internal perception:* the emotional and rational connection buyers have with a product or service—a brand.

A brand resides in the hearts and minds of those familiar with it. It is the visceral reaction that occurs within people when they look at, hear of, or experience that company's goods or services. A brand is formed through impressions that take place on these three levels. The impressions either positively or negatively impact the brand of a business.

To illustrate, what comes to mind when you see or hear reference to the "golden arches?" The fast-food chain, McDonald's®, has an international brand presence. For some, this name makes them hungry for hot fries and burgers, and brings back wonderful memories. Others may have an entirely different perception.

McDonald's has invested millions over the years to establish its brand. The success of its branding endeavors is evident in that the company has retained leader status of an enormous fast-food market. Why? Any business that wants to be successful must be concerned with the message of its brand and that it generates good feelings in the minds of its buyers. The McDonald's *brand* is the *perception* people have of its restaurant chain. The perception is influenced on many levels, including the company's charity foundation, the Ronald McDonald House, its updated fresh alternative menu, and its sophisticated new architectural look. "'McDonald's promises to be a *forever young* brand,' says John Miologos, vice-president of worldwide architecture, design, and construction at McDonald's Corp. 'We have to deliver on that promise.'" (*Business Week* 2006) To be "forever young" is one of McDonald's *brand objectives*. How the company is perceived is its brand. The *visual brand* is the alignment of the company's visual graphic presence with its brand objectives. McDonald's *brand identity* consists of the iconic golden arches and its logo, which are strategically woven through everything the company does.

## WHAT IS BRANDING AND DOES IT REALLY MATTER TO SMALL BUSINESSES?

In its simplest definition, *"branding" is becoming the business that you want to become.* This means, based on a set of objectives (or brand strategy), a business succeeds in creating a *perception* about its products or services. Based on this brand perception, the customer then wants to buy from the company again and again. The customer wants to be part of what he feels good about. Thus when it is time to choose a restaurant, law firm, hospital, plumber, watch, or car, some element of a particular seller's brand has influenced the buyer's decision. This brand loyalty is the result of successful branding.

Now more than ever small businesses need successful branding too. Remember, a company's *brand* is *earned* over time. It is the collection of many experiences and associations and can take years to establish. A company's brand *identity,* however, is *created.* It is the first visual impression, the frosting on the cake, the tip of the spear, the *look* that people see. A vital step toward establishing your brand is first giving your business a professional brand identity.

## HOW TO ACHIEVE A BRAND IDENTITY

The identity is the face of a business. As stated, visual branding is when a company's identity aligns with its brand objectives. Professional visual branding is the successful alignment of a company's brand objectives with its desired graphic personality.

*Brand Objective + Identity = Visual Brand*

In this context, when I refer to a logo or a corporate or brand identity, I am referring to the visual brand of a business. This can be created short-sightedly to save time or money, or it can be carefully designed to reflect and direct the brand objectives of a business.

Especially for smaller businesses, when done properly, a successful visual brand can provide a remarkable advantage over the competition. As stated, a logo is the "tip of the spear." It often is the first impression people have of your business. Properly implemented, the logo is the common thread that unifies all of a company's visual communications.

## THE BENEFITS OF A PROFESSIONALLY CREATED VISUAL BRAND

One major benefit of a professionally created visual brand is immediate perceived credibility. You *look* like you know what you are doing. Like it or not, books are judged by their covers and companies by their logos. If visual impressions appear homespun or outdated, the viewer interprets that the company's products are of the same quality. However, when a visual brand is rendered professionally, the impression communicates a credible business and quality products. This inspires increased consumer trust in the brand.

Another benefit is that the brand communicates quality and professionalism. Unfortunately, homemade and inferior logos are everywhere. Many business owners pride themselves on how much money they saved by doing their own logo. But if they were aware of the damaging repercussions, they would surely find another area in which to be frugal. If the logo is inferior, the subliminal message communicated is that there could be other shortcuts taken within the company. When a business owner invests in a visual brand, the investment will yield perceived respect and identify the company as a leader in its industry.

Further, a professional visual brand is always working to promote the business. People are inundated with thousands of impressions daily, so your logo must quickly and effectively communicate the right message to the right people. It is actually the best workhorse a company has in its employ; anytime it is seen, it creates an impression. These impressions should be positive and memorable.

Finally, a professional visual brand offers tangible competitive advantages. If designed effectively, the identity of a business can make it appear well established. This is especially important for new businesses or for those looking to expand. The right identity enables a company to compete more aggressively with companies at its level and far beyond. Most significantly, a successful visual brand will differentiate a business from its competitors, even in a dense or depressed market.

## DESIGNING A GREAT VISUAL BRAND

After 26 years in this industry, I have outlined four pillars that make a successful identity. A talented graphic designer will balance form and function and render the following four pillars into a dynamic visual brand. (Visit www. IdentityGraphicDesign.com to see a graphic walkthrough of these four pillars defined and how they work together.)

1. *Distinctiveness*: this means that the visual brand must be unique and differentiate a business from its competitors. It is graphically tailored to fit your brand objectives and ties into what makes your business different. Distinctiveness will more easily enable customers to remember your brand when they are ready to buy. A distinctive trademark will capture attention and stand out in a positive way. However, it must be in harmony with the other three pillars. For example, the whimsical image of an animated juggling kitten may get attention, but it would not be the best visual brand for a carpet-cleaning service.

2. *Relevance*: the visual brand should be pertinent to the business in the way of its products, services, or benefits. To align creatively with the other three pillars, relevance is an attribute that requires skill. For instance, the default graphic symbol for an electrician may be a bolt of electricity. Although electricity is a relevant graphic symbol for an electrician, it is sorely overused and, too many times, used poorly. In creating a visual brand, the design must be subtle, relevant, and distinctive. (A creative example of a visual brand that would be relevant *and* distinctive is found in the Turner Electric logo on my website.)

3. *Effectiveness*: as a professor of graphic design at a local university, I tell my design students that because this pillar pertains more to the mechanics of the trademark, it is fundamental to consider its attributes first. Effectiveness means that the trademark works everywhere it is supposed to. For a trademark to be effective, it must be *simple* and *adaptable*.

   Simple means *not complicated*. Too many designers feel compelled to create detailed artwork riddled with thin lines, dot screens, drop-shadows and gradients. These are not logos; these are mini-illustrations and are mostly ineffective when reproduced outside of their original intent. Too many details in a trademark cause image degradation when it is reduced in size, copied, or faxed. A successful company trademark should reduce to the size of a matchbook, or be enlarged to the size of a water tower and still remain impactful.

   Effectiveness also means that the mark is *adaptable* to a variety of media, contexts, and platforms. An effective trademark should be created in such a way that it will look good in black and white or full color. It should embroider or silk-screen well and look great on stationery, a sign, a website, or cut into vinyl and applied to a truck.

4. *Consistency*: this is a quality that is closely linked to effectiveness and speaks to the use of a visual brand wherever it is seen. A logo must be implemented consistently to be successful. Consistency with trademark use is fundamental and critical. Imagine if a sign shop was commissioned to make a sign for a well-known retail chain that uses large circles in a target symbol, and the sign shop decided to squish the red circles into ovals in an effort to fit a rectangular space. Absurd! Believe me, things like this and stories too gruesome to mention happen at logo slaughterhouses like quick-sign shops all of the time. Details like spacing of logo elements, font styles, white space allowance, and colors need to be consistently reproduced. Every rule of use for an identity should be outlined in the *Corporate Identity Standards Guide* of the business. This is an excellent tool for anyone responsible for reproducing the company's logo.

Remember: consistency yields familiarity; this in turn yields impact and, ultimately memorability. When a customer is ready to buy, you want them to remember *your* service or product.

If these four pillars—distinctiveness, relevance, effectiveness, and consistency—are working together in concert, they will yield a memorable logo. This is the core objective: to be remembered. And of course, the objective is to be memorable for the right reasons—not for having a hideous visual brand. Consumers make purchasing decisions on both an emotional and rational level. A professionally designed corporate identity that is distinctive, relevant, effective, and consistent will ultimately lead to customer awareness, confidence, and increased sales.

## CHOOSING A GRAPHIC DESIGNER TO CREATE A VISUAL BRAND

A visual brand is the graphic persona of the business. It is also the most significant investment a business will make in its visual presentation. When beginning your research into a visual branding resource, realize that trusting a designer with this project is no small thing. This is not the area to just go for the lowest price. In addition to looking at a designer's portfolio and discussing his experience, ask for a list of references and interview other clients who have worked with him. With this in mind, there are several things you will want to consider.

A good graphic designer should ask a lot of questions about your business. This person should be a good listener; he should research your company, your industry, and know your target market and your competition. He should become familiar with your business so he can understand your desired brand objectives. If the designer does not provide a thorough interview, watch out! If he asks, "What kind of logo do you want?," it is best to find someone else. A professionally created logo is not just an artsy rendering of a company's name. A knowledgeable designer will determine and clarify the brand objectives of your business, and then graphically render this information into an identity that reflects your brand message.

Consider also a designer's experience. How long has he been in business? Is he doing freelance work on the side? There are many talented graphic designers creating logos, but do they have specific experience in the arena of brand identity development? This is critical. A good visual brand designer will consider the entire scope of the logo's use, including its reproduction into every area, medium, and platform. I have seen logos that looked great on a web page, but wrought nightmares when put into production for signage. An experienced designer will also create work that is not just flashy or trendy, but timeless enough to give the logo a long life.

At the conclusion of the design project, a good designer will give the client everything he will ever need to independently *manage* his new visual brand. This should include the provision of every possible file format available. Too many designers fail to provide the proper files. This forces the client to come back or, even worse, to trust a well-meaning production artist to recreate the logo, which often results in an abject variant of the original design.

In addition, a good branding designer will provide a detailed set of guidelines, definitions, styles, and standards for the logo. This will help the business owner create a *Corporate Identity Standards Guide*. The guide should be provided to any vendor who is expected to reproduce the logo. Any business desiring to grow *must* consistently use its visual brand to be effective.

## THE REMARKABLE ADVANTAGE

The services of an experienced visual brand designer will be an initial investment, but this is one business expense that will yield great returns in the long run. It could mean the difference between competing at the top of your industry and just getting by. Too many business owners do not take this seriously. They do not realize how critical a dynamic visual brand presence is to positioning a business as a serious and competitive player in its respective industry.

Visual branding should be a core part of any business plan from the beginning. Whether reinvigorating an existing company, starting an entirely new business, or launching a new product line, using professional design resources as part of your branding and marketing strategies will give your company a critical edge and a remarkable advantage over your competition. (Learn how to gain the remarkable advantage for your business, visit www.TheRemarkableAdvantage.com.)

### Reference

*Business Week* magazine online. May 15, 2006. http://www.businessweek.com/magazine/content/06_20/b3984065.htm.

\*\*\*

In 1993, Bill Kleist founded Identity Graphic Design. His firm specializes in visual branding for businesses through intelligent graphic design and advertising. This includes creative campaigns, company and product naming, slogan development, corporate identity design development, and full-scope design implementation into print and web.

Bill is also an adjunct professor of graphic design in the College of Architecture & Design at Lawrence Technological University.

You can contact Bill by phone: 586-558-9795, via email: Bill@IdentityGraphicDesign.com, or visit his website: www. IdentityGraphicDesign.com.

# WHY HIRE A BUSINESS COACH?

## by Minesh Baxi, Minesh Baxi and Associates, LLC

"Minesh, I want to let you know that I would have been out of business had you not made that recommendation," Joe said softly.

I distinctly knew what he was talking about. Over a year ago, Joe had asked me for advice on one of his businesses. He had doubts about the business and wanted my opinion. I simply said, "Joe, here are three questions you must ask regarding your business. If the answer is a clear *no* to all of the questions, then you should consider shutting down the business." The answers were all in the negative.

It is never easy making tough decisions but there are times when you need to take a fresh look at your circumstances. In this case, Joe lost some money but he was able to get out of that business without too much of a fallout. If he had not, his other businesses, which were bringing him the revenue and profits, would have become a casualty of the downturn in the economy. He may have had to shut down all of his businesses.

Another client needed to make drastic changes in his business. With entrenched ways of the employees and the officers, they needed new leadership and guidance. For three months I worked closely with them to help them start implementing systems to better monitor the organization and make suitable cuts. Had those changes not been made, the company may have declared bankruptcy.

Let me share another story about a client. He was excited about buying a franchise for about $25,000. He felt that this franchise would help create more cash flow for his business and maybe create a sellable entity in the future. Once we started discussing the pros and cons of the opportunity, I realized that he needed a cooling off period. Have you ever been so excited that you were willing to sign up on the dotted line only to realize later that it was more an emotional decision and not really a wise one? I told him that I would research the details and get back to him. After my research, I found out that he could get access to the same knowledge and tools for $1,500 to start the new business—without the franchise. He did more research too and saw the wisdom in not buying the franchise.

So the question I have for you is, "Who is helping you make the critical decisions in your business?" Quite often, my client is the business owner or an executive who cannot share everything with his or her employees or even a spouse. The client knows that there is a tremendous responsibility on his shoulders. Every decision can either point the organization in the right direction or move it farther away from its goals. Who can you trust then?

The need for professional advice from someone the business owner can trust is the reason why business coaches have become popular. Before making a critical decision, it is wise to run the idea by a board of advisors or a business coach.

## HIRING A BUSINESS COACH

A business coach has two advantages:

1. The coach is much more objective as he has less emotional involvement.
2. The coach has seen similar situations before and can advise accordingly.

Finding the right business coach will take some research. Here are a few things you will want to consider:

- The coach must have been in business for a few years either running his own business before or as a successful business coach. Some things cannot be taught in schools and this is the reason why books like *What They Don't Teach You at Harvard Business School* (Mark H. McCormack, 1984) have become best-sellers.

  Experience gives a first-hand perspective. If somebody has not done marketing himself, he cannot teach you marketing. Thus someone in sales who promotes his marketing ideas but who does not have any track record of having applied the ideas himself will have no clue about what went wrong when his ideas do not work out.

  Yellow Pages™ salespeople come to mind. They do not get clients by putting an ad in their own product, the Yellow Pages. They do cold calling and revisit past clients. Interestingly, they do not use their own marketing tools!

  One of my clients asked me to help design a Yellow Page advertisement. I am not an expert in designing an ad, but I know what components must come into play in every marketing tool.

  The salesperson had been hounding him and my client wanted to be in the next edition, which was up for printing soon. Most salespeople rarely have interest in helping clients with their ads. The salesperson wants to get an ad and earn the commission. He has no accountability whether the client gets results or not. I asked a basic question, "How much business did you get from this ad last year and was it profitable?" We looked into it and the answer was very clear. The ad had not been profitable for him and it accounted for a very small portion of his new business. I saved him over $15,000. In fact, I have saved other clients as much as $50,000 a year in advertising because it did not provide the return on investment. Having helped numerous clients over the last 10 years, I know what works for some businesses and what does not.

- What is the reputation of the coach in the market? Do you want to work with a coach who is relatively unknown or one who is well-known? I was recently referred to a client who heard good things about me from a friend. There was very little selling required on my part for the simple reason that I have built a good reputation.

  If a business coach has been referred to you, then the odds are that he or she is good one. After all, most of us do not recommend lightly. The more reputable the person, the easier it is for you to be comfortable in making the right choice. Ask around and you can get the details easily. Google™ the person and you can find a lot of information.

- Does the coach promise and deliver results? A number of coaches will help clients but do not have a tangible process or result to offer. No coach can really guarantee results. The reason is that a coach can only do so much and the client must be coachable enough to follow through to get results. However, if there is a system being taught and the coach holds the client accountable for his or her own actions, then the client should get tangible and measurable results. I teach such a system to my clients and provide a 30-day, money-back guarantee. I take all the risk. Make sure that you work with a coach who is dedicated to bringing you positive results.

- Can the coach refer you to resources to assist you in your business? A number of my clients have come to rely on my sizable contacts list for referrals to good, knowledgeable experts. It saves them a lot of time and headache in dealing with the wrong people. This fact alone has helped me secure and keep clients. They know that I will help them actually implement solutions, not just give them ideas. (I have posted more "Frequently Asked Questions when Hiring a Consultant" on my website, www.Mbaxi.com/faq.htm. Check them out.)

***

Minesh Baxi is a business coach in his own consultancy, which has been in business for over 10 years. He has authored/co-authored, and published four books: *Network Your Way to $100,000 and Beyond, Stop Hiring Losers, 30-Day Total Business Makeover,* and *You Will Overcome.*

Minesh has also been featured in newspaper articles, radio programs, and TV. He has posted over 300 educational videos online. His TV interview on how to be known as an expert is available online at www.mbaxi.com/ExpertsGetClientsVideoOffer.htm for free viewing. You can reach Minesh by email: minesh@mbaxi.com.

# TIPS TO START YOUR BUSINESS FROM A LAWYER'S PERSPECTIVE

*by Trevor Weston, Falvay, Marcus & Weston, P. C.*

It would be folly to think that one could grasp or explain all of the necessary considerations an entrepreneur must make when forming a business simply by reading a relatively short chapter in a book. That said, the purpose of this chapter is to get prospective business owners thinking about some of the many decisions they need to make to get their businesses off to the right start.

## TIP NUMBER ONE: GET A PLAN!

First, you need to develop a business plan. Most people have never written such a document so, a little guidance could not hurt.

The State of Michigan's Department of Labor and Economic Growth website provides numerous valuable resources for Michigan entrepreneurs. Anyone considering starting a business should spend some time reviewing some of the thoughtful resources that the state has provided. One of the issues that the website can help you resolve is finding a name for your business. A search engine allows you to determine whether the name that you desire has already been taken by an existing business. Believe it or not, on several occasions the name is the only issue that my new business owner client has actually given thought to prior to our initial meeting.

The next step is to sit down by yourself or with the people with whom you are forming this business, and write out the business plan. The State of Michigan's website also provides some literature on how to do this. I would also suggest that you look to inc.com for similar resources.

Your plan does not need to be all encompassing, nor does it need to deal with every possible situation that your business will face from beginning to the end of time; however, it is very valuable to your attorney and to you as the prospective business owner to lay down your vision for this venture on paper. This will help cauterize your ideas about the business, which will in turn help you set the specific goals you need to meet each day to make this dream become a reality.

One thing I would suggest that you incorporate into your plan is a written set of goals. In his book, *What They Don't Teach You at Harvard Business School* (1984), Mark McCormack tells of a study conducted on students in the 1979 Harvard MBA program. Each of the students were asked, "Have you set clear, written goals for your future and made plans to accomplish them?" Only three percent of the graduates had written goals and plans; 13 percent had goals, but they were not in writing; and a whopping 84 percent had no specific goals at all. Ten years later, the members of the class were interviewed again, and the findings should be considered mind blowing for individuals starting a business. The 13 percent of the class who had goals were earning, on average, twice as much as the 84 percent who had no goals at all. And, what about the three percent who had clear, written goals? They were earning, on average, ten times as much as the other 97 percent put together. Despite the fact that this study is often cited by motivational speakers and business experts around the world, still most people do not have clear, measurable, time-oriented goals that they work toward. Do not make this mistake!

When writing your goals, first consider where you want your business to be 10 years from now. What type of life do you want to be leading? Examples could be making a certain level of salary, retiring early, working less, etc. Continue this process, for annual, monthly, weekly, and daily goals. This process will show you exactly what you need to be doing each and every day to make your goals a reality. Be specific as possible and make sure you measure your production against these objectives. Metaphysicist, Robert Collier said that success is the sum of small efforts, repeated day in and day out. This may be true, but the more practical benefit for me is the feeling I have while driving home each day knowing that I met my goal for the day, and knowing what that means for the long-term health of my business and family.

## Important Considerations

Once you have taken the time to develop a thorough business plan and you have set forth specific goals that are aligned with that plan, here are some of the other considerations that you will want to give some thought prior to starting your business. You should know that there are no specific or good answers to any of these questions as each decision depends upon the specific business owner and the type of business he wants to create. However, thinking about these issues will allow progress to be made quickly with regard to these decisions and likely keep some of your formation costs lower.

- If there are numerous partners engaging in this business, will they all be compensated equally? If not, how will they be compensated?
- Will the business be owning or leasing real property? What are the benefits of having a separate entity own the real property?
- Will the business have employees who are not members or shareholders in the business? How will these employees be compensated? Will they be offered stock or cash bonuses as employment incentives?

- Most often the partners forming a business are excited about their new venture and are essentially in a "honeymoon" stage. How will the business address a situation where when the honeymoon is over, one of the business owners wants to leave, or some of the business owners want an individual business owner to leave? Essentially, after the honeymoon, how would we deal with the divorce?

- How will the business deal with the death or disability of an owner?

Often, insurance policies coupled with a Buy/Sell Agreement are simple, cost-effective ways to deal with many of these difficult and complex situations, which if not addressed at the forefront, can bankrupt owners of their life's work. The reason I know that these are important questions to ask is that each one left unaddressed by a business owner has resulted in litigation I've handled over the past several years. In each case, had these issues been addressed by the business owners at the beginning, there would have been no lawsuit.

While the process of forming a business is relatively simple, it is incredibly important that the business owner understands the necessary steps that he has to take to maintain his corporate form. The entrepreneur must understand that once a business is started, from that point forward there needs to be a clear segregation between the business finances and personal finances. Failing to do this can expose the entrepreneur to a situation where personal assets may be used to satisfy debts of the business.

There are also other issues that business owners may have never considered such as worker's compensation insurance should they desire to hire employees, filing business taxes annually, malpractice insurance, retirement accounts and obligations, and premises insurance and liability. Business owners need to have a certain level of understanding of all of these to properly run their businesses.

## TIP NUMBER TWO: GET SOME HELP!

If you do not know it by now, you are not an expert in everything. It is simply impossible. An often cited criticism of business professionals and politicians as proof of their mediocrity is that they are "micro-managers." They will not let go of anything and this is generally a mistake. The trick is to figure out what you are good at, figure out what you need help doing because you are lousy at it, and hire qualified professionals to help you fill in the gaps.

As a business owner, you are going to need a team of professionals to help support you in your field. You will also need a quality assistant or office manager whom you trust and who is dedicated to the business. You also need a good lawyer, a good accountant, and someone who can handle your needs regarding your employees if you have them, i.e. human resources, insurances, 401Ks, etc. Some of the best advice I have ever been given is, get the legal and tax issue right the first time. While you will have to pay for good service, over the course of the life of your business, these people are going to save you more money and headaches than can be measured. If you do not have anyone to fill in this roster yet, ask people you know and trust who are in business for a referral and begin assembling your team from there.

Another point that I make to business owners is that there will always be work that you do for which the bill goes unpaid. This is frustrating, but it happens to every business. The perfect solution is to get paid up front for everything. If you establish this policy, then you do not need to read the rest of this paragraph. But for those of us who have trusted people and then gotten burned, you will need to find someone to handle your collections. Have your lawyer (if he or she does not do this work) recommend a quality collections firm. These people, for a percentage of the debt owed, will take the legal steps necessary to obtain as much of the debt owed to your business as possible through garnishment proceedings or otherwise.

For small debts, you might consider having your office manager handle these claims for you in small claims court. Be sure to figure out how this will affect your relationship with the customer. Generally speaking, this is a road one travels only after the decision is made that this person is no longer valued as a customer.

Another investment that you should consider is whether your business could benefit from creating "standard" or "form" agreements. Any agreement to sell goods or provide services should be in writing. This way everyone knows the rules of the game. As an often "groaned at" attorney, I know that there many business owners who might groan over this suggestion. However, this is the only way to protect your business in each and every transaction. Most businesses provide the same type of goods or services over and over again. My recommendation is to meet with your attorney, describe the types of transactions you engage in regularly, and have some standard agreements drawn up. There are certain terms that should be in every agreement, which can protect you from the costs of litigation should a deal ever go sour. Once you have this document created, you will know with certainty exactly what your rights are in any given transaction. Simply for illustration, here are some issues that should be addressed in every contact.

- How does a party terminate the contract?
- Do the parties agree to arbitrate if there is a dispute, which could save everyone the costs of going to court?
- Does the contract have a term or is it perpetual?

These are only a few of the ideas that your attorney could help you with by drafting a standard agreement.

### TIP NUMBER THREE: GET TO WORK!

There are many rules of thumb that business consultants toss around to define whether a business is going to "make it." The most often cited one is that if a business is still operating one year after its doors are opened then it will most likely survive. Considering this fact only emphasizes the need to have a plan before you open for business.

The most successful business owners that I run into generally do not treat running their business as work. Running their business becomes their life, for better or for worse. They are always looking for a way to fuel their business. Anyone they meet at a dinner party or at a Saturday football tailgate on the weekend is a potential client. They develop a way to let these potential clients know what type of business they run and what type of services they can provide and, perhaps most importantly, they do this without making the individuals they are talking to feel like they are being "sold." Once again, they make their business their life. After all, it is this business that will provide them the personal and financial freedom to live their lives on the terms they desire.

It is important to recognize, however, the duality that resonates from the two points that were just made. One, operating the business becomes a successful business owner's life; and two, he is living his life on his own terms. The important point is as follows: I often laugh when I see commercials on television promoting the sale of products whereby the biggest selling term is "I can set my own hours." I laugh because I assume many people think that this indicates that you can run a successful business and work very little. There are many people in this world, often ones who launch unsuccessful businesses, who believe this. The fact is that this is simply not true. Any successful business owner will tell you, being the driving force behind the business most often means long hours. There is simply no way around putting in time to generate revenue. The old adage in business rings true, action creates reaction.

The important thing for business owners to consider and remember is the value of balance—being the driving force behind your business and still maintaining a life that is one you want to live. The key for me is working efficiently. When you are at work, work hard so that you have time to be with your family. Do not procrastinate; take that awful task head-on, first thing in the morning, even if it is the only thing you accomplish that day. At least the problem you were dreading is done. One other piece of advice is this: every once in a while, as morbid as it might be, imagine being on an airplane that is going down. Imagine what you would be thinking about when looking back on your life. Chances are you will not be thinking about how you should have spent more time at the office. It is this thought that helps me balance my work and family priorities.

## CONCLUSION

As you can glean from this chapter, there is a lot to think about when starting a business. Successful business owners take the time to develop a proper business plan and to address considerations that are outlined in this chapter and brought up by their attorneys. The formation of a business is a classic example of where business owners can be penny-wise and pound foolish. Every day business owners avoid the initial cost of properly setting up a business and consulting with an attorney to set up operating agreements or share-holders' agreements that protect both their interests and the interests of other members, shareholders, and their families. Business owners who skimp on the setup costs often find themselves with ten times the bill when things go wrong.

Not all attorneys are equipped to provide business own-ers with the right advice. Find yourself an attorney who works with business owners exclusively—one who under-stands the pitfalls and can ask you the right questions so that you and your business are properly protected. If you sit down with an attorney and he is not asking you ques-tions similar to the questions outlined in this chapter, or if he is simply having you sign paperwork to be filed with the state without setting up an operating agreement or share-holders' agreement, or fails to discuss the issues outlined herein, you are not being properly served and your legal interests are not being protected. Any individual can simply file the paperwork with the State of Michigan to set up a business; however, consulting with an attorney can make all the difference should trouble arise.

***

Trevor Weston is a graduate of Hope College and Michigan State University College of Law. He joined the firm of Falvay, Marcus & Weston, P. C. in 2008. His focus has been primarily on business formation, estate planning, probate and estate administration, as well as handling the general litigation needs of the firm's clients.

Trevor is admitted to practice in all Michigan State Courts, the Federal District Court for the Eastern District of Michigan, as well as the Sixth Circuit Court of Appeals. He is a member of the State Bar of Michigan, Oakland County Bar Association, the Federal Bar Association for the Eastern District of Michigan, and Michigan Defense Trial Counsel, as well as the Estate Planning Sections of the State Bar of Michigan and Oakland County Bar Association. He is also a member of the Royal Oak Optimist Club.

Trevor has published articles in the *Michigan Defense Quarterly*. He sits on the Construction Code Board of Appeals and Historical Commission and the Acorn Foundation for the City of Royal Oak.

You can contact Trevor by phone: 877-642-5535 or 248-642-5535, fax: 248-594-6235, email: tweston@falvaylaw.com, website: www.falvaylaw.com.

# PERMISSION-BASED MARKETING: EFFECTIVELY USING THE INTERNET

### by Niles D. Crum, NDC Payment Solutions

New, innovative marketing technologies can help you to reach your customers and prospects more effectively and less expensively than the old traditional ways. These technologies can help you to grow your top line. After all, you will make a lot more profit by growing revenue than you ever will by cutting cost. There is an end to the amount of cost you can cut, but there is no end to the revenue growth potential of your business.

It is no secret that business owners are moving away from using traditional media, such as television, newspapers, radio, Yellow Pages™, direct mail, etc. Dozens of newspapers are closing their doors and nobody watches television anymore without their DVRs, which allow them to fast-forward through the commercials. And phone books? When was the last time you opened one? The only thing I use a phone book for now is to prop up my grandkids at the dinner table. And, those ads in the Yellow Pages™ are expensive. So how do you best take advantage of new technology to help market and promote yourself or your company?

## EMAIL MARKETING

Most people do not know that *email is the most effective form of promotion on the Internet*. Yes, and this is the reason you receive so much spam in your inbox. People spend more time on email than on any other online activity. Therefore, it makes sense that this is the place to capture your clients' and prospects' attention.

To effectively market via email, you need the help of a specifically designed tool, which allows you to send permissions-based bulk emails to prospects or existing customers. Such tools have statistics built-in to measure your results. You can measure such things as click rates on links, deliverability, etc.

If you are using one of those free email accounts to try and communicate with your customers or prospects, you are using the wrong tool. To send more than 30 emails at a time, you need a tool designed specifically to do that.

Email marketing is not spam. Spam is illegal and strictly prohibited by the CAN-SPAM Act of 2003. Thus your customers or prospects must give permission to receive emails from you. Using email marketing tools, you can engage with your customers or prospects and measure and refine your results. With a targeted message and approach, it is possible to quickly realize a high return on investment.

## TECHNOLOGY IS THE ENABLER

With current technology, you can create and send professionally designed video emails to capture and attract new customers. Via webinars, you can do live broadcasts with slides and interactive chat so your audience can ask questions—and all information can be archived for later viewing. Engaging with your customers and prospects has never been as rich and rewarding. Multiple targeted email campaigns can be tracked to measure your results in real time. You can see who is opening your campaigns and clicking on the links inside. Follow up to those individuals with a personal video message and see your closure rates skyrocket. Does this sound expensive to do? Not really. There are products that allow you to do all of this and more for under $100 per month.

Fortune 500 companies have been using the Internet for years to market to customers and prospects. You most likely have seen email campaigns that resemble web pages. Media (audio, video) can be easily added to your campaigns to make them even more effective. Place a product presentation video in an email campaign with a "buy now" button adjacent. In the video, tell your prospect to buy the product by simply clicking on the "buy now" button, which goes to your website. Your merchant service provider can help you set up an e-commerce enabled website if you do not have one already.

Another breakthrough technology that allows you to differentiate your business is mobile promotions. How do most merchants attract new customers, get loyal customers to buy more, get customers to try something new, and get customers to come back? Coupons! America is responding to mobile: 94% of text messages are opened and read, 90% of shoppers carry a phone, and response rates are much higher (15:1) when compared to traditional marketing (according to www.LIFTmysales.com).

Mobile marketing is effective for many types of businesses, including:

- Retailers—coupons, offers, deals of the day, etc.
- Restaurants—coupons, specials, new menus, etc.
- Bars and clubs—events, special covers, drink specials, etc.
- Salons and spas—appointment reminders, new services, coupons, etc.
- Doctors/vets/professional services—appointment reminders, new services, notices for checkups.

Moreover, global position system (GPS) technology allows businesses to see where customers are in real time. Of course, a customer must sign up and give permission. For instance, when a customer enters a mall, his favorite retail store knows and can instantly send an offer or notice of the deal of the day right to his phone. How cool is that? It is a win/win for both the merchant and the consumer.

## EMAIL DELIVERY TOOLS

There are many tools on the market with a multitude of capabilities. Your choice of tool should be based on your business needs. I personally use a product called comF5™ for my business. I met a person who sells it at a networking event. All it took for me to be hooked was receiving my follow-up video email message from him. I was immediately impressed and bought the product.

With this new piece of technology, the possibilities for my business became evident. It would enable me to break through the clutter, set myself apart from the competition, and position myself as an expert in my industry. This user-friendly product gave me a sense of cachet in communicating with my prospects and customers.

You would probably agree that many people would rather watch than read and talk than type. Basic text email messages are often misunderstood; but with video email messaging, you can dictate the tone and the message is communicated right every time. I started by sending individual video emails to prospects who did not answer or respond to my text email messages and/or voice mails. In some cases the prospect would call back immediately after watching the video (you also get an immediate email notice when someone watches your video email) and say, "Wow, how did you do that? Your video email message was really cool. I want to do this for my business." Though not the expected response, at least it gave me the opportunity to speak with the potential customer.

This led to using many of the other features of the product and with great results, such as video email marketing campaigns to my entire client list. I developed a website for my business but had no real way to market it and all of my services to my clients. I am now able to embed video in my website and send it out via an email marketing campaign. No longer do I need to wait for traffic to come to my website; I send my website, with a video message, to my clients!

***

This discussion merely scratches the surface of all of the features and capabilities of permission-based marketing. You can be confident that if you invest in the tools and use them properly, they will increase your bottom line. Whether you are a small- or medium-sized business owner trying to increase and sustain your customer base, a church wanting to expand its flock, or a local entertainer trying to keep your fans notified of your shows . . . you will not find anything close to producing the results of these new, innovative marketing solutions.

***

Niles Crum has over 20 years experience in the business-to-business publishing industry, helping companies of all sizes market themselves to their customers and prospects. In 2007, he launched a successful career in the payment solutions industry, focusing mainly on credit card processing.

You can contact Niles at 815-304-4098, cell: 630-935-7416, email: nilescrum@comcast.net, website: www.nilescrum.com.

# WHAT TO LOOK FOR WHEN HIRING A WEB DEVELOPER

## by Steve Hyer, IGD Solutions Corporation

Hiring the right web developer can mean the difference between having your project take more than a year with no tangible results to show and having your project completed on time, on budget, and seeing almost immediate payback.

### DEFINING YOUR PURPOSE

First, you should ask yourself, "What is the purpose of my website project?" There can be any number of reasons why you want to move forward on a project, such as:

- For additional credibility—having a website online can add credibility to your company. This is especially important if you do not have a brick-and-mortar shop or if all of your competitors have websites online.

- To sell something—a website may act as a direct sales tool, allowing customers to browse your products or services and actually buy them online.

- To showcase your portfolio—you may need to showcase your product portfolio, the portfolio of projects you have already completed, or maybe both. Instead of waiting for the customer to receive a piece of mail to review what a certain product looks like or to examine your past experience, you may direct them right to your website to review those items immediately.

- To exchange data—an effective website might provide a method to exchange large files with your clients or it could provide ready access for your in-the-field sales representatives to download product information sheets on demand.

These are just a few of the purposes that you may see your website project fulfilling.

## FINDING THE RIGHT DEVELOPER

You must seek a web developer who understands your purpose and direction. If the conversation starts out with the web developer asking how many pages and how many images you want on your website, you may want to end the conversation and look elsewhere. But if the web developer starts to ask questions about the outcomes and purpose of the website, you are on the right track.

Start out by making sure you are comfortable communicating with your web developer. If you feel that he is using too much jargon and technical acronyms and not taking the time to explain them, this might be a tell-tale sign that the project is not a match. If you feel talked down to or intimidated at any point, it is definitely time to look elsewhere. Do not ever feel ashamed or intimidated to ask questions or get clarification on any point. This is *your* website project and you deserve to be in the loop the entire time. Website projects are almost always done to show a return on investment. If your web developer is not speaking your language, find someone who does.

When you think you have found the right developer, it is time to start digging a little deeper into his qualifications. First, find out if you are dealing with a company or an individual. If it is a company, find out if it is incorporated. If you are dealing with an individual, you should proceed with caution. It may difficult for a single individual to complete your project to your satisfaction within your time constraints. Further, does he have all of the expertise your website will require?

Does the company or the individual have insurance? All companies should carry a general liability policy and web developers should carry an errors-and-omissions policy. This type of insurance coverage guards against mistakes that the web developers make that could ultimately fall back on you, the customer. For example, should the web developer accidentally use a copyrighted image on your website, even without knowing it, there could be fees or damages awarded to its owner by a court of law. An errors-and-omissions policy can protect against this and other types of legal challenges.

You should also find out how many staff members are employed by the company and their range of expertise. How many of them are in sales, customer support, creative design, programming, or clerical roles? What support hours does the company provide? Who will be your main contact throughout the project? Find out which staff members will be working your project and who you will be communicating with along the way. You may be confident that your sales representative sitting in front of you understands the project, but who will you be working with through the technical implementation along the way? Ask about how project communication works and how all the parties working on your web project will communicate with one another and with you.

Find out how long the company or developer has been in business. Ask for references or a client list. How many projects has the website developer successfully completed? It may even be prudent to ask about the backgrounds of the specific staff working on your project. If the website developer is fairly new, you should be cautious that he is not learning industry best practices on your project. You should be looking for someone with at least three to five years in the web development field. Make sure that the company or individual has completed at least 25 distinct projects, and preferably more than 50, to ensure that they will not be using your project as a learning experience.

You also want to delve into similar projects that the developer may have done. These projects do not necessarily have to be for a company in the same industry; however, from a purpose and return-on-investment standpoint, the developer should have worked on similar projects to yours in the past. You can certainly be worried about a web developer who does not post a portfolio or client list on his own website. It may be inferred that by not providing this information the web developer is protecting himself from competitors who are out to steal clients. But the only clients that tend to be at risk of being stolen are those who are not well supported on an ongoing basis. Take the time to call some of the clients and ask about their experience with the web developer. Is their project fulfilling the original purpose that it was set out to achieve? Was the project completed on time and on budget? What was the pre- and post-sale support like? How easy or difficult was it to communicate during the development process and thereafter?

## CREATING YOUR WEBSITE

Once you have chosen a web developer, it is time to get specific about your project. A project that is not well defined up front is one that typically fails along the way. It is imperative to make sure that you and your web developer are on the same page with what is entailed in the project. You should have a clear mutual understanding of what needs to be done.

Generally, when planning a website project, you want to be looking into the future to know what the next steps are, even though they may be a year or more away. These next steps may even change before you get to them. However, it is important to make sure nothing you are doing now in your development will hurt the future scalability and expandability of your website.

If you are building a new website, you should ask questions about the creative look and feel that will be used. How will that be created? How will revisions be handled? How does the pricing work for that? Are there a fixed number of revisions included or is it unlimited? When dealing with the look and feel of a website, it is very difficult to produce a first or second draft that is "perfect." It is usually easy to achieve a functional draft, but it is not as easy to match the client's preferences, which are subjective. And, in most cases, preference is something that cannot be well defined up front. You need to be sure that you do not get "stuck" with a look and feel that you will not be happy with. If you are not proud of your web presence, it is doomed to fail. Part of the success comes from you bragging about your web presence and sending your clients and prospects there every chance you can. If you are not happy with it, that will not happen, and the project's success will be limited.

There must be a clear understanding of the functionality of your eCommerce site as well as any specific application being developed to work with it. Additionally, you and the developer must determine who will provide certain items in the process. Is it your responsibility to add all of your products into the eCommerce shopping cart system or is your developer doing that? Are you going to provide all of the content or is creating that part of the project? Who is going to provide the shipping, privacy policy, and terms and conditions? Every web developer tends to handle these things a different way and it is to your advantage to make sure you understand your responsibilities up front.

Finally, you should make sure that the technologies being used in the development of the project are suitable for the purposes and outcomes that you expect to achieve. For example, if you are looking for search engines to bring traffic to your website, using an abundant amount of images (instead of text for your content) or using flash may be a significant hindrance to achieving that goal. You need to be clear about your expectations and ask if the technologies being used at all limit your ability to accomplish your end goals.

## MAINTENANCE AND SUPPORT

Talk to the web developer about support and maintenance fees. Every web project needs to be hosted somewhere. If you have a large company, you may be hosting your website and email internally. But if your company is a small business, you may choose to outsource your website and email hosting.

Website hosting comprises leasing or renting a small portion of a server where your website will reside. Typically, this is outsourced because a company specializing in this goes to great lengths to make sure that these systems are backed up daily and fully redundant to limit, if not avoid, all down time. Your website needs to be up and running at all times. It should never be down due to technical server issues. Ask if the web developer is providing hosting for you or if you will be responsible for arranging a website host on your own.

You should also investigate whether or not you may need email hosting with the website hosting. If your company uses an in-house email server, such as Microsoft Exchange®, you may not need email hosting. If you are currently outsourcing your email and are happy with the service being provided, you may want to check with that company about hosting your new web project before making a switch. You should find out if your web developer is a reseller or in the business of hosting. If he is a reseller, you should find out if you will be working with him for support or directly with the company he is reselling. Resolving issues in a reseller relationship may take a bit longer because the developer has to work through the original hosting company. If the developer is hosting your website, you should ask about the age and location of the equipment being used to service your web project. If the equipment is more than four years old, I would be very cautious about proceeding. If the equipment is anywhere other than a professional data center with redundant Internet connections and backup power, I would also look elsewhere for my hosting needs.

There must be a clear understanding about how ongoing maintenance and changes will be handled. Is there a maintenance plan or an hourly rate? How is the hourly rate billed (in what increments)? If you will be responsible for making your own changes, you want to be sure that the training and support for the update system is included in your agreement as well.

Ask about what fees you may incur in the first two years—there can be quite a few and you should be sure you are clear on all of them. What is the up-front cost? What does that cost include in terms of revisions? Is there a training or setup fee of some sort? Does the project include content writing or is that being provided? Are there any search engine optimization items included or are those extra? Who is handling the hosting, maintenance (website changes), and domain name renewals along the way?

***

Hiring the right web developer takes some investigation and some planning. Understanding where you are going with your web strategy will ensure that you do not stray off course.

***

In 1999, Stephen Hyer founded IGD Solutions, a website design, application development, hosting, search engine optimization, web marketing, and content marketing company. IGD Solutions was listed in the May 19, 2009 issue of *Forbes* magazine as one of the leading website design companies in the Central United States by Goldline Research.

Besides being president of IGD Solutions, Steve has served in various capacities on the Clarkston School Board, the Clarkston Area Chamber of Commerce board, the state PTA board, and the Oakland County School Boards Association. He is also one of the recipients of the prestigious Champion of

Children award given by the Michigan Association of School Administrators.

You can contact Steve by phone: 248-625-0817, email: sjh@igdsolutions.com, or website: www.igdsolutions.com.

# THE STRATEGIC APPROACH TO ECOMMERCE

*by Steve Hyer, IGD Solutions Corporation*

There are thousands of options for diving into eCommerce. The options vary from something custom designed to something out of the box. Costs vary wildly too, and it can be hard to compare the options.

## DETERMINING YOUR STRATEGY

Before you start an eCommerce project, it is important for you to chart out what you would like to accomplish and how you would like it to work. Once you know what you want to accomplish, you can then explore options to implement that vision.

To determine your eCommerce strategy, you may want to begin by asking yourself some questions, such as:

- What are you selling and who is your intended audience?
- Are you selling one product or hundreds or thousands of products?
- Do you plan to sell products that need to be configured with different options?
- Is your product a downloadable product or piece of software?
- Are you selling a service?

When customers are shopping online, they are sizing you up against your competition. They are looking for any reason to doubt your performance. Internet shoppers are typically hesitant because they have heard horror stories of scams and people being ripped off online. They are almost looking for a reason not to buy from your site. Thus it is vitally important that you give them no reason to question your credibility. The customer's shopping experience on your site should be consistent with the larger websites online that users tend to trust.

The first decision you will need to make is whether you will use an order-form-type transaction or a full-blown shopping cart. If you are selling fewer than a dozen products and you are looking for users to select a quantity and maybe sizes, an order form might work just fine for your purposes. An order form typically lists all of the products on one page and allows the customer to enter a quantity for each item and maybe select the size or color that they are ordering. This approach tends to be a simple and easy way for a customer to see all of your products and easily order them. Further, if customers typically order multiple products at once, an order form tends to work best. With an order form, the payment and contact information is typically added on one page.

If each of your products requires detailed or technical information to be displayed, an order form may not work. Further, if your online store carries more than a dozen different products or requires organization by searchable categories, a shopping cart might be the better way to go.

A shopping cart is a system that allows customers to browse categories and sub-categories of products. Customers can usually search for products or choose a "manufacturer" or "department" to browse products. An order is placed by clicking on a product, selecting the quantity, and choosing "add to cart." At this point, the customer can see the list of items in her cart. She can choose to continue shopping or proceed to "checkout." The checkout procedure usually requires the customer to create an account and enter payment information in a series of steps.

## ECOMMERCE COMPATIBILITY

With either the order form or shopping cart approach, it is prudent to make sure that the eCommerce vehicle you choose fits into your strategy. If you are looking to attract users to the site to buy products, you will require software that is search engine friendly. That is, it should include extra meta keywords and meta descriptions for each product. For example, each product may have a specific page title that you can assign. Most importantly, the product page name should mirror the name of the product and not contain any "? Identifiers." If your site address to a product page is something like this, "http://www.domain.com/productid?=5," your cart is likely not very search engine friendly. Conversely, if your product address is something like this, "http://www.domain.com/nameoftheproduct.aspx," your cart software is likely somewhat search engine friendly. This is definitely something you want to ask the manufacturer or developer of the software about if you are at all unclear.

If you have thousands of products, you will want to investigate the best way to get your products into the eCommerce solution. Will you have to enter them by hand or will you be able to export them from your product management system and import them into your shopping cart system?

The solution you choose must integrate with your eCommerce provider. For example, if you opt for an online gateway, your order form or shopping cart needs to integrate with it.

Another consideration is whether a particular solution is locked into a specific provider or if it is portable to others. If you choose to change your website host, are you losing your eCommerce solution? Or, if you want to change merchant providers, are you able to do that? To make sure your investment lasts far into the future, the solution should be portable to any merchant provider and any website host.

The eCommerce solution you choose should fit your specific group of products and how you choose to offer them to your customers. If you offer options on product configuration, those features must be contained in your solution. For example, if you allow customers to build gift baskets with individual products, the solution should be able to handle it.

## ECOMMERCE SOLUTIONS

If you find that an out-of-the-box solution can meet all of your needs, this may be the least expensive option. However, if you cannot find the features you are looking for, you may need to develop a custom eCommerce application. In this case, you would find a web developer and work with him to clearly lay out the features that you will require in your eCommerce solution.

In a custom solution, do not assume that anything will be included unless it is explicitly listed on your contract. This includes things as simple as shipping and tax calculations. Custom solutions can be a good fit when a company has a large number of products in an existing product management system. A custom online eCommerce application can tie directly into the existing product manager, display products online, and allow customers to order them. Inventory may also be displayed for the customer.

An absolute key to remember with any eCommerce solution is to keep it simple. If you have never had an eCommerce business before and are just looking to test the waters, you can implement a simpler solution before going to a fully customized shopping cart.

To increase the effectiveness of an existing solution, you can certainly use the data you currently have to improve upon the customer experience. When any solution is ultimately implemented, you must put yourself in the shoes of your potential shopper. Will the shopping experience be what the customer is expecting? Will customers have total comfort in purchasing from your website with the solution you are considering? If the solution will at all be inconsistent or confusing, you should look for another. You will end up wondering why you are not getting any sales.

There are cheap solutions that allow your eCommerce solution to be hosted on a separate website. But beware that if a customer feels like he is being bounced to another website from your site, it is an open opportunity for the customer to choose not to continue browsing products. Redirecting from one site to another, especially if the look and feel of the two sites are different, is not a good way to keep your customers engaged.

## SECURITY

Security is a major concern when implementing any eCommerce option. If you are actually hosting the solution on your website, you will need to purchase a Secure Socket Layer (SSL) certificate. This is something that needs to be renewed annually (you can pay for multiple years in advance). The certificate is actually a piece of computer code (128-bit SSL certificate), which allows the browser to connect to your site in a secured manner. This is necessary so that credit card numbers are not transmitted over the Internet without being encrypted. Further, if you are storing credit card numbers in your database with user information, you want to make sure that they are encrypted there as well. It is vitally important that your application be secure and compliant with your merchant provider. Providers and costs can vary significantly. Generally, there are limits on each transaction and you want to make sure that the limit you are purchasing is consistent with the type and size of the transactions you are expecting.

## SUCCESSFUL ECOMMERCE

Once your solution is up and running, it is important to monitor the results. You must get one sale before you can get 10 sales. Compare your pricing and shipping options to other competitive sites online.

It is also important to talk to your customers whenever possible. Many prefer to browse online and call in their orders. If customers are registering and not buying, contact them to ask why. Find out what products they are looking at and where they are spending time.

To be successful online with eCommerce, there is no silver bullet. You should look to make incremental improvements to your eCommerce solution over time. Use the usage data your site generates to make educated decisions about the future of your site in an effort to increase sales. Even if your site is generating what you are expecting, there are certainly ways to increase its effectiveness and generate even more sales. The moment you become complacent and stop improving your site is the moment your competition will overtake you in the competitive Internet marketplace. In the long term, look at eCommerce as more of a marathon and less of a sprint. Making small changes over time can keep you competitive and keep your sales increasing.

Work with a trusted partner who can handle the behind-the-scenes technology, merchant processing compatibility, and optimization so that you can focus on your products, promotions, and marketing efforts.

\*\*\*

In 1999, Stephen Hyer founded IGD Solutions, a website design, application development, hosting, search engine optimization, web marketing, and content marketing company. IGD Solutions was listed in the May 19, 2009 issue of *Forbes* magazine as one of the leading website design companies in the Central United States by Goldline Research.

Besides being president of IGD Solutions, Steve has served in various capacities on the Clarkston School Board, the Clarkston Area Chamber of Commerce board, the state PTA board, and the Oakland County School Boards Association. He is also one of the recipients of the prestigious Champion of Children award given by the Michigan Association of School Administrators.

You can contact Steve by phone: 248-625-0817, email: sjh@igdsolutions.com, or website: www.igdsolutions.com.

# BUILD IT AND THEY WILL COME? GETTING PEOPLE TO YOUR WEBSITE

*Stephen J. Hyer, IGD Solutions Corporation*

It is not uncommon for me to get a call from a potential customer who says, "I set up my eCommerce site and it looks great, it works great, but I haven't gotten even one sale yet. Can you help me?" The world of the Internet is not much different than the traditional brick-and-mortar world we all grew up in. Thirty years ago, you could have opened the best little shop on the planet, but if your store was not located in a mall or near an anchor store, nobody would ever stumble upon it. So, if you wanted any business, you would have to market your store. The same is true today on the Internet.

If you want business from the millions of people searching the Internet every day, you absolutely must market your company there. First, you must come up with your marketing plan. Is there already demand for your product online? Are people already searching your products or services by name or model number? How do you fare on price compared to your competition? How do you fare on credibility, tax, shipping, and other potentially "hidden" charges? Are you selling something that people do not know exists? Did you invent your own product category?

## EXISTING WEBSITES

If the demand already exists for your product, it is somewhat easier to market your offerings online. The first step

---

is to make sure your site contains enough of the "right" content so that you show up in the major search engines. Google®, Yahoo®, Bing™ (MSN), and Ask® make up about 99% of the search engine market. All of these search engines have automated robots that come out and crawl your registered website.

### Optimizing Your Search Ranking

Ten years ago, hidden things within your page called meta tags were vitally important to how your website would rank. Today, they are much less important because your ranking is determined primarily by the content. The content must be all about what it is you are selling or offering on your site. However, you cannot do too much in one block of content. Ideally, each page or section of your website will specialize in just two or three different ideas, phrases, or concepts. You do not want to repeat your keywords too often, nor do you want to dilute them by not mentioning them enough within the context of the larger content blocks. It is also prudent to stay away from flash and frames and other technologies that can hinder search engine placement.

Ideally, to optimize the content on your website properly, you need to tap into an expert. This expert may not be the same expert who designed your website. The first step in any optimization process is to determine the terms that people are currently typing in to find your product or service offering. If your market exists and people are already looking for you, this is easy. You want to narrow your focus to terms that are 100% relevant to your website and that have demand (meaning people are typing them in hundreds or thousands of times per month). The second thing you want to evaluate for each term is how much competition there is. If a term has 20,000,000 results, it will be difficult and nearly impossible to get top-page placement by optimizing content alone. However, if a term has 2,000,000 results, you may be able to get to the top of the search engines by working with your content.

An expert can help you work the key terms into your content in the proper ratio, density, and proximity to other content. The expert can also help you with the technical side of optimization, including embedding the hidden meta tags, site maps, alt tagging, the robots file, custom error pages, and a few other potential items. Each of these things is "behind the scenes" and may be used by the search engines to help rank your site. You want to make sure your process includes all of them.

Always remember, after any content is optimized for the search engine robots, it *must* still be humanly readable and make sense. Even if your content is perfectly optimized for robots, you still must be able to make the sale once the human person ends up on your website. The content has to work for your human audience as well as the robot audience.

Once your site is optimized, you must make sure you are actually listed in all the search engines and that they have picked up your optimized content. Each search engine has a set of submission rules that you should follow. You should not submit regularly unless you have made changes to your website that require re-indexing. Although it may seem like a good idea, you should not use an automated process to submit. You should always submit manually and this is usually an easy process for an expert to handle on your behalf. Ask the expert for a copy of the submission report and make sure it contains your "local" submissions if your business is at all geographically based or if it has a physical location.

If the organic optimization is done correctly, it should be a one-time process. There may be some ongoing reporting and monitoring, but tweaking should only occur to fix certain issues that may arise or when there are changes to what you are optimizing for. There should not be any "tweaking" done to your site on a regular ongoing basis.

## NEW WEBSITES

If the product or service you are selling is new, or people do not know it exists, getting people to your site is going to be a little more difficult. You then need to start thinking about the demographic of the people who may be good target customers for your products. The next step is to determine where those customers may be hanging around online. Are they using Facebook? Are they members of certain organizations? What other services are they currently using? What other challenges may they be looking to solve online? You never want to deceive someone into coming to your website thinking you can solve a problem you cannot solve. However, you can approach your customers with your actual product or service. For example, if you only sell little figurine lighthouses, there may not be a very large market for those online. To expand your reach, you might want to target the collectible market and the lighthouse lover market online. In doing your initial research on how people search, you should be able to find out where you can gain some listing and bring in some interested traffic.

The name of the game in search engine optimization is finding the most relevant and qualified traffic. Ten years ago, bringing any traffic to your site was considered a good thing. Today, you want to target the most qualified people searching online and bring them to your company's website. Working with your expert, you want to be specific in what you are going after and optimizing for.

## BUYING PLACEMENT

Beyond the traditional or organic optimization, there is also a way to buy placement online. You can work by yourself and contact websites directly asking them if they would be willing to host your company's banner ad, which would link back to your site. Banner ads can come in a wide variety of shapes and sizes and can appear all the time or can rotate among several different companies. They can be relatively static or totally animated and completely obnoxious. If you wanted placement on your local chamber of commerce site, you would probably contact someone there directly and strike a deal. If you are looking for broader-based placement on larger sites, you would likely have to contact an agency to help you. Just like radio or television advertising, you want to match the ads to your specific online demographic. If you are targeting senior citizens, getting placement on an extreme sports website would make no sense. For most businesses, paid placement should only be used to supplement an organic strategy or when an offer is extremely time sensitive.

You can also buy placement on the major search engines through a "pay per click" campaign. This allows you to select specific keywords and keyword phrases and actually bid on them on a per-click basis. For example, you could select the phrase, "cheap Jimmy Buffett concert tickets," because you are selling tickets for an upcoming concert. A pay-per-click campaign can get you a response much quicker than the organic options discussed previously. However, when you stop a pay-per-click program, you have almost no residual benefit, whereas the organic optimization can continue to produce benefits for years.

The cost for pay-per-click programs depends on how many people are bidding on the same term or terms and how much they are bidding. In the example above, if you start out bidding at 10 cents a click and someone types the term you are bidding on into the search engine, your ad will show up alongside the search results. If someone clicks on your company's ad, it will cost you 10 cents. If another company wants to appear ahead of yours in the ad list, it may outbid you and pay 25 cents a click. In that case, this company's ad would show up first and your company's ad would be second. Some terms may be higher than $10 per click. If you are considering running a program like this, you definitely want to seek out someone who has experience with this type of campaign. There is a reason Google has billions and billions of dollars. The company makes it easy for individuals and businesses to run their own pay-per-click campaigns. If you try it on your own, it is very likely you will waste money by not being as efficient or effective as possible by either not using the right settings or not using the right keyword phrases. It is definitely worth paying an administrative fee for some professional guidance to make sure your money is well spent.

As with any other marketing or advertising program, you want to measure the return on investment (ROI) from a pay-per-click program. If you are not seeing the return in sales or contacts, you will need to make tweaks or changes to your program until you see results. If you get 1,000 clicks on a certain term and no leads or sales, it is likely that getting 10,000 clicks would result in the same. You may be using the wrong term. Looking at the click-through rates and other usage statistics on your website in addition to the sales and contacts you receive will help you and your expert determine which campaigns or keyword phrases work and which do not.

Generally, someone familiar with running pay-per-click programs can help you select some keyword phrases and establish a budget to get started. It is fairly easy to predict how much the program will cost on a monthly basis by using historical data on the popularity of the terms you are going after.

## GAINING "POPULARITY"

The final piece of the equation in bringing people to your website is popularity, which refers to how many times other people (other websites) are linking back to your website. The search engines can view these links as a recommendation of sorts. The robots are looking at how many times your website is being linked to. They also look at the popularity of the sites that are linking to yours and weigh those accordingly. If popular sites link back to yours, this is more powerful than having a few links from your friends who are linking to you from their websites. A link from the local chamber of commerce website may hold more weight than a link from the local Boy Scout troop because the chamber site is more popular (more people are linking to it).

The way to gain popularity for your website is through content marketing. As I said earlier, content is absolutely the most important element when marketing your company's website online. It is not enough to just post all of your content on your company's website. You must become adept at *content marketing*. That is, using the content you have created and marketing your company on external sites.

The content marketing process could begin by creating optimized unique articles. Each article ends with a byline about the author and a link back to your website. The articles should be educational and information in nature. Do not use a press release or promotional materials—the articles should not be sales oriented. The articles get posted on your website and then you can post them on hundreds if not thousands of other websites. These can be sites that accept article submissions such as e-magazine type sites, article database sites, wiki sites, blogs, social media sites, etc. However, it may be very time consuming to create accounts on hundreds of websites and post articles on a regular basis. That is one reason why this service is usually contracted to someone who is an expert at it. Of course, because of the labor involved, this service is typically not cheap. If you can regularly write and submit articles on a weekly or even monthly basis, you can have a significant impact on your site's popularity over time. Depending on how aggressive you are with content marketing, the benefits of a program like this can last for years. Content does become dated and it will expire, which is why the regular submission of articles is necessary.

Investing in content marketing is a great long-term strategy to build your site's popularity and leapfrog the competition. It will benefit your site in three main ways.

1. Anyone searching on your topic is going to continually see your articles coming up from a variety of different websites. This brands you as the expert in your field and gives you credibility.

2. People who read an article and then click on your website are pre-qualified and you will get more business out of them. If they were not interested in what you were offering, they would not have read the article and they would not have clicked on your site.

3. The increase in site popularity will increase your company's organic search engine placement and you will get more traffic and business from that avenue as well because you will be leapfrogging your competitors who do not have this popularity.

\*\*\*

Bringing people to your website can be challenging. Optimizing the content on your website is a logical first step.

\*\*\*

In 1999, Stephen Hyer founded IGD Solutions, a website design, application development, hosting, search engine optimization, web marketing, and content marketing company. IGD Solutions was listed in the May 19, 2009 issue of *Forbes* magazine as one of the leading website design companies in the Central United States by Goldline Research.

Besides being president of IGD Solutions, Steve has served in various capacities on the Clarkston School Board, the Clarkston Area Chamber of Commerce board, the state PTA board, and the Oakland County School Boards Association. He is also one of the recipients of the prestigious Champion of

Children award given by the Michigan Association of School Administrators.

You can contact Steve by phone: 248-625-0817, email: sjh@igdsolutions.com, or website: www.igdsolutions.com.

# BUSINESS ENTITY CHOICE

by Brian H. Rolfe, Esq., The Kemp Klein Law Firm

## INTRODUCTION

While seemingly basic, choosing a business entity involves a lot of legal issues. This chapter is intended to provide a broad overview of such issues—especially as they relate to a limited liability company (LLC). I will first review non-LLC entities, then LLCs. Finally, the chapter will provide a summary of the distinctions.

## SOLE PROPRIETORSHIP

Where a single person seeks to operate a business, a sole proprietorship may be the appropriate business entity. A sole proprietorship requires minimal formalities and therefore costs less to form. However, some sole proprietors may need to file a form for "doing business as" (d/b/a) a particular entity name with the state or county where he or she does business. In addition, a sole proprietorship must apply for an employer identification number (EIN) if it has employees.

A sole proprietor will own all of the assets of the business. As a result, the owner will also be liable for all of its debts and obligations. Therefore, one of the other business entities discussed below may be a better option.

## CORPORATIONS

There are two types of corporate options: C corporation and S corporation. The main differences between them are how the income is taxed and shareholder requirements. As compared to other entities, a corporation must generally follow the most requirements in terms of formalities.

### C Corporations

*Formation and structure.* To form a corporation, an incorporator must file *articles of incorporation* (Articles) with the state of incorporation. A state generally requires public filings where an entity's liabilities may be limited. Such filing puts the public on notice regarding the potential limits to an entity's liabilities. The Articles provide basic information about the corporation to the public. Once the Articles are filed, the corporation becomes a distinct legal entity separate from the individual shareholders for state law purposes. The advantage of the corporation acting as a separate legal entity is that the corporation, rather than the shareholders, is generally liable for its own liabilities. It is important to note, however, that certain situations may cause a court to "pierce the veil" of a corporation and find a shareholder personally liable for an obligation of the corporation.

*Shareholders* are the owners of the corporation. C corporations are not restricted in terms of the number or types of shareholders. Therefore, a C corporation may provide the best structure for purposes of raising capital through a public stock offering.

The shareholders elect the *board of directors* who oversee the management of the corporation. In turn, the board elects the *officers* of the corporation—generally consisting of a president, vice president, treasurer, and secretary—to run the day-to-day operations.

The corporation must also adopt *bylaws*. Bylaws are an internal document that provides structural and operational guidelines for the corporation. For example, the bylaws may provide information about the board of directors, board meetings, and shareholder meetings. (Please see the "Sample Formation Documents," a PDF file, which is available for free download from www.creditcardprocessingbook.com, for an example.)

Finally, a C corporation may have more than one class of stock that may vary in, among other things, voting rights, dividend rights, and liquidation preferences.

*Operation.* A corporation must follow the statutory guidelines regarding records and meetings.

In regard to records, a state will generally require a corporation to file *annual reports* to keep its public records up to date. If a corporation fails to file its annual reports, a state may find that the corporation is not in good standing. In addition, a corporation generally maintains a *minute book*, which retains records of corporate meetings resolutions adopted by the directors and shareholders.

A corporation must hold *annual meetings* for its shareholders. It is generally during this meeting that the shareholders elect the corporation's directors. The shareholders may exercise other rights provided under the statute or the bylaws and vote on issues brought before them. Directors also hold general and/or special meetings.

Shareholders of a C corporation who are also employees of the corporation, receiving compensation for their services, may generally participate in employee benefit plans.

*Taxation.* As noted previously, a corporation is a legal entity separate from its shareholders for purposes of state law. In addition, it is a separate legal entity for tax purposes. To that end, a corporation must obtain its own *tax identification number*.

Perhaps one of the biggest disadvantages of forming a C corporation is the *double taxation* of income. The first taxation occurs when a corporation files its own income taxes, separate from that of its shareholders (the first taxation). If the corporation distributes any of its income to its shareholders, each shareholder must then include the dividends received in his or her own income taxes (the second taxation). If there is no distribution, there is no income taxation at the shareholder level. It also may be important to note that a shareholder who is also an employee may be subject to tax for unreasonable compensation, resulting in a reclassification of his or her wages to dividends.

Finally, a C corporation with gross receipts of greater than $5 million may be required to use the accrual method of accounting for tax purposes.

### S Corporations

An S corporation is similar to a C corporation, but offers both the advantage of avoiding double taxation and the disadvantage of restrictions on the number and types of shareholders.

*Formation and structure.* Unlike a C corporation, there are restrictions on the number and types of persons or entities that may become shareholders of an S corporation. First, an S corporation may not have more than 100 shareholders. In addition, a shareholder may not be a nonresident alien and must generally be an individual, with few exceptions made for certain trusts and estates. Therefore, if another business entity seeks to be an owner, an S corporation may not be an option unless an exception applies. Although an S corporation may not have more than one class of stock, the stock may be divided into voting versus non-voting stock.

Otherwise, the formation and structure of an S corporation are substantially the same as a C corporation. Like a C corporation, an S corporation is a legal entity that is separate from its shareholders for state law purposes. However, unlike a C corporation and, as discussed later, an S corporation is generally not a separate entity for tax law purposes.

Again, there is always the chance that a court may pierce the veil for liability purposes.

*Operation.* An S corporation operates in substantially the same manner as a C corporation. However, some restrictions apply as to what shareholder-employees may participate in certain employee benefit plans.

If the shareholders of an S corporation later wish to raise capital through a public stock offering, it is possible to convert to a C corporation.

*Taxation.* Other than the restrictions regarding shareholders, the biggest difference between an S corporation and a C corporation is the taxation of income. For federal tax purposes, an S corporation is a *pass-through* (or flow-through) *entity.* As such, its income will pass through to its shareholders. In other words, while a C corporation must pay taxes on its income, an S corporation passes its income on to the shareholders without being subject to tax at the corporate level. The shareholders then pay the taxes owed on such income. For purposes of state tax, some states adopt the pass-through character of federal income tax.

## PARTNERSHIPS

*Formation and structure.* A partnership requires few formalities. It is generally considered to be an association of two or more persons who seek to operate a business for profit. There are two main types of partnerships: *general partnership* (GP) and *limited partnership* (LP). Under either structure, the partners must adopt a partnership agreement.

In the case of a GP, the agreement need not be in writing (although a written agreement is recommended) and states generally do not require any filings. The partners of a GP are all considered general partners and, therefore, may engage in the business equally. In return for such flexibility, the partners of a GP may not seek protection from liabilities by hiding behind the GP's shield and they are personally liable for the debts of the GP.

On the other hand, a state may require filings for a limited partnership. Partners of an LP are divided into *general partners* and *limited partners*. The general partners usually manage the business while the limited partners invest in the business without engaging in management. Regarding any liabilities of the LP, limited partners may be held liable only to the extent of their investments.

*Operation.* Once formed, there are also few operational requirements for a partnership aside from those provided in the partnership agreement. This allows partnerships to enjoy greater flexibility than corporations, including varying the allocation of income and losses among the partners.

*Taxation.* A partnership is considered to be a pass-through entity for tax purposes. Therefore, the partners will be liable for any taxes owed on the income generated by the partnership regardless of whether the partners receive a distribution from the partnership.

## LIMITED LIABILITY COMPANIES

*Formation and structure.* As with corporations, states generally require limited liability companies (LLCs) to file *articles of organization* (similar to a corporation's articles of incorporation). In addition, an LLC generally adopts an *operating agreement* (similar to a corporation's bylaws), which provides internal guidelines regarding the LLC's structure and operations. However, such an agreement may not be a requirement. (Please see the sample operating agreement for a single-member LLC and the sample operating agreement for a multi-member LLC in "Sample Formation Documents," a PDF file available for free download from www.creditcardprocessingbook.com.)

Owners of an LLC are called members (rather than shareholders). An LLC may be structured as a *member-managed*

*LLC* or a *manager-managed LLC*. A member-managed LLC will be managed by its members on a day-to-day basis. On the other hand, members may elect managers to manage the business on a day-to-day basis by forming a manager-managed LLC. If an LLC is manager-managed, some states require the LLC to state this in its articles of organization.

An LLC may have more than one class of membership, permitting different members to enjoy different rights, depending on their class.

If the company provides certain professional services, a state may require an LLC to be formed as a *professional LLC* (PLLC). A PLLC is generally subject to further restrictions.

Finally, an LLC may be a good tool to use in estate planning, especially for purpose of transferring wealth to subsequent generations. Rather than transferring property outright, by contributing the property to an LLC and then transferring the LLC membership interest, the parties may take advantage of a discounted membership interest due to the fact that the interest is a minority interest or lacks marketability.

*Operation.* An LLC is often thought of as a hybrid between a corporation and a partnership. For state law purposes, an LLC acts as a separate legal entity from its members, thereby providing its members with a shield against claims of personal liabilities. An LLC is considered to protect its members against creditors in a manner similar to a corporation—better than a partnership. Although generally not required, an LLC should observe certain formalities to demonstrate that it is, in fact, a separate entity from its members. Some formalities include holding regular meetings and documenting the resolutions passed at such meetings in a records book. The LLC should also use its own name on letterheads, checks, signature blocks and contracts rather than using the name of any of its members. It should also not commingle funds. Despite such formalities, however, it is important to note that a court may pierce the veil of an LLC to find a member personally liable for an obligation. This may be especially true when there is only one, sole member.

*Taxation*. For tax purposes, an LLC is considered to be a pass-through entity (like a partnership). Therefore, its income is passed on to its members and taxes apply at the member level. In these two regards, an LLC is similar to an S corporation. However, whereas an S corporation must distribute income, loss, credits, and deductions to its share-holders in accordance with their ownership percentage, an LLC may enjoy greater flexibility in creating an economic arrangement among the members by providing an allocation method in its operating agreement. It can specifically allo-cate profits and losses or debt (for real estate deduction of losses). Further, members may have unequal distributions.

Finally, similar to an S corporation, certain restrictions may apply as to whether a member-employee may partici-pate in the company's employee benefit plans.

## CONCLUSION

When it comes to selecting a business entity, LLCs have become a popular choice. This is due to the entity's ability to provide both the limited liability advantage of a corpora-tion and the single taxation advantage of a partnership, and yet provide greater flexibility than an S corporation. How-ever, depending on the facts of a given situation, another entity form may be better suited for a business. (Please see the chart that summarizes some of the differences between corporations, LLCs, and partnerships in "Sample Formation Documents," a PDF file, which is available for free download from www.creditcardprocessingbook.com.)

When electing a business entity, it is also important to keep in mind not only the immediate needs of the company, but the future of the company as well. For example, it may be better to convert an LLC to a corporation than to convert a corporation to an LLC. Whereas converting an LLC to a corporation is tax-free, converting a corporation to an LLC may result in a taxable event. Therefore, it may be better to form an LLC rather than a corporation in some situations.

Again, this chapter is intended only to provide a broad overview of some of the issues to be considered when electing a business entity. Every situation brings its own unique set of circumstances and proper legal advice should be sought in terms of electing an entity for each situation.

*** 

Brian Rolfe is an attorney with The Kemp Klein Law Firm, and specializes in business and employment litigation, family law, and business counseling. He handles cases from the State District Court level, involving amounts less than $25,000, to federal and state cases involving millions of dollars, including matters in the Federal Circuit Court of Appeals, the Michigan Court of Appeals, and the Michigan Supreme Court, and has several published opinions in those forums.

Brian has a B. S. from Central Michigan University and a J. D. from the Michigan State University College of Law. He is a member of the State Bar of Michigan and the Oakland County Bar Association. Brian is also a member of the Bloomfield Hills Blue Marlin Chapter of the Local Business Network (LBN) and current chairperson of the Rochester Chamber of Commerce Preferred Networking Group. He has written a number of articles related to employment and business law and lectured on family law issues in a variety of forums. Brian has also appeared on the Business Reality Network radio program. You can reach him by phone: 248-740-5684 or email: brian.rolfe@kkue.com.

# CREATING CUSTOMERS FOR LIFE

### by Michael Wickett, Michael Wickett International

Several years ago, I met a sales representative who was so competent that I modeled him as best I could. Why would I model him? He sold $60 million plus in services for 12 consecutive years. As I got to know him, I discovered that he was brilliant in the basics—asking effective questions, creating/selling value, and using evidence to motivate people to buy.

As you look at your business results, remember that there is no good or bad "luck." There is only the Law of Cause and Effect. Although this has been challenging for me to accept in my life, it *ultimately can be used in your favor to create your ideal life.*

*"If we don't take responsibility for our results, they won't change."* With this in mind, I encourage you to get serious about this book and this chapter. When you implement the strategies explained herein, you will improve your sales significantly.

## ASKING QUESTIONS—THE FOUNDATION OF SALES SUCCESS

After 10 coaches and 35 years of study and self-improvement, I can assure you that the *greatest skill* in life is the art of asking questions. Why? Questions open the lines of communication whereas statements reduce communication and frequently cause people to react defensively. Asking questions gives you clear feedback on what the other person wants or needs. Although you do need to ask *basic* questions of a prospect, it is also essential that you ask questions to discover his "big picture expectation" or desired ultimate outcome.

Here are some "big picture" questions that could be valuable if you adopt them for your business:

- If you could change or improve _____ what would be the result?
- What is your ultimate _____?
- What is your desired long-term payoff?
- What is most important to you in a business relationship?
- If you could wave a wand and create your ideal outcome, what would that be?
- What additionally would you need to know about me or my company before you would consider letting us serve you? (Use this *exact* language and *ask it last*.)

Upon asking these questions (and others, which I challenge you to draft) of a prospect, be sure to write down his answers using his words. This will help you gain insight and uncover ways for you to help your prospect to realize his "big picture."

Also, it is essential that you uncover a prospect's *dissatisfaction*. People will not buy from you unless you can remove a major "problem" by offering a positive, highly beneficial solution. You need to ask enough questions to discover this problem/difficulty and the major objectives of the prospect.

## EVIDENCE DESTROYS DOUBT

Most salespeople have been in a selling situation where a prospect said he was interested in a product or service and then *did not buy it*. Why does this happen? It happens because the prospect did not believe your company, product, or service could give him enough value to justify buying from you. All prospects have to be satisfied with the answers to four questions:

1. Who are you?
2. What does your company offer and is it reputable?
3. What is in it for me? (W.I.I.F.M.)
4. Who says so besides you?

People always want to know who has gotten value or results from your products or service. Thus it is important for you to get testimonials of customers who have gotten successful results from your company's products or services. You must be prepared with *evidence* to show prospects that your company can deliver the value that you suggest. "Evidence" can take many forms, such as:

- testimonial letters from satisfied customers, within which are yellow highlighted benefits that customers say they have received. Ask for testimonial letters from your customers and have them include the exciting/profitable results they received.
- verbal examples. Explain what your customers say about the *value* they receive.
- demonstration. (Make sure it works; check it out in advance.)
- results from other sales people in your company.
- feedback from your corporate headquarters if different from your location.
- statistics—sell your value.
- industry articles highlighting the value of your products or services, which essentially "sell" your company.

If you find that you do not have the specific evidence needed, tell your prospect you will get back with the appropriate evidence—soon.

## WHAT YOU SEE IS WHAT YOU GET

Dr. Charles Garfield conducted the most extensive study ever undertaken on "Peak Performance." He interviewed 1,600 peak performers from business, sports, academia, and entertainment. The process took 15 years and he discovered that an essential characteristic of all peak performers is that they *visualize their ideal outcome in advance.* Further, in their visualizations, *they actually experience the feelings and the joys of having achieved their ideal results.*

Based on Dr. Garfield's findings, it is essential to follow these steps to realize breakthrough sales results:

1. Each morning, before you start your day, get quiet, close your eyes, and visualize your ideal day.

2. See success after success after success. Feel the excitement of a successful sales day.

3. Set a 60-day sales goal and visualize what it will look and feel like when you achieve it. It may be helpful to write it down so that you can reread it each morning. Use "will do," positive, actionable words with emotion. These will help you to visualize the ideal outcome.

4. Plan and visualize attending a special celebration when you achieve your goal.

5. Do not stop here! Continue setting goals, visualizing them, and experiencing the feeling of achievement. The same process can be applied to any area of your life to achieve results.

## THE PAST IS GONE

Learn from your past and move on. The past is certainly no predictor of your future. Since what you *repeatedly* see and feel becomes reality, hold a vision of *your ideal life.*

If you use the strategies described in this chapter and continue to visualize, daily, your desired outcomes—get ready for a new dimension of sales success.

***

Michael Wickett has been a speaker, sales trainer, and success coach for 26 years. His programs have helped companies such as Daimler Chrysler, IBM, State Farm Insurance, 3M Corporation, Siemens/Rapistan, Bosch Corporation, Nestle Corporation, and Metropolitan Title reinvent themselves and create new levels of productivity and growth. Over 1,000 companies have used his audio learning programs to motivate and develop their people.

One of Michael's audio programs on positive attitude has played on American Airline flights around the world. His classic sales program, "Creating Customers for Life," which includes a training workbook, is available on DVD.

You can reach Michael by phone: 248-342-1413, email: michael@michaelwickettinternational.com, or via his website: www.michaelwickettinternational.com.

# SEVEN STEPS TO SUCCESSFUL EXHIBITING

*Anita Mitzel, GraphiColor Exhibits*

You have decided to exhibit in an upcoming trade show and have booked your booth space. Now what do you do? If you are new to exhibiting, this chapter is for you. If you have exhibited in the past and have been unhappy with the outcome, then you might uncover the real reason for your disappointing results in the following pages. Of course, the first rule of the day is to make sure that you have chosen the right show in which to exhibit. Hopefully, you have done your homework and the show you are exhibiting in attracts a good number of prospects for your products and services.

## 1. BOOTH PLANNING

Planning for a successful trade show experience can be a time-consuming process, but it is not "rocket science." It starts with a commitment to plan, execute, and measure the results.

The cost of exhibiting necessitates strategic planning. It is not enough to exhibit because you are expected to be there. You must make sure you are clear about your reasons for exhibiting. Is it to generate sales leads for your products and services? Are you introducing a new product? Is it to build brand awareness? Are you there to recruit employees? Know why you are exhibiting, set specific and measurable goals, and make a plan to achieve those goals.

Start planning early, preferably six months ahead if you have already booked your space. If you have employees, choose one person on your staff to be the exhibit manager, and have this person gather a committee of key people who are focused on sales and marketing objectives. Decide together what you need to communicate at the show and how to best accomplish it. Establish specific goals for the show and design a simple method for tracking them. It is helpful to get your employees' input on the strengths and weaknesses of any prior exhibit programs. Determine your specific needs for the exhibit area, such as plasma or LED monitors, a demonstration area, tables and counters for products, lead handling, and so forth. How much booth space will you need to allow for your activities, display structure, furniture, booth staff, and visitors? What will be the overall look and feel of your booth space?

## 2. STAFFING THE BOOTH

It is important to be selective about who will work the booth. Choose employees who have the skill or personality to interact effectively and make a positive impression quickly with booth visitors.

If you overstaff your booth, there may not be enough room for visitors to comfortably approach. On the other hand, if you are understaffed, you may be missing important prospects who do not have time to wait for someone to assist them. A rule of thumb is to have no more than two staff per 10 × 10-foot booth space. If you have no employees to staff your booth, find a friend, relative, or strategic partner you can train on the basics of your products and services to help you. The individual only needs to know enough about what you do to answer basic questions, qualify visitors to your booth, and record lead information.

## 3. EXHIBITING EXPENSES

An easy way to estimate your total event budget is by multiplying the cost of your space by three. For example, if the floor space costs $21 per square foot, a 20 × 20 booth space would run $8,400 and the budget for the event would be approximately $25,200. Do not forget that you will be dividing the cost of a new display by the number of shows for which it will be used. To determine the display cost per show, estimate how many years you will use the display and how many shows you will exhibit in each year. The average lifetime of a display is five years. For graphics, the average lifetime is one year. Your display and graphic replacement needs may vary depending on how many shows you plan to attend. The more shows you go to, the sooner you may need to purchase a new trade show booth display.

Experienced exhibit professionals can assist you in creating an eye-catching display that is within your budget, meets your needs and goals, and tells your story effectively. Ask your peers or industry contacts if they can give you a good referral. Use local directories or a search engine to find exhibit companies in your area. Look for an established display company that works primarily with companies of your size to ensure good service and reasonable pricing. Go to the facility and look at pictures of other displays that the company has produced. Discuss your goals, challenges, and the budget you have in mind. You should feel comfortable with your choice and confident in the company's abilities before moving forward.

If you are new to exhibiting or are too busy to handle all of the details associated with exhibiting, many display companies can help you with that. Ask the company you choose if it provides booth management services, like storing and shipping, as well as ordering the convention hall services like electrical hookups, hiring labor for the installation and dismantling of your booth (known as I & D), and Internet hookup. Working with a display provider that has this experience can prove to be invaluable—and will probably save you time and money in the long run.

Given the amount of money spent on everything else—space rental, a booth structure and furnishings, shipping, show labor, travel, and other expenses—it is amazing how companies try to cut corners on their booth displays. The most obvious thing your company communicates at the exhibit hall is your image and your message. When you may have only three seconds to catch a person's attention, you had better have a great-looking booth that quickly communicates your message and reflects an image of quality and success. An experienced designer can provide compelling, eye-catching visuals that will stop them in the aisles. By the way, if you are showing photos of your equipment or products, consider having them professionally shot. Nothing detracts from a booth more than using amateur photography. The same applies to using video in a booth.

## 4. PRE-SHOW MARKETING

The whole world of marketing has changed dramatically in the last few years with the increasing popularity of email marketing and the growth of Web 2.0 practices such as Facebook and Twitter™. Never before has it been more affordable to get your name and message in front of millions of potential customers. Study all of the current forms of advertising and marketing to decide which ones would work the best with your type of clientele, and  fit your exhibiting objectives.

It can be beneficial to contact pre-registered attendees ahead of time and invite them to your booth. According to the Center for Exhibition Industry Research, 76% of trade show attendees have a list of "must-see" exhibitors. Use direct mail, phone, fax, or email to invite current and potential customers to come to your booth. Send free attendance passes to good customers or prospects. You may want to offer an incentive for stopping by your booth—a small gift or entry in a prize drawing. Consider running ads in trade journals, on your website, and in other company communications. "Talk up" your participation in the show through social media avenues like Twitter™, Facebook, LinkedIn® or company-based blogs.

If you have a new product, service, announcement, or plan to do something noteworthy at the show, put together a press kit and invite media contacts to stop by your booth to pick up the kit.

## 5. TRAIN YOUR BOOTH STAFF

There are some common rules about good booth behavior, and while they seem simplistic, they are often ignored.

- Those staffing the booth should be well groomed—shoes are polished and clothes are neat and pressed.
- It is a good idea to suggest that staff keep breath mints or spray in their pockets and not forget to use them.
- Eating, reading, sitting, or conversing with fellow staff members while working in the booth is not permitted.
- Using the phone, texting, "Tweeting," or anything else that takes attention away from potential booth visitors is not allowed.
- Be aware of body language. Standing with arms crossed can make booth staff look unapproachable—they should be smiling or at least looking pleasant. Standing near the aisle will allow booth staff to read attendees' name badges. Just make sure staff is not lined up like sentries guarding the castle. There should be plenty of space for visitors to enter the booth.
- Have an ice-breaker or opening line prepared as a way for staff to start a conversation. They should

maintain good eye contact and give a good solid hand-shake.

- Everyone working the booth should use a consistent "company line" when introducing your company.

As a business owner, take the opportunity to check out your competitors' booths while at the show. You can gain some valuable information about what new products or services they are offering as well as observe how they position themselves in the marketplace.

## 6. QUALIFY!

Booth staff should resist the temptation to load customers with information about your company's products and services. Instead, they should ask questions to find out why the prospect stopped by the booth. Attendees want to be listened to, not talked at.

Creating a lead form can help to qualify the prospect's interests. However, the form should be brief or you may lose the patience of the visitor. Here are some items to consider including:

- product interest;
- level of purchasing authority;
- time frame to purchase;
- how they would like you to keep in touch;
- space for adding comments to assist in your post-show follow up activity, such as "John needs to purchase by the end of the year," or "Sally will be on vacation all next week"; and
- contact information, including email address and company website.

You may want to consider asking prospects to complete the lead form as a requirement for entering a drawing or receiving a free giveaway.

Another important tip is for booth staff to rank the priority of each lead. This will help after the show with follow-up so that the strongest leads get attention first. This way, if your schedule is limited, you will have contacted at least your most important prospects.

## 7. FOLLOW UP—QUICKLY!

It is staggering to note an often-cited industry statistic—close to 80% of all contacts made at trade shows never receive a follow-up. Do not be part of that statistic and diminish your chances of finding new business!

In advance, it is helpful to prepare a follow-up letter and any materials you want to include. Send these no more than two weeks after the show so that your company will still be fresh in the prospects' minds. Plan the time to do phone follow-ups, especially when your contact expresses some urgency in making a decision. Get permission to send your prospects an occasional email, if that is in your marketing plans, and keep in touch with them regularly.

## CONCLUSION

There is a lot of helpful information about successful trade show exhibiting to be found in print, online and perhaps even workshops offered through organizations specific to your industry. The more you know, the more effective you will be—and the more you will look forward to exhibiting at your next trade show!

\*\*\*

Anita Mitzel is the president and owner of GraphiColor Exhibits. The company has been in the business of providing trade show displays, corporate signage, and large-format printing since 1984. Before founding GraphiColor Systems with her partner Don, Anita worked at trade shows across the country as a narrator, booth staffer, and supervisor. She helps her clients cover all the bases in preparing for and being successful with their trade shows and events, and has shared her advice and tips with both small and large companies as well as Chambers of Commerce and other business groups.

For more information about exhibit, trade show, or event marketing, or for copies of her other published articles, contact Anita Mitzel by email: anita@graphicolor.com, phone: 866-347-0271, or website: www.graphicolor.com.

# POINT OF SALE (POS) SYSTEMS

## by Debbie Bone, DGB Carolinas

Do you think you want a POS system? When I speak to merchants, I hear many different reasons. The most common is, "My friend has a POS and he likes it." Make no mistake, a POS system can be a valuable asset to your business, but because your friend has one is not a reason for you to buy one.

## THE BENEFITS OF POS SYSTEMS/ELECTRONIC CASH REGISTERS

How can a POS benefit your particular business? First, there must be an understanding that a POS system for a retail store will be different from the POS that works best for the hospitality industry. For example, POS systems for hotels, motels, restaurants, and bars offer the following:

- software that supports the way the establishment does business,
- menu planning,
- inventory control,
- cost per meal,
- one-stroke price change,
- ingredients per dish,
- time clock,
- table setup,

- reservations,
- employee scheduling,
- tracking sales by categories,
- ways to eliminate shrinkage,
- detailed reports,
- the ability to build a customer database,
- gift cards,
- overall improved accuracy and increased efficiency, and
- easily grows with the business.

These are just a few of the reasons why a POS system could prove invaluable for a business in the hospitality industry.

The benefits of an electronic cash register (ECR) include:

- low cost for startups,
- most models are easy to use,
- fewer components than a POS system, and
- basic functions and reporting.

## BEFORE YOU PURCHASE

Depending on the environment and business you are in, there are needs and abilities that need to be addressed before a buying decision is made.

Make a list of the things you think your business needs. Your business is unique to you and your needs will be different than the business next door. Know what you want and how you plan to use the equipment. Examine your business closely; consider all of your immediate needs, and your needs for the future.

There must be a decision made on whether to purchase new or used equipment. A recent survey completed last year cited more business owners prefer new equipment, even in this challenging economy.

Gift cards can be a nice addition to revenue and if you are thinking about offering them, the POS system you choose should be able to accept them.

The amount of bells and whistles needed will vary by type of business. Some questions to ask yourself before choosing a point of sale system or electronic cash register are:

- What tax must your business collect on a sale?
- How many departments are in your store?
- How many products do you carry now?
- How many do you expect to carry in the future?
- How busy will your store be?
- Will you need more than one register?
- Will you accept coupons?
- How will your clerks process refunds?
- What types of payment does your business accept?

Whether you are choosing a POS system or an ECR for your business, be sure to check out the warranty. If the register fails, do you have to pack it up and ship it back for repair or is there a local company with a trained service technician on staff to assist you?

Programming is another huge consideration. If you have multiple departments and multiple tax jurisdictions, who will set the register up to encompass these features? What happens if the tax rate changes? Who will train you and your employees?

There is no one-size-fits-all cash register. There are multiple models with very different capabilities. An example would be one register that may have 10 departments, another 100 departments. One may have a scanner, another may not.

## CHOOSING A VENDOR

Check out references from your local vendors; call them after hours to see if you get a machine or a person who can help you. Above all, know your POS vendor. He can be your best friend when it comes to efficiently running your business. Choose someone who will sit down with you and go over your list and make recommendations as to which system will service your business needs the best.

It is important to understand that the POS system will need to be set up. This is not a job for the faint of heart. These systems come with printers, servers, and displays to network; this does not happen by itself. You must also consider the software before you choose the hardware. Most POS systems have their own requirements for hardware. It is always better to purchase the hardware from the same vendor that you purchase the software from. It also helps to check to see if there is a POS vendor who specializes in your particular business niche.

Then the consideration must be given to service after the sale. It is New Years Eve and your POS stops working! What do you do? You pick up the phone and call the person you purchased your system from, only to find out that there is no answer, only an answering machine. Panic starts to set in. The restaurant is filling up with guests and you cannot even key in an order. The bar and kitchen are at a standstill. You finally resort to paper tickets after you spend 30 minutes digging them out of the closet. By this time, panic has gone to fear as you realize it is going to be a long night. This is a scenario you do not want to be caught up in. How can you avoid it? By simply knowing who you are purchasing from. Buying a POS from the Internet and having it shipped to you leaves you to install and run it.

## EQUIPMENT

### POS Systems

Some merchants try to cut corners and purchase a system as cheaply as possible. But remember, this system is running your business. Cutting corners will only come back to bite you. The average life expectancy of a POS system, with upgrades, is around five to seven years.

You will need a server capable of growing with you. This means it should have enough memory and hard disk space. Skimping on this will cause you more problems and will certainly not be worth the headaches to save a few dollars.

Printers are another item you do not want to skimp on. They are your lifelines to the kitchen, the bars, and your servers. Dot matrix printers work best in kitchens as the ambient temperature in the kitchen may be high enough to prevent a thermal printer from working correctly. Thermal printers are fine in other areas. What happens when the kitchen printer goes down on a busy night? This is another scenario you do not want to be in the middle of! It is always a good idea to keep a back-up printer.

Make sure your POS vendor analyzes your power situation. Most people do not consider the power source or the fluctuations in power that can be caused by meat grinders, blenders, etc. Clean power is essential for POS systems to work reliably. Fluctuating power can wreak havoc on a POS system. A dedicated circuit is always best.

Most of the screens being utilized now are touch screens. Consider the location of the screens and the possibility of spills or breakage.

All of the items talked about here are mechanical or electronic. They break or need service just like anything else. Make sure you have chosen a competent reseller of POS systems to ensure that your business runs smoothly.

### Electronic Cash Registers

The life expectancy of a cash register is six to 12 years, with upgrades usually required around the six-year mark. It is a sound investment if, and only if, it is the right decision for your business.

The electronic cash registers (ECR) of today are not like the mechanical ones your father and grandfather used. They are much more sophisticated and maintenance, for the most part, requires replacing a circuit board. The old mechanical registers were labor intensive and had many moving parts. Typically, I have two kinds of customers: the business owner who went to the deep discounter and bought the least expensive register and the customer who come into our office in search of the right solution for his business. Which customer are you?

## USING THE POS SYSTEM

I have seen retail stores purchase POS systems and then fail to use them to their full potential. One of the reasons for purchasing a POS in a retail environment is to track inventory movement. Opening a new retail store can be a daunting task and, quite frankly, entering inventory in the system is often the last thing in the minds of some store owners. Sure, you can likely get the POS vendor to key in your inventory, but that comes with a price.

A barcode scanner is often utilized in POS systems to track inventory. In liquor stores, all bottles are barcoded and scanned with the barcode scanner to input inventory. Check with your local distributor about this service. If you do not have barcodes, the POS system, in most cases, can print the labels for you, but you must input the information into the system first. If you carry an inventory line from a large vendor, the company may very well have its inventory items on a disk or can email you a file. This is a big time saver.

If you are serious about your business and its success, a POS system can be one of your best investments. In addition to inventory, a POS system can track sales. Tracking sales and understanding the reports you get from your system are critical to effective management of your business.

Most POS systems are connected to the Internet for processing credit cards. This is a much faster way and the most widely used method. However, it can come with inherent risks and these risks need to be examined. In today's world, we have people out there who have become proficient at hacking into computers and stealing information. You need to protect yourself as best you can against these hackers.

The first line of defense is to never use your POS system on the Internet for surfing or browsing. This is one way that hackers can inject a code into your system that would allow them access to your sensitive data. All it takes is one employee visiting a malicious website and you could end up spending thousands of dollars to repair the damage. The bottom line is, do not use your POS system for anything but a POS system.

What merchant processing company will you use to process credit cards? It is prudent to check the type of merchant account you can have with your system. Do not get locked into a vendor who requires you to process credit cards with his company. You should have the right to choose your own processor or use your current one. A lot of business owners think, or are told, that because they bought the POS system, they have to use the vendor for credit cards. This is simply not true. Find this information out up front before you make a buying decision. Most POS vendors have aligned themselves with someone to do the actual processing. Some, however, have their own capabilities. You do not want to get caught up with a POS vendor who locks you into the credit card processing. I am sure some of you are asking, "Why?" Let us put this into perspective using the example of automobiles.

You have one dealer in town that you can buy your car from. You sign a contract with this dealer and now every car you buy for however long must be bought from this dealer. But you find out that the new dealer down the street has the same capabilities, the same car, offers a much better deal, and better customer service. You can not go to the new dealer and buy the car because you are locked into the contract. It is the same with credit card processing; there are POS systems vendors out there who will not allow you to use anyone but them for processing credit cards. Where does that leave you and your business? What costs will there be next month or next year for that processing? Examine all of your options. To further expound on this, I had it happen just today as I write this chapter. A POS vendor told a merchant that my processing partner was not compatible with his POS system software when, in fact, it was certified on the exact same platform. It is a slippery slope, be mindful of the partners you choose.

## MAINTENANCE AND UPDATES

Maintenance agreements are another necessity when you have a POS system, unless you know all of the ins and outs. Programming, network wiring, and equipment repair expertise will be required to maintain and update your system. Look at it like an insurance policy; it is your peace of mind. Maintaining the system that is powering your business will leave less room for headaches down the road.

It is advisable to stay on top of updates and software changes. Updates are done for a reason. Leaving your system vulnerable to attack from the outside or to a crash from corrupt programming puts your business at risk. Ensure that you have a plan in place if your system is breached. Who do you call? What do you do to stop the attack and prevent releasing further information to the hacker?

\*\*\*

Debbie Bone has been in the office equipment industry for 30 years and the merchant processing business for 10 years with DGB Carolinas, a registered ISO for Electronic Payments, Inc. Her family-owned and -operated business carries a complete line of office equipment and services most leading brands.

You can contact Debbie by phone: 888-650-6068, email: dgbcarolinas@gmail.com, or website: www.123processnow. com.

# HIRING AN EXPERT ON NETWORK SECURITY AND REPAIR

## by Todd D. Brady, Kyda Technologies, Inc.

With identity theft radically increasing every year, securing and repairing your computer network is more important than ever. Keeping strangers, employees, or worse, your competition, from knowing your most intimate details about your finances, clients, vendors, sales figures, confidential trade secrets, and even your personal life, is critical. As a small business owner, your time is better spent running your company and performing your craft, not attempting to secure and repair a network. Fierce competition requires attention to every detail. A *revealed company weakness* can cost you a bid on a job; a *network hacker* can cost you lost time and labor; *identify theft* can cost you a much needed loan; *viruses and malware* can cost you time and money; *confidential employee information leaks* can cost you your reputation; and an *unsecure wireless transmission* of client credit card information can cost you your entire business.

## HOW TO HIRE AN EXPERT

Here are some tips on hiring a network security and repair expert:

- Avoid the "jack of all trades, one-person repair show." In this economy, many displaced workers who were successful at repairing their home computer have suddenly opened shop. They lack the education and diverse experiences in multiple strategies for repairing computer networks. Further, they have no personnel to fall back on when multiple emergencies arise. You need someone to be there when you call!

- "Interview, interview, interview." Does the IT firm you are about to trust your network to take the time to learn about your company, your employees, your management style, your security requirements, your products, your mission statement, your business model, and your company's strengths and weaknesses? Repairing computer networks requires more than just inserting parts; the relationship with your network expert is an ongoing, symbiotic one that is critical to your business success. After the interview, ask yourself, did you offer all of the information, or did the IT firm's representative ask first? If it is the latter, you and your company matter to him and that goes a long way.

- "Take some R & R, reputation and referrals." Use multiple sources to check on the company you are about to trust with access to all of your systems. Internet research, the Better Business Bureau, professional networking groups, word of mouth, and vendor interviews are all good ways to investigate a company's reputation. If it is not offered, some things to ask the IT firm's representative about include: Is the company insured and bonded? Who are its current clients? Who has referred business to the IT firm? What are their success stories? And failures? If you have to pry for information, it is because it is negative, or not necessarily important to the representative. Either way, it is probably not a company you want to be relying on for critical IT systems.

- "Shhhhhh, can you keep a secret?" An offer of signing a nondisclosure, or rather the lack thereof, should indicate a problem. Remember, your IT professionals will see every aspect of your business and possibly personal life. You must trust them to keep it confidential, and what is the backup plan if they fail to do so? A smart, proactive IT company has these documents at the ready.

- "What have you done for me lately?" Do you only see your IT professional team when there is an issue? How many times has the representative called you to check on the quality of service or to offer solutions to cut costs, make your employees more efficient, or make your business grow? Failure to do so is a sign of the firm's lack of resources or a "cut and run" methodology, neither of which you need dragging you down when the competition is chasing you in a foot race.

## WHY SECURE/REPAIR A COMPUTER NETWORK?

Imagine if employee A knew what employee B grossed in salary last week. Most companies have enough trouble making employees happy, let alone dealing with this type of information leak. Here is another example. Acme Company hired an IT company. The company satisfied Acme's emergency needs, but failed to proactively investigate its server security. After a little nosing around on the company database by an employee, disaster struck. He discovered all of the future sales leads for the company based upon the expiring vendor contracts in the next two years. The employee quit, opened up a shop in competition with the former employer, and went after and obtained 72% of those leads and turned them into business. To this day, Employee X is in business! And as a result in loss of pipeline sales possibilities, Acme had to lay off employees and downsize.

"Virus attack!" What would you do if you came to work and had no computer? Today, a computer is like a phone; it is critical to business and without it, you and your company are shut down. Hardware is low cost; labor is high cost; and opportunity cost is not even measurable at times. Thousands upon thousands of variants of virus and malware programs are running rampant on the Internet, 24 hours a day, just looking for unprotected victims. Are you next? Although no virus applications are 100% perfect, there are those out there who are better at it than others. A good IT professional can help give you advice on the current threats. Free virus applications are not a bad solution; they provide a moderate level of security. But what is your time worth? If you could spend $40 a year, per computer, to sleep better at night knowing you are protected, and that it would prevent hundreds of dollars in repair fees, possible lost data, employee downtime, and lost sales, would it not be worth it?

Are you compliant? It is a Monday morning, you are hard at work making clients happy, and a court officer walks into your office and serves you with a summons. You are being sued by a former employee because you failed to comply with myriad new laws that govern small businesses. Particularly the ones stating that you must take a "reasonable level of precaution" to ensure that employees' confidential information is protected. You have no idea what this means, but you do know that you will be, at minimum, spending a day in court, away from your clients, losing money, dealing with this. Your IT professional can help you here. Hopefully, he acted before the lawsuit, implementing the "reasonable precautions" that the Supreme Court dictates. This could be anything from adding simple remote access security to your servers, to lockdown of in-house computers to block data extraction by external devices, to more complex monitoring of the Internet line you use to transmit employee data to and from vendors.

"If I only had a few more hours in a day." How many times have you said that to yourself? Well, if your IT contractor is doing his part, you can recoup that every day! Not one computer that comes across our bench is perfect, not one is running at peak performance. Even a two-second delay on the keyboard can translate into hours of lost time. Are you one of those folks that make the joke, "I press a button and go get coffee?" Well, the coffee is getting expensive. Computer maintenance, rather, the proactive inspection and repairs/upgrades, done before something goes wrong, is the answer. Budget $65 per computer per quarter and you can save hundreds a month in lost productivity; multiply this by your number of employees and wow, what a savings! And that does not even account for the downtime and lost productivity when the system crashes because you have ignored the maintenance, and all the employees are being sent home and clients are upset when no product is delivered.

Today, computers are downright cheap, as in inexpensive. Long gone are the days of extensive return-on-investment calculations on computer hardware and software. A good IT professional will assist you in reviewing your current hardware and software to determine if investment in upgrades will give returns in increased productivity. This also applies to employee procedures and processes. Look around the shop. Are you using three pieces of software to track something? Do you have to perform double entry for the same piece of data due to software limitations and or improper setup and usage? We find this sort of misapplication all of the time. It all adds up to lost time and money.

## COMPUTER NETWORK MAINTENANCE

Computer networks are not a one-time purchase. They are an ongoing, budgeted item for your organization. The task of maintenance is not as daunting as it seems when it is broken down by job and priority. Nevertheless, it is critical that a top-down approach is taken to avoid a mismatched collection of equipment purchased without design, over time, which will never work well together as a network. Such behemoths incur more expense and time than they ever save. Even though most small or new companies do not have the budget to design and purchase all network equipment at once, intelligent decisions can be made, over time, to end up with a solid network in the end.

What information, if leaked, or just destroyed, could be disastrous to you and your organization? It is different for every company. Start by listing items in order of importance and then organize them in "need to have" and "nice to have" lists. What can you, and your company, live without if needed? Your IT professional can help you put costs and timelines to the items once they are organized. It is critical that you protect the ones that can do you the most damage first and then work on the others. Some will be one-time fixes only; others will be ongoing expenses in your IT budget.

Computer networks can be secured with multiple methods, hardware based or software based. Which is right? Computer purchases are not made first, and then pushed into an existing organization. They are made based on the type of organization you have. Product A may be the best choice for ABC company, and yet the worst choice for XYZ company. All products have pros and cons, and there are many out there to choose from. Generally, you get what you pay for, and the most expensive solution is not necessarily the best. Computer operating systems have some built-in security, but this has its strengths and weaknesses. It may be appropriate to add, or even take away from a new system to achieve a productivity and security balance.

Do you remember the old school drills? Getting under your desk? Lost data will cost you big time, and it happens all too often. It is not just about backing up religiously, I am talking about pretending that you actually have to use that backup one day. Fake a disaster once in a while! I recall the university trained engineer who backed up his laptop for six years and, sure enough, one day it quit on him. He brought it in to us with his faithful backup and said, "No worries; I backup daily, just restore the backup to a new drive." It did not take one of our bench technicians long to discover that the backup was 100% blank; it had never been written to once, ever. What is my advice? Take a backup set, restore it, and try to work from it. How did you do?

One of the biggest reasons for IT overages in budgets I see is due to missing documentation and software (both media and licensing). Costs can be doubled if there is an attempt to repair a system that has little or no documentation. Ask your IT company for your software CDs and software licenses. Likewise, ask for a history of the repairs made to your systems. You should have in your possession a hardware and software inventory. Next to payroll and Insurance, IT is the third largest budget item for most companies. Why would you not want to know what you have and where it is? And, if you change IT companies, much time and money is saved by having this information. If your current IT company cannot provide this, it is not the right one for your business.

## IT'S ALL ABOUT THE TOOL

Anyone making anything, no matter the product, will tell you that the proper tools, or the lack thereof, will make or break a product. Computers are just tools, no more. They separate you from the crowd, make your products better, deliver them faster, give you a leg up on the competition, make a small business look large, level the playing field, speed up production, and cut costs. Further, if applied correctly, they can make life and business easier and less stressful. The average person only uses 60% of the capabilities of any given hardware or software setup. A little investment in training and education prior to purchase and use of computer systems goes a long way. If your computer systems are keeping you up at night, call your local IT company.

\*\*\*

Todd Brady is owner of Kyda Technologies, Inc., a 15-year-old company providing 24-7 information technology services for small businesses and work-at-home individuals. A former computer programmer for the automotive tiers and author of a patented database software program in the building demolition industry, Todd now offers network design and consulting advice, proactive computer maintenance programs, emergency repair services, and hardware/software purchasing assistance to over 800 clients, large and small, in the Detroit metropolitan area. His support team consists of 12 certified, insured, and bonded field and bench repair technicians. Todd can be reached by phone: 586-307-3511, email: todd@kydatech.net, or website: www.kydatech.net.

# PAYROLL MANAGEMENT

*Theresa Juco, Paychex, Inc.*

If you have just started your own business, congratulations! These next few years will be an important time for your growth and success. Hiring your first employee is just one milestone along the path. In this chapter you will learn what is required from you, as an employer, in regard to payroll administration and taxes.

## HIRING A NEW EMPLOYEE

Depending on the type of employment opportunity you are hiring for, there are some important things to consider. There should be a plan in place for the new position, which includes detailed employee responsibilities and expectations. Evaluate your business finances and establish a base pay (or range) that you want to offer. Depending upon the position, you may want to consider background checks on likely candidates.

You will also have to decide on the type of benefits, if any, which you will offer, such as health insurance. Keep in mind that benefits are just that . . . benefits. You may not have to offer benefits, such as 401k retirement fund, but it is likely that you will have less employee turnover if you are able to provide good benefits. Some benefits, such as supplemental insurances and simple IRAs, have very little administration cost and, in most cases, you may not even have to pay for them. Such plans are inexpensive solutions well worth investigating.

## PAYING YOUR EMPLOYEES

Once you have successfully hired an employee, how do you pay him? According to the IRS, there are two ways to properly pay your employees: as independent contractors or as regular employees.

### Independent Contractors

Hiring a person as an independent contractor is not an option unless he qualifies with the IRS. If you decide to hire someone as an independent contractor, you are essentially hiring an individual who works for himself and who is not an employee. Because this person is not your employee, you will not have to pay employment taxes; however, it is crucial that this individual qualify as an independent contractor under the IRS guidelines. These guidelines are very specific and failing to follow them can result in huge penalties. Some of the rules for independent contractors include the fact that they control their own work schedule and pay. Further, there also should be written contracts. To get more information on independent contractors, visit www.IRS.gov.

### Regular Employees

Typically, as an employer, you have a responsibility to withhold and pay income taxes, Social Security taxes, and Medicare taxes, as well as unemployment taxes to both federal and state for regular employees. There are several different rates, tax tables, and due dates that you will have to abide by. If you plan on operating a successful business that employs staff, then you must become familiar with all of the different types of payroll taxes, especially if you plan on administrating your own payroll.

Many small businesses owners think that having "only a few employees" makes them able to handle the responsibility of administrating their own payroll. What most do not understand is that the number of employees does not matter. It does not matter if you have one, ten, or 25 employees; your tax obligations remain the same. You may have a lesser tax amount to pay with only one employee, but you still have to make those payments just as often as the business owner who has 25 employees.

## PAYROLL PROCESS

When you are in charge of running a business and do not come from an accounting background, you may think that writing a payroll check is simple. But it is the calculations behind it that can give you a headache. Calculating withholding taxes can be time-consuming and double-checking them to make sure they are correct is tedious. Similarly, making payroll tax payments correctly and on time can be a pain.

Further, if you do not know what you are doing, preparing the payroll returns yourself can be disastrous. Fortunately, there are many software packages that you can buy off the shelf to help assist you in this process. However, if you have not ever dealt with payroll taxes or do not have a certified accounting background, outsourcing this responsibility may be the better alternative. Outsourcing payroll is an inexpensive way to ensure that your taxes get paid on time and that you stay out of hot water with the IRS. Most financial advisors and accountants encourage outsourcing.

## PAYROLL OUTSOURCING

Outsourcing involves hiring a qualified third-party vendor to administer your payroll process. Most payroll companies include calculating and writing your payroll checks, paying your payroll taxes, and preparing and filing your returns in their services. Many also provide direct deposit services, bank account reconciliation, and time-clock services. Using a company for these services will make your payroll process seamless and hassle free. It will allow you more time to focus on your business operations and to generate income. It also ensures that your payroll taxes get paid on time, every time. That in itself usually is worth the cost. One late payment penalty can exceed more than 50% of the payroll services cost for the entire year.

Is outsourcing right for you? You must really ask yourself if you want to assume the responsibility for paying payroll taxes on your own. Most payroll companies will assume the liability for your payroll tax calculations and payments. This guarantees that you will not be responsible for any mishaps while using the payroll service.

If you decide to outsource, then choosing a payroll company is the next step. You will find that there are many companies out there that claim to be able to take care of all your payroll needs. You just need to find the one that is the best fit for your business.

### The Secret Six

Choosing a payroll company to work with is no light task. It should be carefully considered and researched. A great way to find a reputable company in your area is to ask your accounting professional for a recommendation. Most will have a company or two that they work with. You can also ask your surrounding business neighbors who they use. Once you establish who you would like to consider, there are probably many questions that come to your mind. Over the years, I have narrowed the number down to the "Secret Six" that will make or break your experience with a payroll company.

1. *Are you insured and bonded?* Believe it or not, there is no law or federal regulation that requires a payroll company to be insured and/or bonded. This can be disastrous for your company if that provider were to suffer a financial loss or bankruptcy, ultimately resulting in loss of your tax money. You should always

make sure that the insurance policy covers employee fraud and/or embezzlement. It may not sound likely, but payroll fraud is a multi-billion-dollar industry and small companies go out of business every day.

2. *Can you send me some references from local businesses in my area?* A good payroll company will be able to supply you with references; a great company should be able to provide you will local references within a ten-mile radius.

3. *Are you a national company and how many clients do you have? Are you publicly traded?* Being publicly traded ensures that a company's financial statements are open to the public. Knowing the size of the company will speak volumes. Payroll companies come and go every day . . . you want one that has been in business for years and has an unlimited amount of resources. However, you do not want to drown in the depth of the company, becoming another number and not a valued client, which leads to the next question.

4. *Who will be handling my account? Will I get a dedicated specialist assigned and will I have her direct number? Will that person be trained in every field (i.e. payroll, taxes, human resources, etc.) or do you have separate departments that handle that?* Having your own specialist makes a huge difference as this person will become familiar with you and your account, as well as make you feel more comfortable with her company's services.

5. *Do you process locally? If so, can I visit your location?* It is always nice to know that you deal with a service locally, meaning that you can talk to someone in the same time zone. Asking to visit is crucial; the response will tell you what kind of company you will be working with. The ones who invite you to visit the office where payroll is processed will be much more organized and

maintained than the company who rents out the basement of a building and has no signs for its location.

6. *How will you set up my account? Will someone come to my place to service me or will it be through phone/fax/email?* This question will define your ongoing relationship. Will this company's representative come to your location when you need something? Or will you have to go there?

\*\*\*

Theresa Juco is a small business payroll consultant and educator with Paychex, Inc. (www.paychex.com), the only payroll provider endorsed by the American Institute of Certified Public Accounts (AICPA). She is also an ambassador of the Greater Farmington Area Chamber of Commerce (Mich.). You can contact Theresa by phone: 248-488-1100, ext. 59047, or email: tjuco@paychex.com.

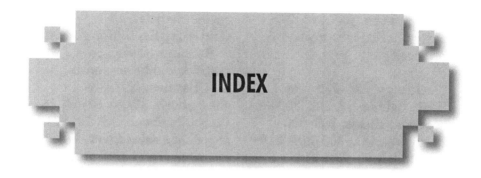

# INDEX

4Access Communications, 95

invalid card, 45–46
issuer, 14
IVR, 26

## J

Japanese Credit Bureau, 8
Juco, Theresa, 311, 316
jury trail waiver, 75, 84

## K

Kemp Klein Law Firm, 269, 277
keyed cards, 67
Kleist, Bill, 211, 220
knuckle-buster, 98
Koze, Kathy, 125, 201, 206
Kyda Technologies, Inc., 303,
309–310

## L

last four numbers of credit
card, 50
law changes, 81–86
lead follow-up, 291
lease, 82
leased equipment, 31–32, 84
leasing terminals, 115–116
level of service, 39–41
lifetime customers, 279–283
limited liability companies,
274–276
limited partnership, 273–274
LinkedIn®, 143–144
loan, 42–43
Local Business Network, 142,
195, 199
local chapter assessment,
189–194

## M

mail order sales, 105
management team, 165
manager-managed LLC, 274–276
manual imprinter, 98, 101
marketing (pre-show), 288–289
marketing plan, 165–166
MasterCard®, 2, 8, 14–15, 119
 /Maestro Worldwide, 70
 Rules, Entire Manual, 48,
 70, 78
 Secure Code®, 44
 Security Rules, 63
 Worldwide Rules, 78
 Worldwide U.S. and
 Interregional Interchange
 Rates, 3
maximum purchase amount,
53–54
McCormack, Mark, 223, 228
McDonalds®, 212–213
member-managed LLC, 274–276
merchant,
 bankruptcy, 76
 checking account, 71
 classification code (MCC), 66
 club, 68
 costs, 17–38
 error, 5, 7, 20, 47–64
 financial statements, 71
 Level Salesperson (MLS),
 13–14
 name (prominence), 62
 needs, 103
 qualification, 118
 signature, 82–83
 site survey, 68
 statement, 83–84